To All Who Revere the Flag and Its History

PUBLISHER'S NOTE: The Publisher acknowledges with gratitude the role of the United States Naval
Academy Alumni Association in supporting this publication

Rear Admiral William Rea Furlong
1881–1976

Commodore Byron McCandless
1881–1967

"One flag, one land, one heart, one hand, One Nation evermore."

OLIVER WENDELL HOLMES

SO PROUDLY WE HAIL
THE HISTORY OF THE UNITED STATES FLAG

WILLIAM REA FURLONG
Rear Admiral, United States Navy (Ret.)
and
BYRON McCANDLESS
Commodore, United States Navy (Ret.)

with the editorial assistance of
HAROLD D. LANGLEY
Associate Curator, Division of Naval History
National Museum of American History
Smithsonian Institution

SMITHSONIAN INSTITUTION PRESS

WASHINGTON, D.C. 1981

Illustrations courtesy of the Smithsonian Institution unless otherwise noted.

Library of Congress Cataloging in Publication Data
Furlong, William Rea, 1881-
   So proudly we hail.

   Bibliography: p.
   Includes index.
   1. Flags—United States—History.
I. McCandless, Byron, 1881-
II. Langley, Harold D.   III. Title.
CR113.F93   929.9′2′0973   81-607808
ISBN 0-87474-448-2   AACR2
ISBN 0-87474-449-0 (pbk.)

FRONTISPIECE: The largest United States flag in the world was made for a permanent display on New York's Verrazano Bridge. The huge fifty-star flag rested on a protective covering near the Washington monument when it was symbolically presented to the nation in 1980.

Photo by Richard Hofmeister

Table of Contents

Preface

This history of the United States flag begins with the exploration, discovery, and settlement of the areas that the nation now embraces. Flags associated with various foreign nations are considered here, not because they had any direct connection with the stars and stripes, but because there is an abiding regional interest in the beginnings of settlement and in the contributions of various nationalities. Next comes a discussion of changes in the English flag and in the evolution of standardized color arrangements in flags for components of fleets and units of the army. This is followed by a treatment of certain aspects of the history of flags in the thirteen North American colonies, as well as of some of the flags associated with European wars that involved the colonies.

Colonial reactions to Parliamentary laws enacted and enforced after the Seven Years War stimulated an interest in various kinds of symbols, including liberty poles and flags. Gradually a flag with thirteen red and white stripes gained popularity. The outbreak of the Revolution led to use of the pine tree, rattlesnake, and Grand Union flags, as well as to a diversity of unit colors. Since this book is concerned with the evolution of the stars and stripes, regimental and unit colors are discussed only insofar as they may have had an influence on the United States flag.

Various designs and uses of the stars and stripes are treated within the context of the Revolution, and then up to the passage of the flag act of 1818. This law fixed the number of stripes at thirteen and provided for the addition of a star for each new state that entered the union. The growth of the union from twenty states in 1818 to fifty in 1960 is treated briefly in order to show the changes in the arrangement of stars. Illustrations or photographs of surviving flags representing various phases of the evolution are noted. Likewise, various laws, regulations, and court decisions pertaining to flags are included as a part of the overall story.

In writing this history of the flag of the United States, the authors sought to produce a work of authenticated fact, one that was as free as possible of conjecture. They wished particularly to avoid confusing fact with legend. The authors also felt it important to indicate the sources of their information in the form of notes—a scholarly method not often used in works about the flag. As a result of these efforts, they believed that they produced a work which corrects many widely held misconceptions about the flag, and which puts the whole subject in a more accurate historical perspective.

As career naval officers, both Rear Admiral William R. Furlong and Commodore Byron McCandless had the duty while assigned to the Navy Department of answering hundreds of specific inquiries on flag matters. These came from congressmen, historians, teachers, and writers, among others. Admiral Furlong was the Navy representative on the committee of patriotic and veterans' organizations that wrote the flag code after World War I. Commodore McCandless was consulted by Presidents Woodrow Wilson, Franklin D. Roosevelt, and Harry S Truman on flag matters. When the forty-ninth and fiftieth stars were about to be added to the flag, many suggestions were put forward concerning the arrangement. President Dwight D. Eisenhower asked Admiral Furlong to submit a design for the arrangement of the stars. The admiral did so, and his design was later adopted by the advisory board appointed by the president. These experiences, plus their discontent with many existing flag books, induced Furlong and McCandless to set out to produce a definitive history of the flag.

Admiral Furlong presented the proposal to the late Leonard Carmichael, then the Secretary of the Smithsonian Institution, and was encouraged to proceed. Secretary Carmichael met with Admiral Furlong, and with Mendel L. Peterson, Chairman of the Department of National and Armed Forces History, Smithsonian Institution, and William Pincus, a representative of the Ford Foundation, to discuss the proposal. The Ford Foundation agreed to make a grant to the Smithsonian to support research on the flag book, the funds to be administered through Peterson to Furlong, McCandless, and Mrs. Lula M. Stephens, research assistant for Admiral Furlong. Under this arrangement the work began in September 1962.

Research was done by Commodore McCandless and Mrs. Stephens. Admiral Furlong organized the material and wrote the narrative. Mrs. Stephens had had a long association with Admiral Furlong on flag matters. She worked with him on the formulation of the first flag code after World War I and in all of his flag work during his years in the Navy. Furlong and Mrs. Stephens prepared the Navy exhibit in honor of the Sesqui-Centennial of the Declaration of Independence at Philadelphia in 1926. She was still working for the admiral when he submitted to President Eisenhower his design for the arrangement of fifty stars in the flag. Long before the Ford Foundation grant was awarded, Mrs. Stephens had done research on the flag at the Library of Congress, the Society of the Cincinnati, the Daughters of the American Revolution Library, the George Washington Masonic National Memorial, the Navy Department Library, the public library of Alexandria, Va., the Scottish Rite Masonic Temple, and the National Archives. During the years of the Ford grant she did research at the New York Historical Society, the New York Public Library, the Bostonian Society, the Boston Museum of Fine Arts, the Massachusetts Historical Society, and the Boston Grand Lodge of Masons. It is therefore understandable that Admiral Furlong believed that the manuscript would have been impossible to complete without her. Admiral Furlong married Mrs. Stephens on November 26, 1969.

Commodore McCandless died on May 30, 1967, before the work was finished. Admiral Furlong continued the task, and the full manuscript of more than a thousand pages was delivered to the Smithsonian in the fall of 1973. The task of preparing it for publication was assigned to Dr. Harold D. Langley, associate curator in the Division of Naval History, National Museum of History and Technology (now the National Museum of American History). Subsequently Admiral Furlong and Dr. Langley determined that a shorter version of the manuscript would be more appropriate to the needs and interests of the general public. They agreed, however, that the original manuscript would be retained by the Smithsonian and made available to flag scholars who might wish to consult it.

As the work progressed, material in the original manuscript was condensed, rearranged, and edited. New information, including textile data, was added. In addition, documentation was updated. Because any discussion of the origin and history of flags has a tendency to be discursive, a chronological narrative was added to provide both a point of departure and a unifying theme to carry the story forward.

Admiral Furlong hoped to live to see this book published. Regrettably, it was not to be. The admiral died on June 2, 1976, at the age of ninety-five. Those who knew this man of great integrity and of relentless energy and intellect, will share in the pleasure of knowing that the results of his long years of labor have been made available to the public.

In completing this work for publication, every effort has been made by all persons involved to be faithful to the ideals and goals of the authors. Research on flags was carried out by Admiral Furlong and Commodore McCandless for many years before there was a thought of a book or a research grant. As a result, no bibliography can reflect everything that they used or learned from. In this book all major citations from the original manuscript have been listed in the bibliography. As far as possible, all source citations at the end of each chapter include recently published works on the subject, even though Mc-Candless and Furlong did not live long enough to use them.

Harold D. Langley
Division of Naval History
National Museum of
    American History

Acknowledgments

The authors and the editor wish to thank the past and present staffs of the following institutions for their help at various stages of this project: Admiralty Library, London, England; Albany Institute of Art, Albany, N.Y.; Alexandria Public Library, Alexandria, Va.; American Antiquarian Society, Worcester, Mass.; American Philosophical Society, Philadelphia, Pa.; the Architect of the Capitol, Washington, D.C.; Anne S. K. Brown Military Collection, Brown University, Providence, R.I.;

Bedford Free Public Library, Bedford, Mass.; Bennington Museum, Bennington, Vt.; Boston Grand Lodge of Masons; Boston Museum of Fine Arts; Boston Public Library; Bostonian Society, Boston, Mass.; British Embassy, Washington, D.C.; British Museum and British Library, London, England; the John Carter Brown Library, Brown University;

Chicago Historical Society; Chicago Public Library, Chicago, Ill.; Colonial Williamsburg, Williamsburg, Va.; Connecticut Historical Society, Hartford, Conn.; Corcoran Gallery of Art, Washington, D.C.;

Danish Embassy, Washington, D.C.; Daughters of the American Revolution Library, Washington, D.C.; Delaware Historical Society, Wilmington, Del.; Detroit Institute of Art, Detroit, Mich.;

Easton Public Library, Easton, Pa.; Essex Institute, Salem, Mass.; Fort Johnson Museum, Fort Johnson, N.Y.; Fort Ticonderoga Museum, Fort Ticonderoga, N.Y.; Flag Foundation, Winchester, Mass.; French Embassy, Washington, D.C.;

Independence National Historic Park, Philadelphia, Pa.; Indiana Historical Bureau, Indianapolis, Ind.;

Library of Congress, including the Manuscript, Map, Newspaper, Prints and Photographs, and Photoduplication Divisions; Librarian of the Ministry of Defense, London, England; Library of Windsor Castle, Windsor, England;

Mariners Museum Library, Newport News, Va.; Maryland Hall of Records, Maryland Land Office, and Maryland State House, Annapolis, Md.; Maryland Historical Society, Baltimore, Md.; Massachusetts Historical Society; Massachusetts State House, Boston, Mass.; Mount Vernon Ladies Association, Mount Vernon, Va; Museum of the City of New York;

Museum of the Confederacy, Richmond, Va.; National Aeronautics and Space Agency; National Archives and Records Service; National Gallery of Art; National Park Service; National Portrait Gallery; National Trust for Historic Preservation, Washington, D.C.; National Maritime Museum, Greenwich, England;

Navy Department Library, Washington, D.C.; Netherlands Embassy, Washington, D.C.; New Jersey Historical Society, Newark, N.J.; New-York Historical Society; New York Public Library, New York, N.Y.; North Carolina Historical Commission, Raleigh, N.C.;

Peale's Museum, Baltimore, Md.; Pennsylvania Academy of Fine Arts, Philadelphia, Pa.; Princeton University Department of Art and Archaeology, Art Galley, and Firestone Library, Princeton, N.J.; Public Record Office, London, England; Rhode Island Historical Society, Providence, R.I.;

William Salt Library, Stafford, Staffordshire, England; Schenectady Historical Society, Schenectady, N.Y.; Scottish Rite Masonic Temple, Washington, D.C.; Society of the Cincinnati, Washington, D.C.; Star Spangled Banner House, Baltimore, Md.; Suffolk County Historical Society, Riverhead, N.Y.; Stonington Historical Society, Stonington, Conn.; Swedish Embassy, Washington, D.C.;

Tennessee State Library and Archives, Nashville, Tenn.; Toronto Public Library, Toronto, Ontario, Canada; U.S. Army Institute of Heraldry, Alexandria, Va.; U.S. Flag Foundation, New York, N.Y.; Valley Forge Historical Society, Valley Forge, Pa.; Washington Crossing Foundation, Washington Crossing, Pa.; West Point Museum, West Point, N.Y.; William Penn Memorial Museum, Harrisburg, Pa.; Worcester Art Museum, Worcester, Mass.; George Washington National Masonic Museum, Alexandria, Va.; the Henry Francis DuPont Winterthur Museum, Wilmington, Del.; Yale University libraries.

Above and beyond their association with some of the aforementioned institutions, several individuals helped in ways that deserve special recognition. Many of these people are retired from their institutions, and some are deceased, but it was the wish of Admiral Furlong that the memory of their help be preserved. They are Richard Carter Barret, Geraldine Beard, Alfred Blair, Lester Cappon, Admiral George J. Dufek, USN (Ret.), Dorothy Eaton, Professor Donald Egbert, James W. Foster, Frederick R. Goff, Robert W. Hill, John Hopkinson, Professor Leonard W. Labaree, Robert Ladd, Wilmer Leech, Colonel and Mrs. Clifton Lisle, USA (Ret.), Barbara A. Lynch, Rear Admiral William P. Mack, USN (Ret.), Captain Dale Mayberry, USN (Ret.), C. Percy Powell, Catherine Power, Russell Quant, Morris Radoff, Stephen T. Riley, Colonel Theodore Sizer, Lawrence Phelps Tower, and David H. Wallace.

In the Smithsonian Institution, the authors wished to remember the late Dr. Leonard Carmichael, a former Secretary of the Institution, as well as a number of people presently or formerly associated with the Institution. These include Robert P. Multauf, Daniel J. Boorstin, and Brooke Hindle, former directors of the National Museum of History and Technology (now the National Museum of American History); Otto Mayr, former acting director; and Silvio A. Bedini, former deputy director of the same museum; former curators Mendel L. Peterson, Edgar W. Howell, and J. Jefferson Miller II; former staff member Otis H. Greeson, and Roger Pineau, formerly with the Smithsonian Institution Press.

While preparing this manuscript for the press, the editor has been greatly assisted by his Smithsonian colleagues: Grace R. Cooper, former curator of textiles; Rita Adrosko and Katherine Dirks of the Division of Textiles; Donald Kloster, associate curator of military history; Donald W. Holst, exhibits specialist; Robert Post, curator of maritime history; Robert S. Harding of the Public Information and Education Division; Philip K. Lundeberg, curator of naval history; Joseph M. Young, museum technician; Harold W. Ellis, museum specialist; Frances Hainer, secretary of the Division of Naval History; Margaret B. Klapthor, curator/supervisor, and Herbert R. Collins, associate curator, Division of Political History. Thanks are also due to the staff of the Research Branch, Naval Historical Center, United States Navy Department.

For their work in expediting payments for outside work and encouraging the editor in the final stages of this project, special thanks are due to Roger Kennedy, director of the National Museum of American History; Douglas Evelyn, deputy director; Luis Del Rio, administrative officer; Joseph Hatch, special assistant; Bernard Finn, chairman of the Department of Science and Technology; and V. Clain-Stefanelli, curator of numismatics and former chairman of the Department of National History.

Over the years the staff of the Photography Branch of the Museum has done wonders in supplying photographs of various flags, sometimes under difficult conditions. Special thanks are due to photographers Richard Hofmeister, Alfred F. Harrell, Jr., and Rolfe M. Baggett, and to Mary Ellen McCaffrey, production control officer in the Photography Branch. Photographing of flags at locations distant from Washington was done by Larry Stevens of Falls Church, Va.

The authors owe a special debt of thanks to Lord Dartmouth for permission to photograph documents relating to Bernard Page in the William Salt Library, Staffordshire, England, and to Mr. F. B. Stitt, the librarian, for his help in overseeing the work.

Color illustrations of various early flags were made by Peter Copeland of Arlington, Va.

The original manuscript of Furlong and McCandless was typed by Mrs. Lulu Stephens (now Mrs. Furlong). Various drafts of the edited version were typed by Catherine Wakelyn, Carol Zarinelli, Patricia Langley. Final drafts were done by Giancarlo Terango and Rosemary E. Regan of the National Museum of American History.

At the Smithsonian Institution Press, Edward Rivinus, now director emeritus, and Felix Lowe, the present director, have given much time and support to the project. Maureen R. Jacoby has been a patient and long-suffering managing editor. Janet B. Stratton and Stephen Kraft of the design staff have been most helpful in resolving the many details associated with the illustrations and the design of the book.

Legal questions have been resolved through the efforts of George S. Robinson and Joseph H. Shealy.

For many years Mrs. William Rea Furlong has urged that this manuscript be completed. Her persistence has made it a reality at last.

Finally, the efforts of many people might have gone for naught had it not been for the financial support of the Naval Academy Alumni Association. Thanks to the efforts of Captain William S. Busik, USN (Ret.) and Commander Mark Tuzo, USN (Ret.), the Smithsonian Institution Press was able to publish this book as Admiral Furlong and Commodore McCandless anticipated.

H.D.L.

CHAPTER 1

Flags of Exploration, Discovery, and Settlement

When Rear Admiral George H. Preble first published his large and precedent-making volume on the *History of the Flag of the United States of America* in 1871, he began his account with ancient flag practices and with flags associated with the discovery and exploration of the western hemisphere. Subsequent writers on the history of flags have commenced their narratives with references to the Vikings, to Columbus, and to other early explorers. The interest of various regions of the United States in their origins has reinforced a tendency to associate the flags of European countries with accounts of early explorations and settlements. In view of this interest, it seems appropriate to take note of some of this lore as a prelude to discussing the direct English influence.

Tales of the voyages and exploits of the Northmen have an enduring fascination. Especially interesting to North Americans have been accounts associated with Leif Ericson's westward voyage from Greenland in the summer of 1001, and the establishment of a settlement at a place called Vinland. For more than a century Vinland has posed an intriguing mystery. Attempts have been made to locate it all along the eastern coast of North America from Newfoundland to the Virginia Capes, and as far westward as Minnesota. This mystery has been of particular interest to flag historians, under the impression that the Northmen carried the first flag into territory that later became part of the United States. A drawing of a black raven on a small white flag has been associated with certain Vikings who raided England. Consequently, the assumption arose that the same sort of flag was carried by the Northmen who reached the Western Hemisphere. But there is no evidence to support this conclusion. Indeed, it seems doubtful that they carried any flag at all, especially in view of the high cost of cloth. As for Vinland, it has now been fairly well established by archeological evidence that it was located in northern Newfoundland at a spot called L'Anse aux Meadows.

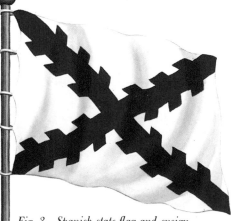

Fig. 1   *Flag of King Ferdinand and Queen Isabella of Spain*

Fig. 2   *A reconstruction of the 1492 expeditionary banner of Columbus*

Fig. 3   *Spanish state flag and ensign, 1516–1785*

The Spanish Flag

When Christopher Columbus made his famous voyage across the western ocean in 1492 under the auspices of King Ferdinand and Queen Isabella of Spain, he landed in the West Indies on what is now known as Watling's Island. Columbus approached the shore in an armed ship's boat that displayed the royal standard of Spain. This was a quartered banner showing a turreted or embattled castle on the field of red, for the house of Castile, and, for Leon, a red lion rampant on a white field (Figure 1). The captains of the other ships displayed the banner of the expedition on their boats—a white flag with a green cross. Below the arms of the cross are two golden crowns, one on each side, and below them the letters F (for Ferdinand) and Y (for the Spanish rendering of Isabella [Figure 2]). In the presence of all who had come ashore, as well as many natives, Columbus took possession of the island, naming it San Salvador (Our Saviour) in the name of the king and queen of Spain. Before returning to Spain in 1493, Columbus reconnoitered the northeastern coast of Cuba and the island of Haiti.

On his second voyage (1493–96) Columbus founded the settlement of Isabela on the north coast of Española (Haiti), and another on the south coast of what is now Santo Domingo. He explored the southern coast of Cuba, passing Guantánamo Bay. He sighted Puerto Rico, which he named San Juan Bautista (St. John the Baptist), and discovered the lesser Antilles and the island of Jamaica. The third voyage of Columbus (1498–1500) resulted in the discovery of the island of Trinidad. On his fourth and last voyage (1502–04) he explored the coast of Central America. A year and a half after his return to Spain, in 1506, Columbus died. To the very end he never realized that the lands he discovered were not near Asia but were a new continent. Many explorers who came after him tried to find a passage through this continent to Asia.

The colony on the southern coast of Santo Domingo became the base from which the Spanish directed further explorations. The military conquest of Puerto Rico was accomplished by Juan Ponce de Léon in 1508–09. In 1513 de Léon explored the entire eastern coast of Florida and the western coast as far north as Charlotte Harbor, and visited the Bahamas before he returned to Puerto Rico.

The reign of King Ferdinand came to an end in 1516. He was succeeded as ruler of Spain by Charles I, the founder of the Hapsburg dynasty. During the reign of King Charles I (1516–56) Spanish possessions in the New World greatly increased. By implication, the flag of King Charles was carried to these regions, but in most of the available accounts there are no specific references to flags. Spanish activities that are especially interesting to Americans are Alonso de Pineda's exploration of the Gulf of Mexico from Florida to Vera Cruz in 1519; the conquest of Mexico by Hernán Cortés in 1519–21; Francisco de Gordillo's exploration of the Atlantic coast from Florida to South Carolina in 1521, and that by Esteban Gómez from Nova Scotia to Florida in 1521, and by Luis Vásquez de Ayllón in North Carolina in 1526. Panfilo de Narváez and his followers searched unsuccessfully for gold in the region of Tallahassee in 1528. Of interest in terms of the later American involvement with the Philippines and the Marianas Islands was the voyage around the world by Magellan and his men between 1519 and 1522 (Figures 3 & 4).

Fig. 4   *A variant form of the Spanish state flag and ensign, 1580–1640*

Fig. 5   *Flag of the Dutch United East India Company*

It is reasonably certain that flags were not associated with the extensive explorations of the southern part of the present-day United States that were carried out by Hernando de Soto between 1539 and 1543, or in those led by Francisco Vásquez de Coronado into the southwest and as far north as Kansas between 1540 and 1542. These expeditions carried only what was necessary, and in the course of their long marches the soldiers and leaders frequently reappraised what they had to carry with them. A flag and a flag pole would most likely be considered unnecessary items very early in the march—if they were even taken along at all. The Indians were sufficiently impressed by the Spaniards—with their horses, armor, and weapons—that a flag would not have been necessary. Nor would it have been needed in claiming any territory for the sovereign.

The Spanish flag may have been flown from the ship of Francisco de Ulloa when he sailed from Acapulco in 1539 into the Gulf of California, around the tip of Lower California, and up the west coast to about 30 degrees north latitude. Further explorations of the California coast were carried out by Juan Rodríguez Cabrillo in 1542 and 1543. Despite these ventures, the Spanish settlement of California did not begin until the eighteenth century, when the Franciscan fathers built a system of missions and presidios at San Diego in 1769, Monterey in 1770, and San Francisco in 1776. Spanish settlements within the confines of the present-day United States were in territories that were on the fringes of the Spanish empire. As a result, occasion for displaying the Spanish flag over any forts or public buildings would have been very limited.

The Dutch Flag

The use of the Dutch flag in the New World is associated with the voyage of Henry Hudson along the coast from Newfoundland to the Carolinas in 1609, as well as with his explorations of Delaware Bay and the Hudson River that same year. His ship flew a flag with three horizontal bands of orange, white, and blue stripes from top to bottom. On the middle white stripe were the letters *OC* for Oost Indise Compagnie or *VOC* for Vereenigte Oost Indise Compagnie (United East India Company), the sponsors of the voyage. Above these initials was the letter *A* for the home port of Amsterdam (Figure 5).

Fig. 6   Flag of the Dutch West India Company

Fig. 7   Swedish state flag and ensign

Sometimes the *A* was inverted, making it resemble a *V*. The company flag was thus the national flag of the Netherlands with the initials added. Hudson's ship may also have flown a flag of the city of Amsterdam, a tricolor with a red stripe on top, a white stripe in the middle, and a black stripe on the bottom.

Subsequently the Dutch East India Company established a trading post on Manhattan Island in 1613, and a settlement near the site of Albany in 1615. This was followed by settlements in Connecticut and New Jersey, and along the Delaware River. The flag of the Dutch East India Company was used until 1622, when the Dutch West India Company (chartered in 1621) took over the government of the colony. This meant that the letters on the middle stripe of the flag were changed to *GWC* for Geoctroymeede West-Indische Compagnie (Chartered West India Company; Figure 6). In 1626 the Dutch West India Company sent out a colonizing expedition under Governor Peter Minuit. After having purchased Manhattan Island from the local Indians, Governor Minuit proceeded to found a settlement called New Amsterdam on the southern end of the island.

The Swedish Flag

Meanwhile, a Swedish settlement had been established on the Delaware River by William Usselinx, the chief organizer of the Dutch West India Company. In 1624 Usselinx organized a new corporation called the Swedish West India Company (or South Company) and secured a charter from King Gustavus Adolphus of Sweden. Territory purchased from the Indians between Bombay Hook and the mouth of the Schuylkill River, and later considerably enlarged, was called "New Sweden." Acting on behalf of the South Company of Sweden, Peter Minuit established a settlement at what is now Wilmington, Delaware, in 1638. It was named Christinaham in honor of Christina, the infant queen of Sweden. When the Swedish settlers landed near Wilmington they planted a coat of arms on a pole. Over the settlement flew the blue and yellow flag of Sweden (Figure 7).

In 1641 the Swedish bought out the Dutch interest in the South Company of Sweden. Two years later a new governor was sent out and plans were made for further colonization. Settlements were established on an island near present-day Chester, Pennsylvania, near the mouth of the Schuylkill River, and at the mouth of Salem Creek in New Jersey. A third governor arrived in 1654 with a large contingent of colonists. They proceeded to expel the Dutch from their settlement at Fort Casimir at New Castle. The Dutch retaliated by sending an expedition that conquered New Sweden and made it a dependency of New Netherland. The Dutch flag now replaced that of Sweden over the settlements in Delaware, Pennsylvania, and New Jersey. In 1656 the Dutch West India Company, in payment of debts, transferred what had been New Sweden to the city of Amsterdam. By 1663 all of Delaware was under the jurisdiction of the city of Amsterdam. It is not known whether the flag of that city was used in these territories.

The New Netherland flag changed slightly after the death of William II of Orange in 1650. The top horizontal stripe of the flag was changed from orange to red. Thereafter the flag of the Dutch West India Company carried red, white, and blue stripes.

Fig. 8   French state flag and ensign, c. 1370–1600

Fig. 9   French national flag at sea, 1661–1790

The French Flags

French flags are associated with the voyages of Giovanni de Verrazano, an Italian in the service of King Francis I of France, who in 1524 explored from the South Carolina coast to Newfoundland. His ship probably carried the ensign of the King of France, gold fleurs-de-lis on an azure field (Figure 8). A decade later King Francis I sent Jacques Cartier on three voyages of discovery between 1534 and 1542. Cartier carried the French flag from Newfoundland, Labrador, and up the St. Lawrence River. This was probably a blue flag with a white cross in its middle. Superimposed over the center of the cross was the blue shield bearing three gold fleurs-de-lis. He discovered the Gulf of St. Lawrence, the Gaspé Peninsula, and Prince Edward and Anticosti Islands, and founded Montreal. An attempt to establish a settlement on the island of Orleans between 1541 and 1543 failed. This ended French efforts to colonize Canada until the end of the century.

By the middle of the sixteenth century many European countries were experiencing religious and political disruptions that were the outgrowth of the Protestant Reformation. Protestant Huguenots found the policies of the Catholic king of France intolerable, and in 1562 they made an unsuccessful attempt to establish a Huguenot colony near the present site of Beaufort, North Carolina. The color of the French Protestants was white, and a white flag may have flown over this settlement. Another unsuccessful effort to plant a colony was made on the May River in Florida in 1562. This settlement possibly flew a square blue flag bearing three fleurs-de-lis.

Between 1562 and 1598 France was in the throes of a civil war between Huguenots and Catholics. When the Protestant leader, Henry of Navarre, emerged victorious and became King Henry IV, the white flag of the Protestants became the royal flag of France. During his reign the first permanent French settlement in America was made at Port Royal, Nova Scotia, in 1604. Between 1603 and 1609 Samuel de Champlain explored the coast of Newfoundland, built a trading post at Quebec, and discovered the lake that bears his name. This was a commercial venture and his ships carried a blue flag with a white cross in the middle. But in his drawing of the settlement at Quebec, Champlain depicted a pennant with three fleurs-de-lis flying over the settlement. When King Henry IV was assassinated in 1610, French exploration and settlement lapsed for about sixty years.

Once again France became the scene of conflict. When this conflict ended a ten-year-old boy emerged as King Louis XIV, but the actual power was in the hands of Cardinal Mazarin, the regent. King Louis came to power in his own right in 1661, and stimulated a fresh wave of exploration that brought the French settlements in the Western Hemisphere to their greatest volume. The flag of King Louis XIV was white, strewn with the gold fleur-de-lis.

It had long been the custom in France for kings to use a design of their own choosing as a royal ensign. As a result of this practice, there was no ongoing design of a national color, and there was to be none until the French Revolution. To distinguish between navy and merchant ships, in 1661 Louis XIV gave a white flag to the ships of war and to the merchant service a blue flag with a white cross and the crest of France in the middle (Figure 9). Later, in November 1669, King Louis decreed that the ensign worn at the stern of a warship be blue with a large white cross in the middle and sprinkled with yellow fleurs-de-lis. Under the new regulations, merchant ships wore the same

*Fig. 10   French state flag and ensign, c.
1643–1790*

ensign as warships except that the escutcheon of their province or town was in
one of the corners and bordered with two white bands. There was hardly time
enough to implement this order before the king superseded it with a new one.
In December 1669 the king said that in all cases the ensign worn at the stern
of a ship was to be white. For more than a century afterward French ships
carried the white flag in all naval battles.

Meanwhile, in 1664, the king made a concession of Canada to the French
West Indies Company. This company enjoyed a trading monopoly in America
and in Africa. By royal privilege it received the right to use a white flag bearing
the arms of France. To expand the company's holdings in New France, Robert
Cavelier, Sieur de La Salle, established a trading post at the outlet of Lake
Ontario in 1669. He also discovered the Ohio and Illinois rivers. The following year Detroit was settled by the French. It is believed that the white flag
with the gold fleur-de-lis and the arms of France flew over this settlement. The
company's flag may or may not have been flown over the mission established
by Jacques Marquette at Mackinac in 1671. Two years later Marquette and
Louis Joliet left Michilimackinac and explored the Mississippi River as far
south as the Arkansas River.

In 1674 French Canada was removed from the company's administration and
placed under the crown. Thereafter it is believed that the white flag of France
flew over all or most of the French forts and settlements in America. Sometimes the flag had gold fleurs-de-lis, with or without the royal arms (Figure
10). Many times convenience dictated that a plain white be used.

Whatever the flag, French territory and influence continued to grow in
America. In 1674 Marquette established a missionary station at the site of

Chicago, and the following year he built a mission at Kaskaskia, Illinois. La Salle made a second expedition into the interior to explore lakes Erie, Huron, and Michigan. He launched the first vessel to sail on the Great Lakes. In 1680 he sent Father Louis Hennepin to explore the Mississippi River from the mouth of the Illinois River to the Falls of St. Anthony at Minneapolis. La Salle led another group, in 1682, to explore the Mississippi River from the Illinois River to the Gulf of Mexico. La Salle took possession of this vast territory for his king and named it Louisiana in honor of Louis XIV. Sailing from France in 1684, La Salle headed an expedition that landed in Matagorda Bay, Texas. Enroute to Canada in 1687, he was murdered by his men near the Brazos River. With his death a great era of French exploration came to an abrupt end.

Meanwhile, France had watched the steady spread of English colonization in America. Englishmen were already in competition with Frenchmen for the fur trade. English trappers were making their way into western lands claimed by the French. To secure their territory from English encroachment, the French established a mission at Cahokia, near present-day East St. Louis, in 1699 and another religious outpost at the junction of the Kaskaskia and the Mississippi in 1700. The route to the west was protected by forts built at Mackinac in 1700 and Detroit in 1701. A settlement originally established at Biloxi Bay in 1699 was moved to a fort on the Mobile Bay in 1702. The city of Mobile was founded in 1710, and New Orleans in 1718. The white flag of France waved over an array of settlements and forts that were established at various points to mark its control of vast acres of wilderness.

By the middle of the eighteenth century, France and Great Britain were locked in a struggle for the control of the Ohio country. Before considering that struggle and its impact on flags, we must first examine the development of flag consciousness in England and Scotland, and in the English North American colonies.

English and Portuguese Explorations

The first English flag associated with the mainland of North America was that carried by John Cabot, who sailed under the sponsorship of King Henry VII of England. King Henry had turned down the chance to sponsor the first voyage of Columbus. Opportunity knocked again in the form of John Cabot, an Italian, and probably a Genoese, who proposed to seek a higher latitude route to the Indies than that which was followed by Columbus. Cabot offered to sail at his own expense, and this made his proposition even more appealing. In March 1496, King Henry issued letters-patent to Cabot and his three sons granting them authority to sail "under our banners and ensignes" to seek out islands, regions, provinces, or countries in unknown parts of the world. Cabot set sail from Bristol in the *Matthew* on May 2, 1497, and reached the coast of Newfoundland thirty-five days later. On June 24, he landed, perhaps at what is now called Griquet Harbor. The formal ceremony of claiming possession of the land was carried out with a crosier, the flag of St. George for King Henry, and the flag of St. Mark in remembrance of Cabot's years as a citizen of Venice.

The flag of St. George was a red cross on a white field. This red cross was in use during the Crusades, and it was one of the national emblems of

Fig. 11   English flag with the Cross of St. George

England as early as 1277 (Figure 11). The flag of St. Mark consisted of a winged lion and the book of St. Mark.

Cabot explored the eastern coast of Newfoundland before returning to England with the news that he had found a passage to the Indies. King Henry was pleased and sent Cabot out again in 1498 with five ships. One ship returned shortly, but the rest were never heard from again.

Some information about Cabot's two voyages must have been known to Gaspar Corte Real, an adventurous Azorean. He had served King Don Manuel I prior to his accession to the throne of Portugal in 1481, and continued as a gentleman of the court while looking after his property in the Azores. Corte Real had already made one voyage about which nothing is known. In May 1500 he received a patent from the king to discover islands and a mainland over which he would be granted extensive privileges. It is now believed that Gasper Corte Real reached Newfoundland in the summer of 1500. After a second voyage in 1501, he sent home by other ships fifty-seven Indians to the court of King Manuel as proof of his discoveries. Corte Real's brother made another voyage to Newfoundland in 1502 from which he never returned. Information from the voyages of Corte Real was incorporated in a world map made in Lisbon in 1502 for Ercole d'Este, Duke of Ferrera, which is still preserved in the Estense Library at Modena. This Cantino Mappenmode shows the flag of Portugal, a red flag with five white circles, planted at Greenland and Newfoundland.

João Alvares Fagundes of Portugal sailed to the south coast of Newfoundland and into the Gulf of St. Lawrence about 1520 or earlier. In 1521 he successfully petitioned the King of Portugal for property rights and privileges in this region.

Colonists for the venture were recruited from families in the Azores. Fagundes established a settlement at Ingonish on Cape Breton Island. Within a year to eighteen months the colony was being harassed by Indians and by French fishermen who resented the intrusion into their fishing area. Deprived of help from Portugal, Fagundes was forced to abandon his colony.

The next voyage to North America under English auspices was that of John Rut in 1527. He reached Nova Scotia and followed the coast down to some point in New England. Frequent landings were made to explore the region. Rut then changed course and nothing further is known about his whereabouts until his ship turned up in Spanish-held Puerto Rico. He returned to England in 1528. From the point of view of King Henry VIII, who sponsored the voyage, it was a failure. But the king gave Rut a yearly annuity for his efforts. The flag that John Rut carried was the white flag with the red cross of St. George.

Fifty years elapsed before the next English contribution to exploration. This time the motivation came not from a desire to discover new lands, but from English jealousy and envy over the amount of treasure from the New World that was being sent to Spain. England and Spain were in a state of undeclared war when Sir Francis Drake set sail from England on December 13, 1577. Officially, Drake was on a voyage to Alexandria, Egypt. Actually, he was to prey on the Spanish ships operating in the Pacific. This activity had grown to considerable proportions since the Spanish conquest of Peru in 1530–32.

Drake sailed through the Straits of Magellan, reached the Pacific, and began raiding Spanish possessions along the west coast of South America. He continued to sail northward until he reached about 43 degrees north, then he turned south. A heavy cargo of silver, acquired during his raids, was causing a number of leaks and Drake needed to find a quiet locale to careen his ship and repair the hull. He found an ideal location in a shallow estuary, now known as Drake's Estero, in the northern bight of Drake's Bay. Here his men spent five weeks while the ship was being repaired. Before departing, Drake had a metal plate engraved with the record of his taking possession of the region for Queen Elizabeth I. This plate, along with a sixpence bearing the queen's profile, were nailed to a post. There is no mention of a flag being used in Drake's ceremony in claiming Nova Albion for England, but the Mellon-Drake map of 1587 shows the flag bearing the red cross of St. George planted on the coast of California to make the English claim.

Drake now sailed eastward across the Pacific and the Indian Ocean, and rounded the Cape of Good Hope. He reached Plymouth, England, on September 26, 1589, thus completing a memorable voyage around the world. He brought home to England a quantity of Spanish treasure. Queen Elizabeth knighted him on the deck of his flagship. Drake's act of defiance, and the attitude of Queen Elizabeth toward his deeds, led to Spain's decision to send a mighty Armada against England in 1588. The defeat of that force led to the decline of Spain as a world power.

Other Englishmen continued to explore the northern coasts of North America and adjacent regions in the hopes of finding a passage to Asia. Sailing from England in 1576, Martin Frobisher sighted Greenland, reached Baffin Land, and discovered the bay that now bears his name. He made two other voyages, one in 1577, the other in 1578, in which he reached Baffin Land and Hudson Strait. Between 1585 and 1587, John Davis made three voyages in search of the northwest passage that brought him to the west coast of Greenland, Baffin

Land, Baffin Bay, and the northern coast of Labrador. Further exploration of Baffin Land, Frobisher Bay, and Hudson Strait were carried out by George Weymouth in 1602. Under the sponsorship of the East India Company and the Muscovy Company, John Knight explored the shores of Labrador and Newfoundland in 1602.

By this time the English were hoping to plant a colony in the New World to use as a base of operations against Spanish possessions. Sir Humphrey Gilbert made an unsuccessful effort to establish a settlement in Newfoundland in 1583. When Gilbert was lost at sea on the homeward voyage, his half brother, Sir Walter Raleigh, was granted a renewal of the royal patent to colonize. Raleigh planted a colony on Roanoke Island, on the North Carolina coast, in 1585. Indian troubles and the tension with Spain led the settlers to accept Drake's offer to take them home when he stopped there in 1586, after a raid on the West Indies. A few weeks later a supply ship arrived at the colony and found it deserted. Fifteen men were left behind to hold the settlement. When a new expedition arrived at the settlement in 1587, it found no survivors. A new shipload of supplies for the colony was expected the following year, but its departure was delayed due to the growing problems with Spain. It was not until after the Spanish Armada was defeated in 1588 that it became possible to proceed with the dispatch of the supply vessel. Even then, it did not reach Roanoke Island until August 1590. No trace of the settlers was ever found. Only the word Croatoan carved on a tree, evidently the name of a nearby island held by friendly Indians, suggested that the colonists had departed of their own accord. During its brief life, the colony was protected by a fort which may have flown the flag bearing the red cross of St. George.

The merchants of London and Plymouth now petitioned the English crown for a patent to establish a colony. Under the terms of the royal patent of 1606, two Virginia companies were established. The London Company was authorized to settle the area between 34 degrees and 41 degrees north latitude. The Plymouth Company was to establish a settlement between 38 degrees north and 45 degrees north, except that neither group was to settle within one hundred miles of the other. When each group made its first settlement, it was to be awarded all lands fifty miles to the north and south and one hundred miles into the interior of the country.

The London Company established the first successful English colony in America at Jamestown, Virginia, in 1607. The Plymouth Company made an unsuccessful effort to establish a colony at Popham Beach, Maine, in 1607–08. A group of English separatists who had settled in the Netherlands now opened negotiations with the London Company for permission to establish a colony within their domains. But when they arrived off Massachusetts in 1620, they decided to settle there even though it was outside of the company's boundaries.

The settlement at Plymouth was followed by others in what were to become known by 1662 as Massachusetts Bay (which included present-day Maine), New Hampshire, Rhode Island, Connecticut, and Maryland. By 1650 it was estimated that the English colonies in America had a population of 52,000.

Notes

The basic source for information on the exploration and discoveries in North America is Samuel Eliot Morison, *The European Exploration of America: The Northern Voyages, 500-1600* (New York, 1971) and *The Southern Voyages* (New York, 1974). In *The Northern Voyages*, Morison makes a distinction between the Northmen, who were mainly peaceful traders, and the Vikings, who were armed raiders, pirates, and freebooters. They also used different kinds of ships. That distinction is used in this text when we refer to Leif Ericson and his followers as Northmen. For background on the Northmen and the Vikings see Knut Gjerset, *History of the Norwegian People* (New York, 1932). A popular account on the finding of the site of Vinland at L'Anse aux Meadows is Helge Ingstad, "Vinland Found," *National Geographic Magazine* 126 (1964): 708–34. For a more scholarly and more complete account see his book, *Westward to Vinland: The Discovery of Pre-Columbian Norse House-sites in North America* (New York, 1969).

Columbus and his voyages are described in Samuel Eliot Morison, *Admiral of the Ocean Sea* (Boston, 1946). Morison's *Portuguese Voyages to America in the Fifteenth Century* (Cambridge, 1940) is still useful for the contributions of that nation to the knowledge about the Americas. Information on some of the famous aspects of Spanish exploration may be found in Cleve Hallenbeck, *Alvar Nunez Cabeza De Vaca: The Journey and Route of the First European to Cross the Continent of North America, 1534–1536* (Glendale, 1940); Herbert E. Bolton, ed., *Spanish Exploration in the Southeast, 1542–1706* (New York, 1911), and his *Coronado, Knight of Pueblos and Plains* (New York, 1949). An old but enduring study of the Coronado expedition is George Parker Winship, *The Coronado Expedition, 1540–1542*, originally published in 1896 as a part of the annual report of the Bureau of American Ethnology, Smithsonian Institute. This work was reprinted with a new introduction (Chicago, 1964).

Henry Hudson's voyage for the Dutch is described in Morison's *The Northern Voyages*. Material on the settlements of the Dutch East India Company and the Dutch West India Company may be found in Edmund B. O'Callaghan, *History of New Netherlands*, 2 vols. (New York, 1846–48). For descriptions of the flags see George H. Preble, *History of the Flag of the United States of America* (Boston, 1880), pp. 223–24.

Information concerning the flag used in New Sweden was sent to Admiral Furlong by Gerhard Albe, the foremost Swedish authority on the subject, in a letter of April 6, 1960, and by Amandus Johnson of the American Swedish Historical Foundation in a letter of October 3, 1967. Both are in the Furlong Flag Files, National Museum of American History, Smithsonian Institution. Supplemental information came from Amandus Johnson, *Swedish Settlements on the Delaware, 1638–44* (Philadelphia, 1914).

The basic work on French flags is Gustave A. Desjardins, *Recherches sur les drapeaux francais* (Paris, 1874). More recent works relating to North America are Milo Quaife, "Flags Over Detroit," *Detroit Historical Museum Bulletin* 7 (1951): 5–9; and René Chartrand, "Les Drapeaux en Nouvelle-France," *Conservation Canada* 1 (1974): 24–26. This article has been translated into English and reprinted in *The Flag Bulletin* 15 (1976): 13–21.

For earlier accounts of Sir Walter Raleigh's efforts to establish a colony on Roanoke Island see Increase Niles Tarbox, *Sir Walter Raleigh and His Colony in America* (Boston, 1884); and Conway W. Sams, *The Conquest of Virginia: The First Attempt* (Norfolk, 1924).

Fig. 12   A contemporary engraving of the Ship of the Line,
The Ark Royal, *built in 1587*
The British Museum

CHAPTER *2*

English Flags on Land and Sea

In 1588 Spain launched its formidable Armada against the British Isles. Its defeat (and subsequent destruction in a storm) marks the emergence of England as a major power. To meet the threat of the Armada, Queen Elizabeth I supplemented her force of 34 ships with 163 belonging to her subjects—a maritime equivalent of what had been common practice for raising medieval armies. While no permanent maritime fighting force emerged in England until the time of Cromwell, by late medieval times a distinction was drawn between ships belonging to the crown (the forerunners of flagships) and ships and crews temporarily in the service of the sovereign. A contemporary engraving of the *Ark Royal,* built for the queen in 1587, shows it festooned with various flags, including the Royal Standard at the mainmast (Figure 12).

It was Queen Elizabeth's father, King Henry VIII, who first built a private "navy" of ships designed expressly for fighting. The existing administrative structure had included a minor official whose title was Keeper of the Shippes. But King Henry greatly expanded the responsibilities of the official concerned with the jurisdiction, command, and administration of the navy, and endowed him with the title of High Admiral or Lord Admiral. He also insisted that the high admiral should personally command the fleet during any major engagement. So it was that when the English forces went out to fight the Armada— although the actual fighting leader was Francis Drake—Lord Charles Howard of Effingham went along as the lord admiral.

Given this arrangement, it was only natural to designate the ship that carried the lord admiral. The situation became more complex when a combined English and Dutch fleet was sent against Cadiz in 1596. The fleet was divided into five squadrons, four English and one Dutch. A contemporary account of the expedition contains a series of colored diagrams of the flags of the admirals in charge of the various squadrons, flags that appear to have been stern ensigns designed for this special occasion.

About 1574, during the reign of Queen Elizabeth I, a green and white ensign was adopted. Toward the end of Elizabeth's reign, the stripes were sometimes diagonal.

27

Fig. 13 The Ark Royal *about 1588: note
the striping on flags on the mizzen
mast and at the stern
The British Museum*

The Lord High Admiral, Howard, flew the Royal Standard at the mainmast
and the Cross of St. George flag at the foremast. The vice admiral under him
flew a green and white striped ensign at his foremast. The rear admiral in the
lord admiral's squadron flew a similar flag at his mizzen mast (Figure 13).

The squadron under the Earl of Essex flew only the Cross of St. George at
the mainmast of the flagship. The flagships of his vice admirals and rear
admirals flew the Cross of St. George with horizontal blue bars at the fore and
mizzen masts respectively.

Lord Thomas Howe, the vice admiral of the fleet, flew the flag of St. George
at the foremast. At the main mast, as admiral of his own squadron, he flew a
flag with the Cross of St. George in the canton and a field of green and white
horizontal stripes. The vice and rear admirals of this squadron flew a similar
flag at their fore and mizzen mastheads respectively.

The rear admiral of the fleet, Sir Walter Raleigh, flew the Cross of St.
George at his mizzen mast, and he and the vice and rear admirals of his own
squadron flew plain white flags at the main, fore, and mizzen masts respectively. So it was that early in the history of the maritime fighting force of

28

Fig. 14   The Cross of St. Andrew flag

England there existed both uniformity and diversity in designating the ships of the various admirals and their subordinates within a squadron.

After James VI of Scotland took the throne as King James I of England in 1603 it became appropriate to have a flag representing both Scotland and England. The flag of Scotland was the white Cross of St. Andrew on a blue field (Figure 14). Although probably used by the Scots much earlier, the earliest extant record of this X-type cross dates from July 1, 1385. Other evidence indicates that the contrasting background of the white saltire was of more than one color, but predominantly blue.

Despite being joined in the person of King James, the kingdoms of Scotland and England each had their own Parliament and national jealousies were strong. Seeking a symbolic manifestation of unity, in 1606 King James issued a proclamation joining the flags of St. George and St. Andrew in a national standard (Figure 15). This order applied to merchantmen and to ships of the king.

Instead of promoting unity, however, the proclamation stirred up great opposition in both countries. The English did not propose to give up the old

Fig. 15   The British or Union flag

flag of the Cross of St. George without a struggle. Even more than the English, the Scots wanted their own flag. But if the two crosses had to be joined at all, the Cross of St. Andrew should pass in front of the Cross of St. George. Some Scots went so far as to fly such flags. Scottish shipmasters appealed to the king, but to no avail. So the mariners worked out their own compromise—to fly either the English or the Scottish flag as well as the combined flag. When the *Goodspeed,* the *Susan Constant,* and the *Discovery* arrived off Virginia in 1607 to plant the first permanent English settlement in America, they all carried the Cross of St. George flag (Figure 16). In addition, the *Susan Constant,* the flagship of the expedition, carried the new "British" flag at its mainmast. It was not until the funeral of King James I in 1625 that one finds the first use of the term "Union" to describe the combined flags of St. George and St. Andrew.

In 1634 King Charles I, the son of King James I, proclaimed that the Union flag should be flown only by ships of the Royal Navy or ships employed in the king's service and pay. The proclamation also stipulated that ships belonging to the king's subjects from the south of Great Britain should carry the flag of the Cross of St. George (Figure 17), while those from Scotland should carry the flag of the Cross of St. Andrew. Unlike King James's proclamation of 1606, King Charles's order made no mention of hoisting flags at the masthead. This may have been due to the introduction a year or two before of the "jack," the king's colors placed on the bowsprit.

When King Charles I was executed in 1649, a victim of the English Civil War, the union between England and Scotland came to an end and the Union flag was discontinued. The English Commonwealth government decreed that all ships in the service of the state should fly the old Cross of St. George flag. After Scotland was reunited with England in 1654, it again became mandatory for the St. Andrew Cross to be borne on the arms of the Commonwealth. In addition, the arms of Ireland were placed in the center of the new Union Jack.

30

Fig. 16

The Godspeed, Susan Constant, *and* Discovery *at Jamestown in 1607; painted by Lieutenant Commander Griffith Bailey Coale, USNR (Ret.) in 1949 after eighteen months of intensive research on the period*

Virginia State Museum, Richmond, Va.

Fig. 17   The Cross of St. George flag

In 1660, at the invitation of Parliament, the son of Charles I returned to be proclaimed King Charles II. On May 5, 1660, three days before Charles's return, the Council of State ordered the Commissioners of the Navy "to take care that such Standards, flags and Jacke Colours for the ffleete be forthwith prepared as were in use before 1648. . . ." The Commissioners were also ordered to send painters and carvers to change any ornamentation on ships that might be inappropriate. Under the restored monarchy the Union flag reverted to its original form, and the right to fly it remained the special prerogative of ships in the service of the state.

Owners of merchant ships fought for many years for the right to fly the Union colors in a jack flag* on the bowsprit. Why did they want this right? A ship that flew the Union flag received greater respect. In the Channel foreign ships were obliged to salute those colors, and in foreign ports customs duties could often be avoided. There was also an aesthetic reason. The Union flag was more striking and more visible at sea than the Cross of St. George with its white background. So the misuse of the king's flag by merchants continued into the twentieth century before it finally was stopped.

On May 11, 1666, during the reign of King James II, orders were issued to seize any ship and master who "shall presume to Wear the Kings Jack." After merchant captains began contriving imitations of the forbidden flag that were sufficiently accurate to deceive the representatives of foreign powers, a new proclamation was issued in 1674 that called for seizing such illegal flags and punishing those who used them. Merchant ships were permitted to fly only "the Flag and Jack White, with a Red Cross (commonly called Saint George's Cross) passing right through the same; and the Ensign Red, with a like cross in a Canton White, at the upper corner thereof next to the staff." Yet, despite this proscription, merchant mariners continued to fly the king's jack.

---

* A jack flag is one corresponding in appearance to the union or canton of the national ensign.

Fig. 19   An eighteenth century engraving of the British Red Ensign

During the War of the League of Augsburg (1689–97) a question arose as to what flag should be worn by armed vessels that operated under official licenses as privateers. The British Admiralty decided in 1694 that they would be allowed a special "burgee jack" or the Union flag with a red border on the bottom and the fly edges. The name was an allusion to Bugia in Algeria, a seventeenth century haven for pirates. This flag therefore became associated with piracy. Perhaps the Admiralty thought that privateers were rather close to pirates. Yet, despite the undesirable connotations, the combination made for an attractive jack.

In July 1701 the Admiralty complained to the Privy Council—which reviewed legislation passed by the various American colonies—about the practice of colonial governors in commissioning vessels for public service duties. Captains of vessels commissioned in this way felt entitled to use the Union Jack. The Privy Council instructed the colonial governors that vessels they commissioned were to use the same jack prescribed for warships—the Union Jack—but with a large and distinctive white shield superimposed in the middle of the flag. From July 31, 1701, until 1707 this was the official flag flown by merchant ships in British North America while engaged in the public service (Figure 18).

In 1702, during the reign of Queen Anne, another proclamation forbidding the use of the Union flag by merchant ships was issued. For the most part it repeated the language of that of 1694. The new document did nothing to stop the practices, and despite the special arrangements made for them, ships from the British North American colonies were now being found among the offenders.

While the use of a distinctive flag or ensign at the stern of the ship had become common during the sixteenth century, there was no uniformity of design. Both merchant ships and warships flew a flag that featured the Cross of St. George in the center; sometimes the red St. George Cross was placed in the corner of the flag as a canton, and stripes of various colors were added. When William Baffin, in the service of the English Muscovy Company, sailed up

Davis Strait in 1616 and established a new record in the penetration of the far north, he carried a distinctive ensign with red, green, and blue horizontal stripes. A list of ensigns stored at the royal shipyard at Deptford, near London, in 1633 shows ten different types of flags, including a white ensign with the king's arms, a white ensign with a rose and crown, and one with a red and white rose. Despite this diversity, however, by this time a movement toward uniformity was already underway.

In 1625 the red ensign came officially into use. This consisted of the Cross of St. George in a white canton on a field of red. Merchant ships were formally given the right to fly this ensign in 1663, and public and private vessels both used it until 1707. In that year the Union flag in a square design replaced the Cross of St. George as the canton of the red ensign. This change had a special significance, for in 1707 the separate parliaments, councils, and navies of England and Scotland were dissolved and superseded by those of the United Kingdom (Figure 19).

While these changes were taking place with respect to the royal and national flags and jacks, the Navy had developed an elaborate protocol of flag usage. In 1620, for the first time in British history, a fleet was distributed into organized squadrons before it set out for the Mediterranean. The senior squadron under the admiral of the fleet was allotted red flags which were carried on the mast of his ships. The vice admiral's squadron had blue flags carried on the fore masts. The rear admiral's squadron had white flags on the mizzen or rear masts. This precedent became established custom.* (Figure 20).

Later, during the Commonwealth period, the squadrons were further divided into three divisions. The main masts flew the flags of admirals, the fore mast flew those of vice admirals, and the mizzen masts were for the rear admirals. Now, instead of three admirals there were nine—one for each division and three for each squadron. These officers were known as flag men and later as flag officers or as flag ranks. During the Restoration period the squadron in the van became the White, the center was the Red, and the rear was the Blue.

By the early part of the eighteenth century the single great fleet with its three squadrons, each subdivided into three divisions, had given way to smaller fleets which usually had three squadrons but no divisions. But, even though the posts normally occupied by admirals of the blue, rear admirals of the white, and similar ranks, ceased to exist, the ranks themselves persisted, as did the term flag officer. By the middle of the eighteenth century the Royal Navy was a very flag conscious service (Figure 21).

Military Flags of the Colonial Period

For the defense of their settlements in the New World, the English colonists had to rely primarily on their own militia companies. Such units drew upon English military precedents in establishing their colors.

In Cromwell's time the flags carried by military companies were called "colours." There was no regimental color as such. Instead, the flag carried by the first company was the flag of its commander (in those times a colonel). If the flag of the first company or colonel's company was red, then the flags of all

---

* See above, p. [27], for an earlier example of a division of a fleet into squadrons.

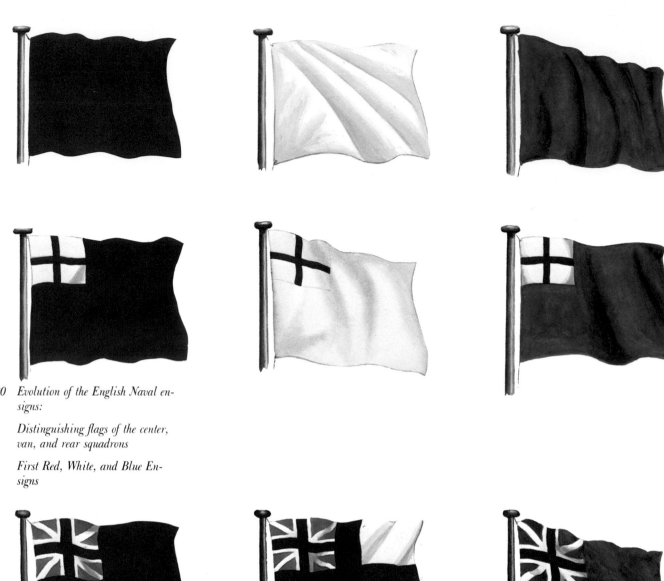

Fig. 20 Evolution of the English Naval ensigns:

Distinguishing flags of the center, van, and rear squadrons

First Red, White, and Blue Ensigns

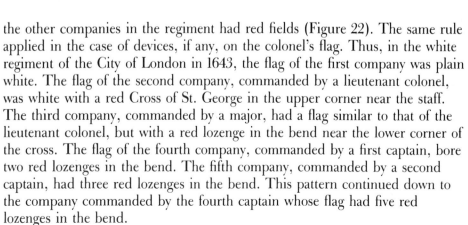

Fig. 21 The British Red, White, and Blue Ensigns of 1707

the other companies in the regiment had red fields (Figure 22). The same rule applied in the case of devices, if any, on the colonel's flag. Thus, in the white regiment of the City of London in 1643, the flag of the first company was plain white. The flag of the second company, commanded by a lieutenant colonel, was white with a red Cross of St. George in the upper corner near the staff. The third company, commanded by a major, had a flag similar to that of the lieutenant colonel, but with a red lozenge in the bend near the lower corner of the cross. The flag of the fourth company, commanded by a first captain, bore two red lozenges in the bend. The fifth company, commanded by a second captain, had three red lozenges in the bend. This pattern continued down to the company commanded by the fourth captain whose flag had five red lozenges in the bend.

34

Fig. 22 British Infantry colors of the Crom-well era:

Colonel's; Lieutenant Colonel's; Major's; First Captain's; Second Captain's; Third Captain's; Fourth Captain's

Fig. 23   Flag of a captain's infantry company in Boston, 1679

In the case of the red regiment of the City of London, the colonel's color was a plain red flag. The lieutenant colonel's company had a red flag with the red Cross of St. George in a white canton. The flag of the major's third company was like that of the lieutenant colonel's except that it added a white flame—or *pile wavy* in heraldic terminology—emerging diagonally from the corner of the canton. The fourth company's flag had two flames, and so on through the other companies.

In the other color regiments—blue, green, yellow, and so forth—differentiations were made with trefoils and other heraldic devices. In time the flame as used by the red company became recognized as the device used on the flag of the major. The design, though not the colors, of the colonel's, the lieutenant colonel's, and the major's flags became fixed. Likewise, the flags of the captains were distinguished by different devices in regular numbered arrangement. The British army discontinued the system of designating regiments by the color of the field in its flags after the reorganization of 1661, except for those of the Guards.

The old system also persisted in various colonial militias. As late as the mid-1690s Maryland assigned the colors of Horse, Foot, and Dragoon companies in the various counties on the following basis: St. Mary's, red; Kent, blue; Anne Arundel, white; Calvert, yellow; Charles, orange; Baltimore, green; Talbot, purple; Somerset, the Union or Jack Flag; Dorchester, buff; Cecil, crimson. Prince George's county was assigned the St. George's Cross, a red cross on a white field.

In the American colonies there was a comparatively small number of men in each settlement. Usually there was no need for units larger than a company, commanded by a captain.* Thus, in the absence of such officers as colonels and majors, the first captain commanded the first company and the company's color would then be his flag (Figure 23).

The flag of the military company of Saybrook, Connecticut, in 1675 was red with a red cross in the white canton. It also carried a blue ball or bullet, probably in the field, as a mark of distinction, possibly of the first captain's company. In another case, the flag of the company at Newbury, Massachusetts, in 1684 had a green field with a red cross in the white canton. The order for making this flag reads: "The number of bullets [musket balls] to be put into your colors for distinction may be left out at present without damage to the making of them." This omission suggests that marks of distinction may have been left off in earlier times because there were fewer companies. Also the need for one town to distinguish another town's company was slight.

As far as we know, the English system for company colors was first adopted in the colonies in December 1636 when Massachusetts Bay ranked its militia companies into three regiments. A portrait of Captain Thomas Savage of Boston, painted in 1679, also shows the English system of company flags. Three flags may be seen in front of a regiment: a plain red flag, a red flag with a red cross in a white canton, and a red flag with a white canton and red cross as well as a white flame or blaze extending from the lower outer corner of the canton across the field toward the opposite lower corner. These flags were the colors of the colonel, the lieutenant colonel, and major, respectively.

---

* In seventeenth century America the first lieutenant of each of the first three companies was often called captain-lieutenant. He drew the pay of a captain and commanded the company when the field officers were busy with other duties. See Howard M. Chapin, "Colonial Military Flags," *New England Quarterly* 4(1931):451.

Fig. 24   Flag of the Three County Troop

We also have a description of flags used during a mock battle in Boston on October 19, 1685. In his diary Judge Samuel Sewall told of "White colours with a red cross, and Red Colours." These may have been the flags of the lieutenant colonel of one regiment and a colonel of another regiment. It is also possible that they reflect the new system of company colors adopted in England in 1661. This was introduced by the king's soldiers in Virginia in 1676, and by soldiers who came to New England with Governor Andros. If the flags seen by Sewall were a preview of the new system, then the colors were those of the lieutenant colonel and colonel, respectively.

Under the terms of the reorganization of the British army in 1661, the colors of the colonel remained unchanged. In all the other companies, the red cross in the white canton was superseded by a red cross extending from edge to edge on the flag's vertical and horizontal axis. In cases where the field was not white, the red cross was edged in white. With the flag of the major's company, the flame was retained, but placed in the first quarter. The company's number was often designated by roman numerals instead of repeated symbols. During the time of King James II, the colonel's color sometimes had a device in the center. Distinctive devices also were used on the colors of the lieutenant colonel and major.

The five companies of British soldiers that arrived in Virginia in 1676 carried five different flags. These were: a red cross on a white field, with a lion passant crowned in gold on the cross; a red cross on a white field with the royal oak crowned in gold on the cross; a red cross with white edges on a blue field; a red cross on a field of white and lemon, equally mixed, and the cipher I D Y, for James, Duke of York, in gold on the cross; and a red cross edged with white on a green field.

The so-called Andros flag, associated with the arrival in New England of Governor Sir Edmund Andros in 1686, had a white field with a red cross

37

interlaced by the king's cipher, *J.R.* (James Rex), and surmounted by a crown. This same design appeared on the first captain's colors of the First Foot Guards of 1685, a company of which was sent to serve under Andros. Thus a unit flag mistakenly became identified as the flag of a hated governor.

In colonial America there was some use of flags by mounted units. A Massachusetts Bay cavalry company raised in 1659 in the counties of Essex, Suffolk, and Middlesex was known as the Three County Troop. Its flag or "cornett" was made in England of red damask on which was painted in gold, black, and silver an arm coming out of a dark cloud and holding a sword upright. Across the flag was a ribbon that was supposed to bear the inscription: "Three County Troop." Instead, the artist misspelled or misread what he was to copy and painted "THRE COUNTY TROM" (Figure 24). Many members of this troop served in the campaign against the Indians known as King Philip's War (1675–76), but there is no evidence that they participated as a part of the troop.

During the early years of the reign of King Charles II (1600–85), the cavalry used a square flag, often called a cornet after the rank of the officer who held it. Later, during the reign of King James II, the cavalry carried two flags. The square one, now called a standard, was accompanied by a second flag or guidon that was slit to produce a two-tailed effect.

The Crossless Flags

One of the most intriguing stories about flags during the colonial period concerns Roger Williams and the cross in the English flag. For most of the details we are indebted to the Reverend William Hubbard, who arrived in New England in 1635, a year after the controversy began. Hubbard, who became a close friend of many of the persons involved, subsequently published an account of the episode in his *General History of New England*.

Williams, the acting head of the church at Salem, Massachusetts, was concerned about eliminating symbols of superstition, in fulfillment of the spirit of the Reformation. He contended that the red Cross of St. George in the English flag, given to the king of England by the pope as an ensign of victory, was a relic of the antichrist.

Inspired by Williams's views, John Endicott, an associate or member of the governor's council in 1634, ordered the ensign bearer at Salem to cut the red cross out of the king's colors. This prompted Richard Browne, the ruling elder of the church of Watertown, to complain in the name of the rest of the freemen to the governor's council, which considered itself comparable to an upper house of a legislature and also functioned as a court in certain circumstances. Browne declared that defacing the king's colors might be interpreted as an act of rebellion. The council, or Court of the Assistants, heard arguments from both sides but did nothing about the matter except to order the ensign bearer to appear at its next session. Apparently the case against him was dropped.

By the time of the next meeting of the council the controversy had spread. Several soldiers had refused to follow the defaced flag in their training. A newly formed group, the Commissioners of Military Affairs, had been granted power over life and limb, but were unable to proceed on this matter. The Assistants decided to write to a Mr. Downing in England, presumably the

Fig. 25   The Crossless Flag

brother-in-law of Governer John Winthrop, to present the facts of the case and to solicit British opinion. In this letter they expressed their dislike of the action and their determination to punish the offenders. At the same time, they expressed doubts about the use of the cross in the flag. The letter was apparently written with an eye to protecting themselves in the event that the news of the removal of the cross created any difficulties in England.

The flag question was presented to a group of ministers who met in Boston in January 1635, but they could not reach a decision. At the meeting of the legislature or General Court in March 1635 the matter was again discussed without reaching a decision. Meanwhile, the Commissioners of Military Affairs ordered the defaced colors laid aside.

A committee, chosen by the people and the magistrates, reported to the legislature in May 1635 that Endicott had acted without authority in ordering the cross cut out, and that his action risked incurring the ill will of the English government. It recommended that he be admonished and disqualified from holding office for a year.

This disposed of that matter, but Endicott's action and the views of Roger Williams had raised the question of a proper flag for the colony. It was decided that this matter would receive further consideration from the legislature. In the meantime, the ministers promised to seek advice from England while the citizenry tried to agree among themselves as to what should be done. Some were already proposing that the flag be adorned with a red and white rose.

Apparently no decision was reached by this means, for in March or April 1636 the legislature ordered the military commissioners to decide on the colors of every militia company. The commissioners decreed that the units would carry a flag without a cross (Figure 25). A decision was also made to use a flag with the king's arms on the fort on Castle Island in Boston Harbor. Whether this was actually done at this time is doubtful, but the strong feelings engendered by these events emerged in two controversial incidents connected with the fort.

The first of these took place in May 1636 when a lieutenant in charge of the bastion, or projection from the fort, went on board the merchant ship *St. Patrick* while it was anchored below the fort and compelled the master to strike his flag. The master complained and the lieutenant was forced to make a public apology. A second incident, a few days later, was the result of statements made by the master's mate of the ship *Hector* to the effect that failure to show the king's colors at the fort marked the local people as traitors. The master, ordered to appear before the Court, was found guilty and allowed to go free after making an apology.

Governor Winthrop then asked the other masters of vessels if they had any grievances. The masters said that they wanted to see the king's colors displayed at the fort. The governor and two of his advisers decided that since the fort was the king's property it was appropriate that his colors be displayed there. Therefore, in June 1636, Governor Winthrop issued an order that the fort should display the king's colors when ships passed by.

As for the rest of the colony, the red flag with a white canton and no cross was the ensign used for some time after 1636—during the Pequot War (1636–37), for example, and during King Philip's War (1675–76). If New England troops carried any colors at all during the Indian campaigns, which seems doubtful, it would have been this flag.

Fig. 26   The flag of Captain Noyes's company

Fig. 27   The New England Flag

When the English Parliament revived and adopted the old standard of the Cross of St. George as the colors of England in 1651, the General Court, the legislative body of Massachusetts, ordered:

as the Court conceive the old English colors now used by the Parliament to be a necessary badge of distinction betwixt the English and other nations in all places of the world, till the state of England alter the same, which we very much desire, we, being of the same nation, have therefore ordered that the captain of the Castle [the fort] shall advance the aforesaid colors of England upon all necessary occasions.

This appears to mean that the king's colors were again displayed from the fort on Castle Island, and by inference that the flag without a cross was still used elsewhere.

In 1665 the Royal Commissioners proposed to the General Court of Massachusetts that the laws of the colony be revised to read "that all the masters of vessells & captaines of foote companjes doe carry the true colours of England, by which they may be knowne to be his majesties legittmate subjects." This suggests that the ships and militia of Massachusetts were still carrying the flag without a cross. In any case, nothing seems to have been done to implement the suggestion of the commissioners on any wholesale basis.

One indication that the crossless flag was still being flown in 1680 comes from the account of two Dutchmen, Jasper Dankers and Peter Sluyter, who visited Boston in July of that year. In his journal Dankers wrote: "I observed that while the English flag or color has a red ground with a small white field in the uppermost corner where there is a red cross, they have here dispensed with this cross in their colors, and preserved the rest."

Apparently some militia companies did replace the cross in their ensigns, if the 1679 portrait of Captain Thomas Savage is accurate. In any case, Judge Samuel Sewall noted in his diary that the subject of restoring the cross to the militia flags was discussed with company officers in 1681. Most opposed the change, though one did restore the cross to the flag. Also, in the town of Newbury in 1684, the militia adopted a green flag with a white canton and a red cross (Figure 26). Despite the strong objections of Judge Sewall, the cross was restored to all flags in Boston in August 1686, and throughout the colony shortly thereafter.

The story of the crossless flag between 1634 and 1686 suggests the rise and decline of strong religious feelings in Massachusetts. Eventually, people like Judge Sewall became a minority. With the passage of time there was less public interest in the origin of the cross, and the flag in its entirety was viewed simply as a political emblem.

The New England Flag

During the reign of King James II (1685–88) some New Englanders wished to use a flag that had a distinctive association with their region. They chose a pine tree and added it to the canton that already carried the cross of St. George (Figure 27). The choice of this symbol may have been related to the minting of the flat, square pine tree shilling by Massachusetts between 1652 and 1680. Actually, though the mint was closed in 1680, the colonists continued to make these shillings using the older (and legal) date. Their actions were prompted by the acute shortage of circulating currency in the colonies.

Fig. 28   The New England Flag on the Covens and Mortier flag sheet. Furlong Flag Files

The use of the tree may also have appealed to those who were weary of the discussion of the appropriateness of using the cross on the flag. A pine tree, added to the first quarter of the canton, presumably helped to secularize the flag. Just when the practice started has not been determined. The earliest known reference to it is in a manuscript flag book belonging to a Lieutenant Graydon, dated 1686, in the Pepysian Library at Magdalen College, Cambridge, England. This contains color sketches that were presumably drawn and painted by Graydon. Among the sketches is one showing a white flag with the red cross of St. George in the canton. In the first quarter of the canton is a green oak tree outlined in black and sprinkled with gold dots.

Another reference to a New England flag appears in *Le Neptune François* (Amsterdam, 1693). It is illustrated as a red flag with a white canton and the red cross of St. George. In the first quarter of the cross there is a green tree that resembles a pine rather than an oak. The text confirms this color arrangement.

In 1701 an Englishman, John Beaumont, published the third edition of *The Present State of the Universe*, which carries an illustration of the "New England Ensign." This shows a flag with a red field and a white canton bearing a red cross. In the first quarter of the cross is a green oak tree outlined in black. This illustration is not the same as the one that appeared in *Le Neptune François*, thus suggesting the use of different sources for the same information.

Additional evidence comes from the work of Alexander Justice, another Englishman, who published *A General Treatise of the Dominion of the Sea and a Complete Body of the Sea Laws* (London, 1705). Here the New England ensign is shown with a red field and a white canton bearing a red cross. In the first quarter of the canton is a crudely drawn tree resembling a palm more than a pine, but possibly intended as an oak or willow.

A Dutch book by Carl Allard called the *Ship Builder* (Amsterdam, 1705) says that the New England flag is blue with a white canton and a red cross, and that in the first quarter of the canton is a globe showing the Western Hemisphere. It is likely that this design is the result of a mistake in copying the illustration in *Le Neptune François*. In that case the text called for a red field, but the hatching lines on the illustration indicated blue. Perhaps the Dutch publisher took his cue from the illustration and not the text. On the matter of the globe, the absence of any contemporary American or English source for such a design suggests that the artist misjudged the sketch of the tree shown in *Le Neptune François* and thought it looked like a globe on a stand.

The situation was further confused when Pieter Schenck published his flag sheet in Amsterdam in 1711. Entitled *Schouw-Park aller Scheeps-Vlaggen*, or pictures of all the ships' flags, this sheet shows the New England flag with tincture lines indicating a blue flag with a white canton and a red cross. Again, a globe is depicted in the first quarter of the canton. No color is given for the globe, but it was outlined in black.

In this case the design was apparently based on a French sheet, *Table des Pavillons*, published by Covens and Mortier in Amsterdam about 1711 (Figure 28). Later D. Mortier published *Les Pavillons on Bannieres . . .* (Amsterdam, 1718) in which the New England flag was again illustrated with a globe. But this time, after describing the colors of the flag, the editor added a note on the significance of the globe. It was, he said, an allusion to the fact that America was called the New World.

41

The Covens and Mortier flag sheet was copied by a German publisher. This time the vertical or longitudinal lines were left off the globe but the horizontal or latitudinal lines were included. In a subsequent reprint another German publisher mistook the horizontal lines for tincture lines and the globe on that sheet was colored blue. From time to time various copies of the Covens and Mortier flag sheet were issued by various publishers until the first English version appeared in 1783 in a book by Carrington Bowles. Here the globe is uncolored but outlined in black and the flag appears under its original French caption: "Pavillon de la Nouvelle Angleterre en Amerique." By this time the American Revolution was ending, and there was no attempt to depict this New England flag other than as something that had been in use in earlier times.

Despite its long publishing history, there is no evidence that the flag with the globe was ever used. There is also no evidence to indicate how extensively the flag with a tree in the canton was in use either in New England or on the ships of New England. It seems a likely possibility that the tree flag was used at least in its jack form during the reign of King James II (1685–88), and as an ensign during the years when King William III was on the throne of England (1689–1702). In 1707, during the reign of Queen Anne, a proclamation was issued regulating the use of the British flags. It required that the Burgee flag, or red ensign with the two crosses of union in the canton, be used on merchant vessels. Not only was this proclamation published in the Boston *News-Letter* on January 26, 1707, but a woodcut of the proper flag was also included. This was the first illustration printed in an American newspaper. It is assumed that the Queen's proclamation put an end to the use of the New England flag in 1707.

Infantry Flags

Following the Act of Union of 1707 there was a change in infantry flags. The colonel's colors now had the union introduced in the canton. The Union flag itself, frequently with a device on it, now became the colors of the lieutenant colonel, as well as the basis for the major's flag. Presumably the union was introduced into the cavalry standards about this same time. It is known that the cavalry standards were square or rectangular as late as 1720 and that they sometimes carried a union in the canton. Before 1727 the number of cavalry standards was reduced to one per squadron.

Under the terms of a warrant issued on September 14, 1743, the number of colors of the infantry was reduced to two. The first color was to be a Union flag. The second was to be the same as the uniform facing of the particular regiment and the union in the canton. In cases where the facings were red or white, the second color of the regiment was to be the red Cross of St. George in a white field and the Union flag in the canton. The first flag came to be called the "King's Colours" and the second the regimental color. Also, in the center of each color the number of the regiment was to be painted in gold roman numerals. This was to be surrounded by a wreath of roses and thistles on one stalk except in the case of those regiments authorized to wear ancient badges or royal devices. After 1743 these regulations governed all English infantry regiments, including those stationed in the North American colonies.

The British system appears to have influenced the Continental Congress's Board of War, which in 1780 decreed that each American regiment should have two flags: the flag of the United States and another with a field of the same color as the facing of the regimental uniform.

Fig. 29   Flag of the British East India Company

East India Company Flags

Other flags that are of interest because of their similarity to the later Continental or Grand Union flag are those used by the British East India Company (Figure 29). In 1600, near the close of Elizabeth's reign, a royal charter was granted to a joint stock company described as "the Governor and Company of Merchants of London Trading into the East Indies." It became more popularly known as the East India Company. The charter given by the queen awarded the company a monopoly on the trade of the east between the Cape of Good Hope and the Strait of Magellan, as well as full political and military power in the posts it might establish. It was expected that the company would exploit the rich colonial empire established by the Portuguese in the East Indies and India. Portugal was then temporarily under the throne of Spain, but since the defeat of the Spanish Armada Spain was not able to protect all of its own possessions.

There is evidence that as early as 1616 the company had a flag with a cross on it, for in that year the Japanese objected to the use of this symbol of Christianity. There is also a sketch of a striped flag dated 1656 in a travel account by Peter Mundy.

When Edward Barlow, a seaman, made a voyage to India in 1670, he kept a journal and illustrated it with colored sketches that have been preserved. Three of these sketches show ships at Bombay, Calicut, and near Surat that carry flags with red and white stripes and the St. George's Cross. The number of stripes is usually nine, eleven, or thirteen. Barlow made another voyage and additional sketches in 1683. The later sketches show flags with seven and even one with nineteen stripes. Barlow's pictures also indicate that in addition to the company's flag the ships carried a red ensign with the Cross of St. George in a white canton.

In 1676 the Admiralty called to the company's attention the proclamation of King Charles II of two years previously that forbade merchant ships to wear more than two flags, the red ensign and the Cross of St. George as a jack. The result was a compromise formula whereby the company was forbidden to fly its flag north of St. Helena Island.

The East India Company's flag is illustrated in the third edition of John Beaumont's book, *The Present State of the Universe*, published in London in 1701. This shows a flag with seven red and white stripes and a white canton bearing the red Cross of St. George.

After the legislative union of England and Scotland in 1707, Queen Anne ordered that the Union flag be substituted for the Cross of St. George in navy and merchant vessels. There is some evidence that the company followed the same rule in regard to its own flag. A painting of the harbor at Bombay, one of six paintings purchased by the company in 1732 for its London offices, shows four vessels with the red ensign, and a striped East India Company flag with the Union jack as its canton. Especially interesting is the fact that the company's flag is shown with thirteen red and white stripes, and that both the first and the last stripe are red. When Ireland was incorporated into the Union in 1801, the company changed its flag to show the new Union Jack.

On the basis of pictorial evidence and reasonable inference from extant company records, Sir Charles Fawcett argued in the *Mariner's Mirror* in 1937 that the East India Company's flag was identical with the Continental or Grand Union flag flown in the early years of the American Revolution. Despite the proclamation forbidding its use north of St. Helena, it was certainly known to colonial seamen as a result of their wide-ranging voyages. Fawcett wrote that Esek Hopkins and Benjamin Franklin must have known of the East India Company flag. Since the company's administration of India was not directly controlled by the king's ministers, it might have been regarded almost as an ally. Its flag symbolized a type of independence from royal control. Fawcett argues further that the company's flag was deliberately copied by those who designed the Grand Union flag. Yet, in the last analysis, all this must remain simply fascinating conjecture.

But it is true that for over one hundred and fifty years the East India Company had enjoyed extensive privileges. Its power reached a peak at the end of the Seven Years War when French power was eliminated and the authority of the native rulers was undermined. The company took on additional aspects of sovereignty, and at the same time it had to work out its relationship with the government in London. After the Seven Years War the North American colonies also found themselves obliged to work out new understandings with the mother country. But before treating that problem we must first examine the influence of the intercolonial wars on American flag making.

Notes

On the general subject of the history and usage in the British isles see W. G. Perrin, *British Flags* (Cambridge, 1922). For details on the army aspects see Major T. J. Edwards, *Standards, Guidons and Colours of the Commonwealth Forces* (Aldershot, 1953), and Samuel M. Milne, *The Standards and Colours of the Army, 1661-1881* (Leeds, 1893). A description of the naval flags used in the expedition against the Spaniards in 1596 is in Sir Julian Corbett, ed., *Naval Records*

Society: Miscellany, vol. 1 (London, 1902). On the history of the navy see Michael Lewis, *The Navy of Britain* (London, 1949), and his work *The History of the British Navy* (Harmondsworth, Middlesex, 1957). For the role of the officers see Michael Lewis, *England's Sea-Officers: The Story of a Naval Profession* (London, 1948).

Information on military usage in North America may be found in Howard M. Chapin's articles: "The Early Use of Flags in New England," *Old Time New England* 21 (1930): 60–73; "Colonial Military Flags," *New England Quarterly* 4 (1931): 448–59; "Notes on Colonial Flags," *Old Time New England* 24 (1934): 135–141; and "Colonial Military Flags," *Transactions of the Colonial Society of Massachusetts* 32 (1937): 306–07. See also Whitney Smith, *The Flag Book of the United States* (New York, 1970), pp. 33–36. The portrait of Captain Thomas Savage is in private hands.

The controversy over the crossless flag is treated in detail in Howard M. Chapin, *Roger Williams and the King's Colors: The Documentary Evidence* (Providence, R.I., 1928). A briefer account, but one set in the political context of the times, is in Charles M. Andrews, *The Colonial Period of American History* (New Haven, 1934), 1:414–16. A clergyman who knew many of the participants in the controversy later published his account of the episode. See William Hubbard, *A General History of New England, From the Discovery to MDCLXXX*, 2d ed. (Boston, 1848). The observations of the Dutch visitor to Boston are in Bartlett B. James and J. Franklin Jameson, eds., *Journal of Jasper Danckaerts, 1674–1680* (New York, 1913; 1952). Judge Samuel Sewall's views can be found in M. Halsey Thomas, ed., *The Diary of Samuel Sewall, 1674–1729*, 2 vols. (New York, 1973).

A brief account of the Three County Troop may be found in George H. Preble, *History of the Flag of the United States of America*, 2d ed. (Boston, 1880), pp. 182–83.

The East India Company's flag is discussed briefly in Preble's *History of the Flag*, p. 221, and in detail in Sir Charles Fawcett, "The Striped Flag of the East India Company and Its Connection With the American Stars and Stripes," *Mariner's Mirror* 23 (1937): 449–76.

Brief descriptions of the military flags of Maryland in the colonial period may be found in William Hand Browne, *Proceedings of the Council of Maryland, 1693–1896/7* (Baltimore, 1900), p. 154.

CHAPTER 3

The Intercolonial Wars

The various political, dynastic, and commercial rivalries between the major European powers that resulted in warfare in the late seventeenth and eighteenth centuries had increasingly important implications for the American colonies. One might assume that with the intensification of national feelings, and the impact of battles, there would have been an increased interest in flags. But, for the most part, this did not occur. Wars and national rivalries continued, and flags remained as utilitarian objects that were rarely subjects of comment or description.

During the War of the League of Augsburg (1689–97) the French in Canada and their Indian allies made raids on English settlements in New York, Massachusetts, Maine, and New Hampshire. English colonists from Massachusetts Bay, Plymouth, Connecticut, and New York captured the French settlement at Port Royal on the Bay of Fundy in 1690, but abandoned it soon afterward. An attempt to capture Quebec failed.

The War of the Spanish Succession (1702–13) was fought by Great Britain to prevent the union of the French and Spanish crowns. In the American colonies, Queen Anne's War, as it was known, was highlighted by a second capture of Port Royal. This time it remained in British hands and was renamed Annapolis in honor of Queen Anne. A colonial expedition against Quebec again failed, as did an attempt by South Carolinians to capture the Spanish settlement at St. Augustine in 1702.

Commercial rivalry led to a new outbreak of warfare between Spain and England in 1739. This conflict was soon absorbed into the War of the Austrian Succession (1740–48) in which Spain, France, and Prussia were allied against Great Britain and Austria. In America, King George's War, as it was known, was notable for three important expeditions. The first was an unsuccessful attempt to capture St. Augustine in 1740. A second and more ambitious enterprise had as its goal the capture of the Spanish cities of Cartegena, in present-day Colombia, and Santiago, Cuba, in 1741. The effort was not successful.

The third and in many ways the most remarkable expedition was that which resulted in the capture of the French fortress of Louisbourg in Cape Breton Island in 1745. Under construction for twenty-five years, the Louisbourg fortress was a prime strategic base for the French forces. The news that it had fallen to a force of some four thousand untrained New England farmers and fishermen was greeted with astonishment in both France and England. The Louisbourg expedition also drew attention to three distinctive flags that were carried by the colonial forces.

One of these flags is associated with Sir William Pepperell, who not only commanded the expedition but helped finance it as well (Figure 30). It was Pepperell who supplied the motto for the expeditionary flag: *Nil desperandum, Christo duce* ("Never despair, Christ leads us"). That sentiment gave the enterprise the air of a crusade. The Pepperell flag no longer exists, but two other flags used on the expedition still survive.

Fig. 30   A portrait of Sir William Pepperell. Essex Institute, Salem, Mass.

Fig. 31   The Britannia Louisbourg flag canton. New-York Historical Society

Fig. 32   The Moulton Flag as it appeared in 1980

The painted canton of a camp color is preserved in the New-York Historical Society. This shows a female figure in a flowing gown and a helmet seated near the seashore. Her left hand rests on a shield that bears the red Cross of St. George and the white Cross of St. Andrew on a blue background. Her right hand holds a pole over which flies a white streamer bearing the word "Britannia" in blue letters. Beyond her a British ship is observed sailing on the seas. The lower edge of the canton is torn, but the other three sides show fragments of red where the canton was attached to a flag (Figure 31).

The second surviving Louisbourg color is known as the Moulton flag, after Colonel Jeremiah Moulton, the commander of the Third Massachusetts Regiment, whose unit carried it (Figure 32). The flag is made of white linen and measures 26½ inches square. In the center is an oak tree pierced with a dagger and surmounted on a scroll, all painted with oil colors. The design is painted on only one side, and it is thought that the original flag consisted of two similar designs on linen pieces that were sewn together back to back. Two parallel bands of light blue about two inches wide can be discerned across the top of the field in the surviving fragment. These may have been intended to represent clouds. The motto, *Bello Pax Quaeritur,* means literally "Through war peace is sought," or more loosely, "In war our quest is peace." This sentiment is said to have been uttered by Oliver Cromwell, the Lord Protector of England, at the time of his second investiture. The letters of the motto are painted in black on a white scroll. The scroll is outlined in crimson, and crimson is used to shade its folds. An examination of the border of the fragment suggests that there may have been a border or fringe attached to the flag. If so, this would bring the dimension to about thirty inches square, or the size of the Bedford flag of Revolutionary War fame (see Figure 43).

Aside from its association with the Louisbourg campaign, the flag is of interest for two additional reasons. First, colors for individual companies were rare in colonial times. Second, the use of the oak tree on a public symbol such as a flag was unusual. The British prohibited the use of the oak tree as a symbol after 1707, but it may well have survived in some forms such as this until revived at the time of the Revolution.

Another incident in King George's War that had wide repercussions stemmed from raids by a French privateer on two plantations near Bombay Hook in Castle County, Delaware, in July 1747. Three days later the privateer seized a ship off Cape Henlopen. In October of that year the president of the Provincial Council told the Pennsylvania Assembly that Philadelphia might be the scene of the next visitation of the privateer, and that the city should provide for its defense. The Assembly was dominated by pacifists who were unwilling to spend money for defense. This attitude prompted Benjamin Franklin to publish a pamphlet entitled *Plain Truth, or Serious Considerations on the Present State of the City of Philadelphia, and Province of Pennsylvania.* The two thousand copies that were printed were widely read, and a second edition of one thousand copies in German was printed and sold. Under the pen name "a Tradesman of Philadelphia," Franklin appealed to the citizens to act in their own defense: "At present we are like the separate Filaments of Flax before the Thread is form'd, without Strength because without Connection: but UNION would make us strong and even formidable." The news that such a strong union existed would deter enemies: "The Way to secure Peace is to be prepared for War."

Franklin called upon like-minded citizens to meet and to form an association

Fig. 33 The flag of the first company of the Pennsylvania Associators (1747), designed by Benjamin Franklin Smithsonian Institution, courtesy Historical Society of Pennsylvania

for the common defense. Four days after the pamphlet appeared five hundred men had been enrolled in a unit known as the Associators. The government raised no objections to this development. Each man who joined promised to supply his own musket, cartridge box, and twelve rounds of ammunition. Lottery tickets were sold to raise money for cannon and ammunition.

Along with other preparations, the Associators prescribed distinctive flags for each of its ten companies (Figure 33).* These descriptions were published in the *Pennsylvania Gazette* of January 12, 1748. The *Gazette* of April 14, 1748, carried an account of a review of the thousand-man Associators as they marched up Philadelphia's Market Street. Commenting on the colors of the various companies, the *Gazette* said: "Most of the above Colours, together with the Officers Half-Pikes and Sponto[o]ns, and even Halberts, Drums &c. have been given by the good Ladies of this City, who raised Money by Subscriptions among themselves for that Purpose."

Franklin became a common soldier in the Associators, and the organization maintained a nightly guard throughout the rest of the war. In order to devote himself more to public affairs, Franklin took on David Hall as a partner in his printing business in January 1748.

Public rejoicing over the end of King George's War in 1748 was tempered by the news that under the peace treaty Louisbourg was given back to the French in return for the British possession of Madras in India. The American colonists found it hard to believe that such a strong military fortification would be returned to a nation that had been the source of periodic threats to the safety of their settlements. In New England, where there was an additional rivalry with the French in the coastal fishing grounds, the decision to return Louisbourg was greeted with chagrin, dissatisfaction, and bitterness.

Within five years after the end of King George's War, the French and English were engaged in a rivalry for the control of the Ohio country. Governor Robert Dinwiddie of Virginia sent Major George Washington with a letter to the commandant of the French forces in Ohio asking them to withdraw from lands claimed by the king of England. Washington delivered his letter to the French commandant at a fort near Venango at the headwaters of the Allegheny River. In his diary Washington noted: "We found the French Colours hoisted at the house from which they had driven Mr. John Frazier, an English subject." This may have been the white French flag strewn with the gold fleur-de-lis, but more likely it was a plain white flag.

The French had no intention of leaving the Ohio country, and Governor Dinwiddie received this unsatisfactory reply through Washington on December 16, 1753. Washington also gave the governor his observations on French activity west of the Appalachian mountains. These observations in journal form were published by the governor and copied by virtually every newspaper in the English colonies as well as in Great Britain. Washington's account gave authentic information on the designs the French had against the English colonies. It was apparent that the French would attempt to contain the British east of the mountains. If they succeeded, British penetration of the west would be stopped.

To meet this threat, the Virginia House of Burgesses voted funds to raise a military force of three hundred men. Washington accepted the rank of lieuten-

---

* For descriptions of all the flags carried by the Associators see the Notes and Queries section of the *Pennsylvania Magazine of History and Biography* 10 (1887), p. 479.

Fig. 34 Wood engraving of a snake in the
Boston Weekly News Letter, *1754*
Historical Society of Pennsylvania

ant colonel and went with an advance party of one hundred and fifty men to occupy a fort then being constructed at the junction of the Allegheny and Monongahela rivers. Enroute to the site he was met by Ensign Ward, who was in charge of the building party, who told Washington that the French surprised them and forced them to surrender. The French were now completing the fort for their own use. Ensign Ward was sent on to report these developments to the governor of Virginia. Washington moved on, fought a successful skirmish with a French reconnaissance party, and built Fort Necessity at Great Meadows, east of present-day Uniontown. Here he was attacked by a larger French force and was forced to surrender.

News of the two surrenders of Virginia troops reached the various colonies within weeks. It also became known to the delegates from seven colonies who were assembled at Albany, New York, to make a treaty with the Iroquois Confederacy, which claimed title to the Ohio country and whose loyalty to the British was wavering. Benjamin Franklin, a delegate from Pennsylvania, had been very much impressed by the need for a stronger union among the English colonies. When the news of Ensign Ward's surrender to the French reached Philadelphia, Franklin printed the report and called public attention to the dangers of the French activity. He added:

The Confidence of the French in this Undertaking seems well-grounded on the present disunited State of the British Colonies, and the extreme Difficulty of bringing so many different Governments and Assemblies to agree in any speedy and effectual Measures for our common Defense and Security.

Illustrating this theme was a woodcut of a rattlesnake cut into eight pieces, each segment labeled with the initial of a colony, and with the head and a large segment labeled with the initials of New England. In reproducing this cartoon, *The Boston Weekly News-Letter* added the caption "Join, or Die" (Figure 34). The idea that a dismembered snake could join its parts again was a part of the folklore that confused snakes with some long lizards that had regenerative capacity.

At the Albany Congress Franklin presented a plan for the union of all the colonies except Georgia and Nova Scotia under a president general appointed and supported by the crown. He also proposed a Grand Council to be elected with the approval of the president general and the crown. This ambitious plan was discussed and a modified version of it was approved by the Albany Congress delegates. But the plan was not approved by the crown nor by a single colonial legislature. Nevertheless, the discussion helped to prepare the minds of the colonists for a closer union twenty years later.

Having failed to achieve its goals by diplomacy, the British government decided to use force to eliminate the French influence in the territory it claimed. As the first step in this policy, a strong military force under Major General James Braddock was sent to recover the command of the Ohio country. About ten miles from Fort Duquesne, the site of present-day Pittsburgh, Braddock's force was surprised and routed by a force of French and Indians. Braddock was killed. George Washington, his personal aide, rallied the forces and got the remnants safely back to Virginia.

Meanwhile, a large force of Massachusetts troops captured two French forts in Nova Scotia, and resettled six thousand French settlers among the thirteen colonies. The English launched unsuccessful attacks against French forts at Fort Niagara on Lake Ontario and at Crown Point on Lake Champlain, but they did capture Fort William Henry at the southern end of Lake George, New York.

51

These military actions were a prelude to the formal declaration of war between France and Great Britain in 1756. The Seven Years War, as it was known, found France allied with Austria and Great Britain fighting alongside Prussia. The war was fought in Europe, India, and America. When it ended in 1763, France had lost all of her colonial possessions on the mainland of North America.

After setbacks early in the war, the British forces captured Louisbourg and Fort Duquesne in 1758, Fort Niagara, Ticonderoga, Crown Point, and Quebec in 1759, and Montreal in 1760. The British flag replaced the fleur-de-lis on all lands east of the Mississippi River.

Concerned about what the defeat of France would do to the European balance of power, Spain decided to join France and Austria late in the war. An offensive-defensive alliance was signed in August 1761. Anticipating an attack by Spain, Great Britain declared war on Spain in January 1762. Martinique, St. Lucia, and Grenada soon fell to the British. The cities of Havana and Manila were also taken. This string of disasters prompted France to compensate Spain by ceding Louisiana and all territory west of the Mississippi to Spain. In those areas the white flag with the gold fleur-de-lis was replaced by the Spanish flag—white field with the royal arms of the house of Aragon in the center.

Although the final victory in the Seven Years War tended to make most people forget the difficult times during the conflict, British officials could not overlook the fact that there had not been a great deal of colonial cooperation during the war. For the most part, the colonists had been willing to let the British do the fighting for them. With the French menace removed, it soon became apparent that the British soldiers would now have the job of defending the colonial frontiers from Indian attacks, since there was no disposition among the colonies to do this for themselves. The war had revealed weaknesses in the administration of the colonies, and British officials were now disposed to correct those deficiencies.

Notes

The main outlines of the struggle for North America are set forth in standard textbooks and encyclopedia accounts. A detailed account may be found in Lawrence H. Gipson, *The British Empire Before the American Revolution*, 14 vols. (New York and Caldwell, Idaho, 1939–68), vols. 4–8.

The Pepperell flag is described in George H. Preble, *History of the Flag of the United States of America* (Boston, 1880), pp. 190–91. The Britannia camp color was presented to the New-York Historical Society by a member, John Stark, in 1846 or 1847. The society has no other information about the flag or its donor. There is a description of the Moulton color in H.W. Williams, "The 'Moulton' Flag," in *Old Time New England* 24 (1934):132–35. The genealogy of the owners of the flag was given by Colonel Clifton Lisle, a descendant of Moulton, in a letter to William R. Furlong on Jan. 9, 1964.

A concern about the activities of the French and Spanish privateers on the Delaware Bay is reflected in the *Colonial Records of Pennsylvania, 1683–1790*, 16 vols. (Philadelphia, 1852–53), 5:80–82, 89–93, 111, 117–18, 226. The erection of a battery by the Associators is recorded on page 322. On a flag of the Associators, see Francis O. Allen, "The Provincial or Colonial Flag of Pennsylvania," *Pennsylvania Magazine of History and Biography* 17 (1894):249–52. A description of the devices and mottos for the various company flags is in Franklin's pamphlet *Plain Truth*. The quoted segment was reprinted in the Notes and Queries section of the *Pennsylvania Magazine of History and Biography* 10 (1887):479–80. Franklin's experiences with the Associators are described in his autobiography, published in several editions.

Washington's experiences with the French are recorded in John C. Fitzpatrick, ed., *The Diaries of George Washington*, 4 vols. (Boston and New York, 1925), 1:43, 54–55. Franklin's call for union is from the *Boston Weekly News-Letter* of May 23, 1754, which reprinted it from the *Pennsylvania Gazette*.

CHAPTER 4

Preliminaries of the Revolution

The French and Indian War had convinced the British government of the need for more effective control over colonial affairs. The expulsion of the French from North America had also brought increased responsibilities to Great Britain. The prosecution of the war had entailed a great deal of expense, and the British believed that the colonies should help to pay off this debt.

From the point of view of the colonists, the tightening of administrative controls infringed rights that they had enjoyed for many years. They also argued that, since they were not represented in Parliament, that body could not levy taxes on them. For a dozen years after the end of the French and Indian War the British and colonial leaders argued about the proper relationship of the colonies to the British government. In the process of defining their liberties and protesting abuses to them, the colonists resorted to symbols that dramatized their sentiments. One of the symbols that gradually gained acceptance was the use of flags with slogans or mottos that expressed the unity of the colonies.

Various laws enacted by Parliament provoked great controversy, especially the Stamp Act, passed on March 27, 1765. This act required the colonists to buy a special stamp for legal documents, bills of lading, liquor licenses, pamphlets, newspapers, almanacs, advertisements, and playing cards. Vice admiralty courts were given jurisdiction to punish offenses against the act.

When the Stamp Act was brought up in the House of Commons, Charles Townshend spoke in favor of it. He concluded by asking if "these Americans, children planted by our care, nourished by our indulgence" and "protected by our arms," would "grudge to contribute their mite to relieve us from the heavy weight of that burden [of taxation] which we lie under?" Townshend's question was answered by Colonel Isaac Barre, who had participated in the capture of Quebec in the French and Indian War. Barre said that the colonies had not been planted by the care of the British government, but had been established by people fleeing from its tyranny. The colonies had not been nourished by indulgence, but had grown up despite the government's neglect. When the government began to pay attention to the colonies, it sent out as rulers people who misrepresented colonial actions and preyed upon the colonists. As for protecting them by British arms, Barre said rather that they had "nobly taken up arms" in the defense of British territory.

Barre's speech did not prevent passage of the Stamp Act, but it did win him many friends in the colonies. In Boston his portrait was hung in Faneuil Hall. In his speech, Barre had referred to the colonists as "Sons of Liberty." This designation was to be adopted by many colonists who opposed the Parliamentary legislation.

Meanwhile, John Wilkes, a member of the House of Commons and the owner and publisher of the newspaper *The North Briton*, who had been arguing for reforms in the constitutional government of Great Britain, published a bitter criticism of the king's message to Parliament. It appeared on April 23, 1763, in issue No. 45, a supplement to *The North Briton*. Seven days later Wilkes was arrested and imprisoned in the Tower of London. Friends rallied to support him, and gifts and letters poured in to him in prison. One of his letters came from a group in Boston that identified themselves as "The Friends of Liberty, Wilkes, Peace and Good Order assembled at the Whig Tavern to the number of forty-five and upwards."

In May 1763 Wilkes was discharged on a writ of habeas corpus. The following January he was expelled from the House of Commons. The court of the King's Bench then entered a judgment against Wilkes for libel, and he fled to France and was outlawed. By his enemies he was considered a libelous and morally worthless person. His friends saw him as a man of wit and courage, and his prosecution and outlawry made him a popular idol in Britain and America. "Wilkes and Liberty" became a party cry in both Great Britain and America, as did the use of the number forty-five. One manifestation of his popularity was the production of porcelain bowls bearing his portrait and the legend "Wilkes and Liberty" (Figure 35). A better known manifestation is the decision in 1770 of an eastern Pennsylvania town to change its name from Fort Durkee to Wilkes-Barre. This change also points up the fact that the climax of the Wilkes case and the passage of the Stamp Act came at about the same time. In Great Britain the Wilkes case was well known, but the Stamp Act was not. In America the two issues were united. The Sons of Liberty were identified with both causes.

News of the passage of the Stamp Act led to a storm of protest in the colonies. In October 1764 the New York Assembly appointed a committee to correspond with several colonial assemblies on the subject of opposition to the Stamp Act. The committee urged upon colonial assemblies the necessity of holding a convention of delegates from the various colonies to remonstrate against the continued violation of their rights and liberties. Acting on this suggestion, the General Court of Massachusetts sent a circular letter to the other colonies proposing that representatives of the colonies meet in New York City in October 1765 to consult together and "to consider a general and united, dutiful, loyal, and humble representation of their condition to his Majesty and to the parliament, and to implore relief."

During the summer of 1765 the Sons of Liberty were busy violently demonstrating to the stamp distributors that no stamps should be sold and that the stamp agents should resign. The agents were burned in effigy and in some cases their property was destroyed; they were also threatened with physical violence to force them to resign. In Boston an effigy of Andrew Oliver, the

Fig. 35   Chinese export porcelain bowl design commemorating "Wilkes and Liberty." Smithsonian Institution, courtesy J. Jefferson Miller II

provincial secretary and a stamp distributor for Massachusetts Bay, was placed on a large tree on Newbury Street, a well-traveled thoroughfare of the city. The tree became known as the Liberty Tree. The sheriff was ordered to take down the effigy. He sent men to do the job but they reported that it would be unsafe to attempt such an action. That night the mob destroyed the stamp office, burned the effigy, and smashed the windows and frames in Oliver's house. The next day he resigned his office as stamp distributor.

The action of the Boston mob indicated to other colonists a method of resisting the hated stamp tax. If petitions and memorials could not stop the passage of the act, terroristic methods could nullify it. Rioting against stamp distributors and the Stamp Act broke out in Newport, Rhode Island. In Connecticut a loose, semimilitary secret organization called the Sons of Liberty allegedly had ten thousand armed men ready to take action against the enforcement of the act. The Sons of Liberty apprehended a stamp distributor enroute to a meeting of the Connecticut Assembly and forced his resignation. In New York the Sons of Liberty placed an effigy of the local stamp distributor in the carriage of the lieutenant governor and burned both. They also destroyed the interior of the home of Major Thomas James, the commanding officer of Fort George at the Battery, who had made disparaging remarks about the Sons of Liberty. When the people threatened to storm the fort and seize the stamps that were stored there the stamps were taken to City Hall and placed in the custody of the municipal council. After this action the New York Sons of Liberty proceeded to organize themselves along formal military lines and to bring about a close alignment of other such groups.

In Maryland a newly appointed stamp distributor arrived at Annapolis where he found himself treated with contempt by many of his former acquaintances. After a mob hanged him in effigy and destroyed a house he had leased, he decided that the best course of action was to go to New York and place himself under the protection of Major General Thomas Gage, the commander-in-chief of the British forces in North America. But soon after he arrived in New York the local Sons of Liberty forced him to resign. The Sons of Liberty celebrated this victory by carrying a flag described as the Flag of Liberty, which bore the words "Liberty, Property and No Stamps." No complete description of this flag is available. Red was the traditional flag of protest, but there are indications that some Liberty flags were blue or green. The letters were most likely painted on in white.

In Charleston, South Carolina, the hated stamps were deposited in Fort Johnson. A volunteer force took the fort and captured the stamps. While they held the fort they displayed a flag with a blue field on which there were three crescents. This flag seems to have been improvised by the three companies of volunteers who took the fort.

A determined resistance by the people in the thirteen American colonies prevented the stamp distributors from operating and effectively nullified the act. On October 7, 1765, the Stamp Act Congress met in New York City, adopted a declaration of rights and grievances, and sent petitions to the king, and to the House of Commons and the House of Lords. The Congress adjourned on October 25, and awaited the results of their appeals.

When the Stamp Act went into effect on November 1, 1765, there were no stamps and no distributors. Since only stamped paper was legal, and the people would not use it, business was suspended. Merchants in New York, Philadelphia, and Boston agreed not to import certain enumerated articles from Great Britain. Fearful of the loss of trade from the colonies, commercial and manufacturing towns in England petitioned Parliament to repeal the Stamp Act. After a long debate in Parliament it was finally repealed on March 18, 1766.

News of the repeal brought rejoicing in London and in the colonies. In New York citizens erected a Liberty pole in an area known as The Fields, and raised on it a flag inscribed "The King, Pitt, and Liberty." There is no information known on the colors used in this flag; it might well have been red or blue with white or gold letters. The people of New York ordered the erection of a statue of William Pitt, who had fought for the repeal of the Stamp Act in the House of Commons, and another statue of King George III to be erected at Bowling Green. Overlooked in the celebrations was the fact that along with the repeal Parliament had passed the Declaratory Act, claiming the right to make laws and to bind the colonies in all cases.

The American colonists now turned their attention to the Mutiny Act, passed in 1765, which gave British officers in the colonies the right to quarter troops in towns and in certain cases to demand such things as bedding, cooking utensils, fire, candles, cider or rum, and wagons. The law was motivated by the shortage of barracks in the colonies, but was regarded by the Americans as an attempt to destroy their liberty. Even after the law was amended so that the quartering took place only in empty houses and barns when no barracks were available, the colonists were suspicious. American assemblies were required to provide barracks. The colonists now believed that if Parliament could compel them to supply the troops with necessities, it would still violate the principle of no taxation without representation. Massachusetts took the lead in 1766 in nullifying the Mutiny Act. Other colonies followed its example. Soon New York City, the headquarters of the British army in North America, became the storm center of oppostition to the Mutiny Acts. These actions alienated supporters such as William Pitt, and further angered those persons in Parliament who argued that the repeal of the Stamp Act was a mistake and that a firm policy was in order.

The result was the passage of new revenue measures, known as the Townshend Acts, which laid duties on glass, lead, paint, paper, and tea. The specific amount of duty on these items was small, and it was hoped that Americans would not object. Once the precedent was established, revenue from the colonies might eventually ease the burdens on the British taxpayer. But this was not to be. The colonists recognized the taxes for what they were, and a fresh outbreak of opposition followed.

The Massachusetts legislature endorsed a Circular Letter, drafted by Samuel Adams, that set forth the idea that the power of the crown and of Parliament over the colonies was limited. Copies of the letter were sent to the other colonial legislatures and to the British government. The secretary of state for the colonies sent a harsh reply, calling upon the Massachusetts assembly to disavow the Circular Letter and threatening to dissolve any colonial legislature that adopted it.

By a vote of ninety-two to seventeen the Massachusetts legislature refused to rescind the Circular Letter. A group of the nonrescinders hired Paul Revere to make a silver punch bowl commemorating their action. The bowl, now in the Museum of Fine Arts in Boston, includes an engraved circular device enclosing a "No. 45" and the words "Wilkes & Liberty" on one side. Below them is torn paper marked "General Warrants," referring to the warrants used to search Wilkes's house. An engraved Liberty Cap and banners marked "Magna Charta" and "Bill of Rights" complete the design. On the other side of the bowl is an engraved Liberty Cap under which is an inscription honoring the ninety-two nonrescinders (Figures 36 and 37). As for the rescinders, only five of the seventeen were reelected, and only two of those took up their duties.

In the wake of the legislature's action, the governor of Massachusetts dissolved the body. Boston was now under the control of a mob led by the Sons of Liberty. Customs officers in the city fled to the safety of Castle William in the harbor and to a British warship anchored nearby. King George III then ordered two British army regiments from Halifax, Nova Scotia, to Boston. One was to be stationed at Castle William and one in the city of Boston. The stage was being set for further clashes between the royal authority and the people of Massachusetts.

Meanwhile, the other colonies followed the lead taken by Massachusetts. By the end of 1769 only New Hampshire was without a nonimportation covenant.

It soon became obvious to the British government that the cost of collecting the Townshend duties was far greater than the revenue involved. The Townshend Acts were repealed in April 1770, except for the tax on tea. This was left in order to uphold the principle that Parliament had the right to tax the colonies. With the repeal of the Townshend duties the colonists' nonimportation agreements collapsed, except for the ban against tea. The Sons of Liberty in the various colonies were opposed to the return of tranquil times, for they believed that there were still other grievances to be resolved. Nowhere was the continued opposition to British tyranny more pronounced than in Boston.

Events such as the Boston Massacre in 1770 played into the hands of the

*Fig. 36   The Liberty Bowl made by Paul
Revere, 1768
Boston Museum of Fine Arts*

radical leaders of the Sons of Liberty there. They used the incident to inflame further the hostile feelings of the people toward the British government. In November 1772 the Boston town meeting organized a committee to correspond with similar committees in other towns, thus establishing a system of communication outside normal political channels. Other colonies followed the example of Massachusetts in establishing committees of correspondence. In March 1773 the Virginia House of Burgesses adopted resolutions calling for the creation of a standing committee of correspondence. This committee was to obtain all information concerning actions of the British government that affected the American colonies and to share it with other colonies. A copy of the Virginia resolutions was sent to other colonies, with the request that they appoint similar standing committees or persons who would communicate with Virginia. The other American colonies responded and a cooperative arrangement came into being. The goal of the intercolonial committees of correspondence was to establish a unity of mind and purpose among the leaders of the colonial assemblies in opposing British efforts to subordinate them.

In many American towns the opposition to the acts of the British government was symbolized by raising a flag pole, sometimes adorned with a Liberty cap, that became known as the Liberty Pole. As hostile feelings between the Sons of Liberty and British officials increased, the latter often attempted to remove such poles as provocative symbols. In New York City, British soldiers twice cut down a Liberty Pole that bore a flag with the motto: "The King, Pitt, and Liberty." After the second destruction, the Sons of Liberty erected a new pole that was sheathed with iron around its base, bearing the inscription: "To his most gracious Majesty George III, Mr. Pitt, and Liberty." After standing

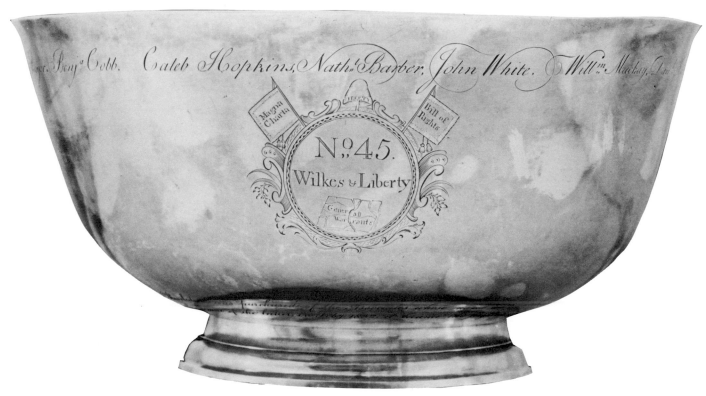

Fig. 37   Opposite side of Paul Revere's Liberty Bowl showing flag designs
Boston Museum of Fine Arts

almost three years, this pole was attacked by British soldiers in January 1770 and brought down. The Sons of Liberty prepared a new pole, but the city officials refused to let them raise it again on public ground.

The Sons of Liberty then purchased a strip of private ground nearby. A large pole, transported to the new location by a team of six horses adorned with ribbons inscribed "Liberty and property," was planted in a base twelve feet deep, and girded with iron for two-thirds of its length above ground. On it they shipped a topmast twenty-two feet long inscribed with the word "Liberty." This pole remained standing until the British cut it down in 1776.

In Charleston, South Carolina, the Sons of Liberty met under a tree that became known as the Liberty Tree. The actions associated with this tree were so unpleasant for the British that when the city was captured in 1780 Sir Henry Clinton ordered the the tree cut down.

The Liberty Tree in Boston was the largest in a grove of beautiful elms that stood in Hanover Square at the corner of present-day Washington and Essex Streets. It became known as the Liberty Tree because of the meetings held under it by the Sons of Liberty beginning in the summer of 1765. The ground under the tree was called Liberty Hall. From a pole fastened to the trunk of the tree and rising far above its branching top a red flag was occasionally flown as a signal to the people. Placards and banners were also suspended from the limbs or affixed to the body of the tree.

When Sir Francis Bernard, the governor of the Massachusetts Bay Colony, was ordered home to England on July 31, 1769, the people of Boston manifested their joy by congratulating each other, lighting bonfires on the hills, firing salutes from Hancock's wharf, and raising a union flag above the Liberty

59

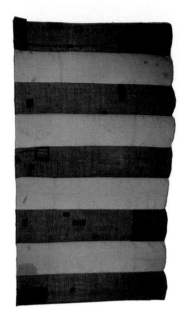

Fig. 38   Flag of the United American Colonies

Fig. 39   Boston Liberty flag fragment
The Bostonian Society

Tree. This union flag consisted of thirteen red and white stripes. Flags of such a design were popular before, during, and after the American Revolution (Figure 38). When the Boston Sons of Liberty celebrated the anniversary of their opposition to the Stamp Act on August 14, 1773, they flew the union flag over the tent in which they had their entertainment.

In the collections of the Bostonian Society there is preserved a portion of a Liberty Flag that flew over the Liberty Tree in Boston. This remnant consists of nine alternate red and white bunting stripes made of single worsted yarns of the early type. Each stripe is hand sewn with two rows of linen thread. The fragment measures approximately 17 inches long, selvage to selvage, and 12¾ inches wide. When a Smithsonian textile expert examined this flag in 1976, she found nothing in the physical evidence that would refute the claim that this flag dates from the period of the American Revolution (Figure 39).

On November 23, 1773, a large flag was raised above the Liberty Tree and the town crier summoned the people to assemble. The reason for the meeting was the arrival at Boston of ships carrying tea to be sold to the American colonists under the Tea Act. The governor would not permit the ships to return to England, and the tea agents would not resign. The people of Boston were determined that the tea would not be landed. Two mass meetings were held. After the second, a mob of fifty or sixty men, dressed as Indians, boarded the ships and threw the tea in the harbor. Parliament decided to punish Boston by passing four coercive measures known to the colonists as the "Intolerable Acts." These actions led to the calling of the First Continental Congress in Philadelphia in September 1774 and to the organization of a United Resistance. In the winter of 1775–76 British soldiers cut down the Boston Liberty tree and used it for firewood.

Fig. 40   The Taunton Flag

In other cities and towns, colonists also raised flags of protest. At Taunton, Massachusetts, in October 1774 a new type of union flag was raised on the top of a Liberty pole. This consisted of a red field with the British Union Jack as a square-shaped canton and the words "Liberty and Union" in white letters on the red field extending across the lower portion of the flag beneath the canton (Figure 40).

Early in March 1775 the citizens of New York City manifested their discontent by raising on the Liberty Pole on the Common a regular English red ensign with the union. But added to the red field were the words "George Rex" and "Liberties of America" on one side and "No Popery" on the other. The "No Popery" slogan had to do with the efforts of the Archbishop of Canterbury to establish bishops of the Church of England in the American colonies—a move that was resisted by other Protestant denominations.

In Poughkeepsie, New York, on March 21, 1775, liberty-minded individuals raised a flag which bore on one side the words "The King," and on the other "The Congress and Liberty." We do not know its colors, but it may well have been the regular English red ensign with white letters. The flag was cut down by the authorities on the grounds that it was a public nuisance.

Fig. 41   *The Schenectady Liberty flag*
          Smithsonian Institution, courtesy
          Schenectady Historical Society

Fig. 42   *The Schenectady Liberty flag (de-*
          tail)
          Smithsonian Institution, courtesy
          Schenectady Historical Society

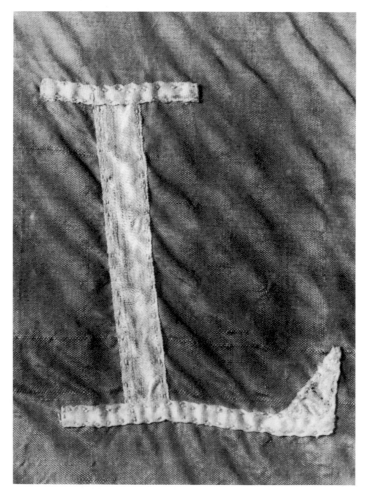

Another flag associated with the early protests against Great Britain is the Liberty flag preserved at the Schenectady Historical Society in Schenectady, New York. The flag is of plain woven silk, or taffeta, and measures approximately forty-five inches square. It is now a brownish color, but a fragment removed from its staff in 1951 shows a blue-green color. Originally it may have been blue or green. The word "Liberty" is made of white silk tape in block letters and is sewn on with linen or coarse silk thread. This flag is associated with the Sons of Liberty in upstate New York in 1774 and perhaps later (Figures 41 and 42).

During the ten years that followed the passage of the Stamp Act, colonial dissatisfaction over the actions of Parliament had taken the form of demonstrations, the calling of an intercolonial congress, the passage of nonimportation agreements, and the organization of committees of correspondence and of secret quasi-military units, the Sons of Liberty. The symbols of their discontent evolved from a hero worship of John Wilkes and the adoption of the number forty-five, to the emphasis on the word "Liberty" and its use in connection with trees, poles, and flags which bore that sentiment. A basic loyalty to the crown and to the empire was evident in the use of the British flag as a device for expressing their sentiments. But a sense of common purpose was also emerging with the use of a flag with thirteen red and white stripes symbolizing the American colonies.

So, by the fall of 1774 there was a great feeling of resistance to British authority in the American colonies. Attempts to reorganize the empire after the French and Indian War had led to much discussion of the nature of the relationship of the colonies to the mother country. Taxation was but one of the issues that helped to bring about the eventual separation. In Massachusetts the coercive measures against Boston were regarded as threatening rights guaranteed by charter.

In Great Britain there was a belief that irresolute action had brought affairs to this head, and there was general support in the country at large for a policy of coercion. Lieutenant General Thomas Gage, the commander-in-chief of the British forces in North America, was sent to Boston to assume the functions of governor-in-chief of the Massachusetts Bay Colony as well as those of a military commander. He assured the king that four regiments of British soldiers would be sufficient to prevent further disturbances. But the people of Boston had a hatred for British officials, and especially the customs officers. After the destruction of the tea, some of the leaders of the Sons of Liberty in Massachusetts Bay were making secret plans for armed resistance. By March 1774 activist citizens had chosen their own military officers and were taking military training. The spring of that year saw the Boston town meeting openly assume the functions of a local government. Pressures were building on both sides and an armed clash was approaching.

Notes

For details on the Stamp Act protests see Edmund S. and Helen M. Morgan, *The Stamp Act Crisis: Prologue to Revolution* (Chapel Hill, N.C., 1953), and Lawrence Henry Gipson, *The British Empire Before the American Revolution*, 15 vols. (Caldwell, Idaho, and New York, 1939–74), vol. 10, chaps. 12–17. On the role of John Wilkes and his influence in the American colonies see Gipson, vol. 11, chap. 7. Details on other sources of colonial discontent and the pattern of resistance are to be found in Gipson, vols. 11 and 12. The silver punch bowl commemorating the action of the Massachusetts legislature in refusing to rescind its circular letter is described in an article by Edwin J. Hipkiss in the *Bulletin of the* [Boston] *Museum of Fine Arts* 47 (1949):19–21. Various Liberty flags are described in George H. Preble, *History of the Flag of the United States of America* (Boston, 1880), pp. 193–96; in Samuel G. Drake, *The History and Antiquities of Boston, 1630–1770* (Boston, 1856), p. 716 n.; and in the *Proceedings of the Bostonian Society, 1894* (Boston, 1895), pp. 36-37. Grace Rogers Cooper's reports on the Liberty Tree flag in the Bostonian Society and in the Schenectady Historical Society are in the files of the Division of Naval History, Smithsonian Institution. The Liberty flag hoisted in New York City in March 1775 is described in Isaac J. Greenwood, *Captain John Manley* (Boston, 1915), p. 79 n.

CHAPTER **5**

Flags and Symbols of Armed Rebellion, 1775–1776

The spring of 1775 was a time of unrest in Massachusetts as a result of the British coercive measures against Boston in the wake of the Boston Tea Party. Evidence of the rising tension was published in British newspapers and magazines. Under the date of April 17, 1775, two days before the battle of Lexington, *The Gentleman's Magazine* said: "By a ship just arrived at Bristol from America, it is reported, that the Americans have hoisted their standard of liberty at Salem."

What was this standard of liberty? The Massachusetts legislature formally adopted the pine tree flag on April 11, 1776, but it is said to have been in use for a year before that. It is also possible that the reference might have been to a British flag with the word Liberty on it similar to the one raised at Taunton, Massachusetts, in the fall of 1774. In any case, the sentiment expressed in the flag was clearly understood.

The Gentleman's Magazine predicted that fighting would break out between the colonists and the British troops before the news of the battle of Lexington had reached England. Under the date of April 29, 1775, it declared:

Letters of good authority from America affirm, that the militia of Massachusetts bay and Connecticut are actually embodied, have magazines ready prepared, and are assembled to the number of 12,000 effective men; that Salem was the headquarters when the letters were written; but that a considerable body were on their march to Boston; so that there is not a doubt but that the next news will be an account of a bloody engagement between the two armies.

The account was prophetic indeed.

Reports reached the British headquarters in Boston that the colonials were collecting gunpowder and arms at Concord. General Gage decided to send a small force to destroy this materiel and to arrest colonial leaders in the area. But word of the expedition reached the colonials, and their leaders went into hiding. An armed body of colonial "Minute Men" assembled on the village green at Lexington on April 19, 1775, where it was met by the advancing British column. Shots were exchanged. According to a colonial report, the Minute Men were fired upon as they were obeying a British order to disperse. They fired back in defense as the shooting continued. The British report said that the order to disperse was met by a shot from the colonial side which was

*Fig. 43   The Bedford Flag
Bedford Free Public Library*

answered by a British volley. At any rate, the battle of Lexington resulted in eight killed and ten wounded on the colonial side and one dead and two fatally wounded on the British. A detachment of survivors marched to Concord to dispute the British passage.

There is no record of a flag being carried by the Minute Men at Lexington, but at Concord the diary of a British lieutenant mentions that "we marched into the Town after taking possession of a Hill with a Liberty Pole on it and a flag flying, which was cut down; the Yankies had that Hill but left it to us; we expected they would'd have made a stand there, but they did not chuse it." There is no description of this flag.

At Concord bridge the British advance was disputed by the Minute Men of Bedford, a town lying midway between Lexington and Concord. Organized by the townspeople in March 1775, the company had promptly elected its officers and chosen its flag. The Bedford flag was square in shape and crimson in color (Figure 43). Next to the staff is a vertical group of clouds from which an arm grasping a sharp pointed sword extends. Partly surrounding the arm is a large scroll with the words *Vince Aut Morire* (Conquer or Die). This flag is of the type originally designed in England between 1660 and 1670 for the three county troops of Massachusetts militia. It is similar to the flag used by the Dutch while withstanding the siege of Ostend by the Spaniards between 1601 and 1604, and to the flag of the seventeenth century Polish kings. The arm and sword design was also used by both sides in the English Civil War (1642–46).

News of the fight at Lexington was carried by post rider Israel Bissel through Connecticut, New York, New Jersey, and Pennsylvania as he made his way to Philadelphia, arriving there on April 24. Others carried the word through Massachusetts and New Hampshire. Militia units were called out. By June many colonies had authorized the formation of regiments. Volunteers came forward, including many veterans of the French and Indian War. They armed themselves as best they could and proceeded to Boston. These loosely organized groups, numbering about fifteen thousand men in all, placed themselves under Major General Artemus Ward, the commander of the Massachusetts forces. They were encamped around Boston in a semicircle from Dorchester through Cambridge to the Mystic River.

Meanwhile the Second Continental Congress had met in Philadelphia on May 10, 1775. Hostilities had already begun at Lexington and Concord, and on the day the Congress met a small force under Ethan Allen captured Fort Ticonderoga in upstate New York. On May 26, the Congress resolved "that these colonies be immediately put in to a state of defense." This was followed by a resolution to send another petition to the king for a redress of grievances in the hope that harmony might be restored. While waiting for the return of peaceful relations, however, they continued preparing to fight. The Congress decided to support the provincial troops before Boston on May 31, and voted that twenty thousand men of this Continental Army should be equipped immediately. George Washington of Virginia was unanimously elected as the commander-in-chief of the army of the United Colonies on June 15.

Three days earlier, in Boston, the governor of Massachusetts issued a proclamation imposing martial law and declaring that those in arms and those aiding them were rebels and traitors. Pardon was offered to all who would lay down their arms, except Samuel Adams and John Hancock. The response of the colonists came in the form of a meeting of the committee on safety on June 15, which recommended that Bunker Hill on the isthmus across from Boston

Fig. 44   *The Flag of the Second Connecticut Regiment*

be fortified. The settlement of Charlestown, containing about three or four hundred houses, lay on the isthmus across from Boston. Beyond it were three major hills, Morton's, Breed's, and Bunker's, with elevations of 35, 75, and 110 feet, respectively. On the night of the sixteenth the digging of entrenchments and the building of a redoubt on Breed's Hill were begun, on the grounds that it was nearer to Boston and the shipping. Covering works were to be constructed on Bunker Hill.

The British had also planned to seize the isthmus, and at daybreak H.M.S. *Lively*, seeing the American entrenchments, brought its guns into action against them. The rest of the British fleet in Boston joined in. According to the nineteenth century American historian Benson J. Lossing, "At twelve o'clock (noon) the men in the redoubt ceased work, sent off their entrenching tools, took some refreshments, hoisted the New England flag, and prepared to fight."

At 3:00 P.M. on June 17 between 2,200 and 2,500 British troops attacked the American force, estimated to be about 1,400 to 1,700 men and boys with six cannons. The British seized the hill after three assaults, but at a fearful cost: 1,054 killed or wounded. The American loss was 100 killed, 271 wounded, and 30 prisoners.

There has long been a question as to whether the Americans displayed any flags during the battle. Benson J. Lossing reported that a pine tree flag was flown. His authority was an old woman, a Mrs. Manning, whose father was in the battle and allegedly raised the flag. Thirty years later, in his *History of the Flag of the United States*, George Preble said that there were probably no colors displayed on the American side during the battle of Bunker Hill, but that immediately afterward Connecticut troops had standards bearing the arms of that colony and the motto *Qui tran*[*stulit*].*sust*[*inet*]: (He, who transported us hither, will support us; Figure 44).

John Trumbull, the Connecticut artist, observed the battle of Bunker Hill from a distance of about four miles; even with the aid of a spyglass he could not tell the result. Eleven years later, in March 1786, he completed his painting of the battle. In it he drew a large red flag with a red fly and a white canton with a tree in the middle of the canton, a plain red flag without a canton, and a part of a flag of indistinct design. There is no contemporary evidence that any of these flags were in use at Bunker Hill during the battle, but flags of these designs were used during the Revolutionary War.

Finally, the narrative of an officer of the Royal Marines, published in 1775, says of the battle: ". . . nor did I see any colours to their regiments on the day of action." Thus, on the basis of the best evidence at hand, we can conclude that there were no American flags at Bunker Hill.

While the battle of Bunker Hill was being fought, the Continental Congress picked George Washington as the commander-in-chief of the army, chose four major generals and eight brigadier generals to assist him, voted to raise fifteen thousand troops, and made arrangements for paying them in Continental currency. In addition, the Congress appointed Horatio Gates as adjutant general with the rank of brigadier general; Thomas Mifflin was made quartermaster general and Colonel Joseph Trumbull became the commissary general. Washington arrived at Cambridge on July 2, 1775, and assumed command of his army the following day. Two days later, on July 4, he issued a general order informing the troops that, in view of their adoption by the Continental Congress, they were now "the troops of the United Provinces of North America."

The Flag of the Philadelphia Troop of Light Horse

Washington's army was made up of a variety of militia units, many of which carried their own flags. The richness and diversity of these regimental colors have been described elsewhere* and need not be detailed here. Of particular significance, however, are those regimental flags which may have influenced the design of the stars and stripes. The first of these is the flag of the Philadelphia Troop of Light Horse.

This troop originated at a meeting of twenty-eight wealthy Philadelphia gentlemen on the evening of November 17, 1774. It was a time when the American colonies were trying to secure a redress of their grievances against Great Britain. The first Continental Congress had met in Philadelphia from September 5 to October 26. One of its most important resolutions pertained to a ban on importing British goods. The enforcement of this nonimportation resolution was left to the individual colonies, and in Philadelphia the citizens chose a committee of correspondence to ascertain how best to implement it.

Among those who concluded that a military unit would make an ideal enforcement body were three members of the committee. One, Abraham Markoe (1733–1806), a Danish-born Philadelphia merchant whose firm carried on extensive trade with the Virgin Islands, was unanimously elected captain of the Philadelphia Troop of Light Horse. The troop was made up of well-to-do individuals who supplied their own horses, military equipment, and uniforms. Captain Markoe decided to contribute a flag to the unit and hired John Folwell to design it and James Claypoole to paint it. The flag consisted of a yellow silk

---

* See Gherardi Davis, *Regimental Colors in the War of the American Revolution* (New York, 1907). An updated and enlarged version, prepared by Edward Richardson, is now in press.

Fig. 45 Flag of the First Troop of Philadelphia Light Horse
Officers and Gentlemen of the First Troop of Philadelphia City Cavalry

field with a silver fringe. Along the three outer edges of the field there is a silver leaf design (Figure 45). In the center is an elaborate shield-like device of dark blue with a white decorative edging; the center of the shield is adorned with a gold device with petals. Flanking the shield is an Indian on the left and an angel on the right. Below their feet is a white ribbon bearing the words: "For These We Strive." Above the shield appears the head of a brown horse; above its head are the intertwined initials of the troop. The British union was originally painted in the upper left hand corner, but with changing times and sentiments, the artist was instructed to paint thirteen silver stripes over the union to represent the United Colonies.

This colorful flag was displayed by the troop in its movements about Philadelphia, about three months before the Continental Union* flag was hoisted on the *Alfred* in Philadelphia on December 3, 1775. When George Washington left Philadelphia to assume command of the army before Boston, the Philadelphia Troop of Light Horse escorted him as far as New York City. The troop also escorted Martha Washington into Philadelphia on November 21, 1775. Some writers have suggested that Washington saw the flag of the troop as he was being escorted and was inspired by it when the Continental Union flag was later being designed. No one knows, of course, but as has been noted this was not the first use of a thirteen stripe design.

* Although it is customary to refer to the flag of thirteen red and white stripes with the British union in the canton as the Grand Union flag, Admiral Furlong preferred the term Continental Union flag.

69

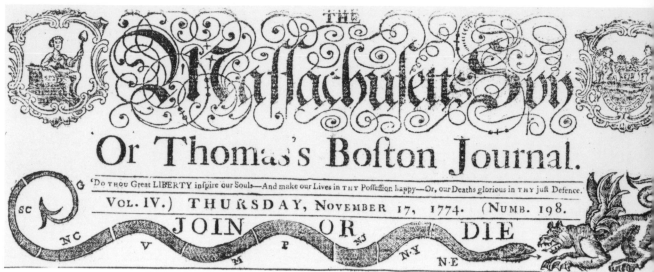

Fig. 46   Woodcut of the snake in the Massachusetts Spy of 1774
Library of Congress

Fig. 47   Snake and pillar design from the
New York Journal or General Ad-
vertiser, 1774
Library of Congress

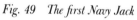

Fig. 49   The first Navy Jack

Fig. 48   Flag of the United Company of the
Train of Artillery; recent research
suggests this flag probably dates
from between 1830 and 1837
Rhode Island Historical Society.
Photograph by Robert P. Emlen

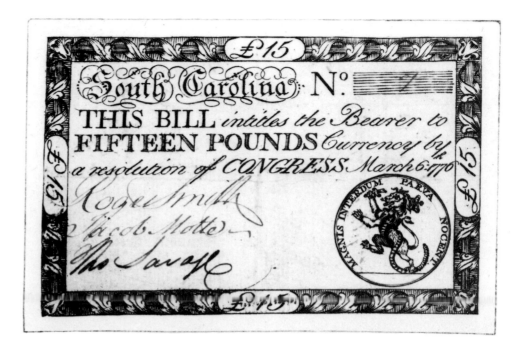

Fig. 50 South Carolina note showing a snake attacking a lion

The Rattlesnake as Symbol

The use of a rattlesnake as a symbol of American unity dates from the origins of the Seven Years War. It was used again about twenty years later during the agitation against the Stamp Act. On November 17, 1774, two months after the meeting of the First Continental Congress, the *Massachusetts Spy* newspaper used the divided snake symbol. This time it extended across the width of the page above an article addressed to "The Inhabitants of the Province of Quebec," urging them to join the colonies in opposing Great Britain. The snake was divided into nine pieces, with the head section representing all the New England colonies (Figure 46); its tail was shaped like an arrowhead.

In December 1774, *The New York Journal* used a snake device on its masthead. The woodcut shows a column standing on the Magna Charta (sic) and supported by twelve outstretched arms. Encircling it is a snake with two concentric coils. The outer coil shows the snake holding its own tail in its mouth. Lettering, beginning on the right side of the outer coil and continuing around the inner coil and the left side of the outer, reads: "United Now Alive and Free / And Thus Supported Ever Bless Our Land / Firm On This Basis Liberty Shall Stand / Till Time Becomes Eternity" (Figure 47).

After the outbreak of fighting between the British and the colonists, the rattlesnake symbol was used extensively. It appeared on newspapers, paper money, uniform buttons, and on a great number of military and naval flags with or without the warning: "Don't Tread on Me" (Figures 48, 49, 50). A coiled rattlesnake was also depicted on the stern of the Continental brig, *General Gates*.

In December 1775 an anonymous Philadelphia correspondent wrote to *Bradford's Pennsylvania Journal* concerning the symbolic use of the snake. The Continental Congress had authorized the raising of two battalions of Marines on November 10, 1775. While these men were being enlisted, this Philadelphia gentleman noted that one of the Marines' drums had a rattlesnake painted on it and the words "Don't Tred on Me" beneath it. Curious, he consulted with a man familiar with heraldry who told him that as a rule only the "worthy" parts of an animal were considered in making a heraldic symbol. Among the ancient peoples the serpent was considered to be an emblem of wisdom, and in some positions to represent time without end. The Philadelphian recalled that the rattlesnake was common only to America. After pondering the properties of the rattlesnake that might make it a worthy heraldic symbol, he sent his conclusions to the editor of the *Journal* in a letter dated December 27, 1775. As to the suitability of the rattlesnake, he said:

I recollected that her eye excelled in brightness that of any other animal, and that she has no eye-lids. She may, therefore, be esteemed an emblem of vigilance. She never begins an attack, nor, when once engaged, ever surrenders. She is, therefore, an emblem of magnanimity and true courage. As if anxious to prevent all pretensions of quarreling with her, the weapons with which nature has furnished her, she conceals in the roof of her mouth, so that, to those who are unacquainted with her, she appears to be a most defenceless animal; and even when those weapons are shown and extended for her defence, they appear weak and contemptible; but their wounds, however small, are decisive and fatal: conscious of this, she never wounds till she has generously given notice, even to her enemy, and cautioned him against the danger of treading on her. Was I wrong, sir, in thinking this a strong picture of the temper and conduct of America? The poison of her teeth is the necessary means of digesting her food, and at the same time those things which are destructive to our enemies. This may be understood to intimate that those things which are destructive to our enemies, may be to us not only harmless, but absolutely necessary to our existence. I confess I was wholly at a loss what to make of the rattles, till I went back and counted them, and found them just thirteen, exactly the number of the Colonies united in America; and I recollected, too, that this was the only part of the snake which increased in numbers. Perhaps it might be only fancy, but, I conceited the painter had shown a half-formed additional rattle, which, I suppose, may have been intended to represent the Province of Canada. 'Tis curious and amazing to observe how distinct and independent of each other the rattles of this animal are, and yet how firmly they are united together, so as never to be separated but by breaking them to pieces. One of these rattles singly, is incapable of producing sound, but the ringing of thirteen together is sufficient to alarm the boldest man living. The Rattlesnake is solitary, and associates with her kind only when it is necessary for their preservation. In Winter, the warmth of a number together will preserve their lives, while, singly, they would probably perish. The power of fascination attributed to her, by a generous construction may be understood to mean, that those who consider the liberty and blessings which America affords, and once came over to her, never afterwards leave her, but spend their lives with her. She strongly resembles America in this, that she is beautiful in youth, and her beauty increaseth with age; "her tongue also is blue, and forked as the lightning, and her abode is among impenetrable rocks."

Having pleased myself with reflections of this kind, I communicated my sentiments to a neighbour of mine, who has a surprising readiness at guessing at every thing which relates to publick affairs; and, indeed, I should be jealous of his reputation in that way, was it not that the event constantly shows that he has guessed wrong. He instantly declared it as his sentiments, that the Congress meant to allude to Lord North's declaration in the House of Commons, that he never would relax his measures until he had brought America to his feet, and to intimate to his Lordship, that were she brought to his feet, it would be dangerous treading on her. But, I am positive he has guessed wrong, for I am sure the Congress would not condescend, at this time of day, to take the least notice of his Lordship in that or any other way. In which opinion I am determined to remain, your humble servant.

A modern naturalist, Dr. Laurence M. Klauber, confirms the description of the anonymous Philadelphia correspondent and gives other characteristics of the

Fig. 51 *An adult timber rattlesnake in its*
light phase
New York Zoological Society

rattlesnake. He states that rattlesnakes occur only in the Western Hemisphere and that the snake used as an emblem in colonial times was the timber rattlesnake (*Crotalus horridus*). The number of rattles on the snake varies as does the color (Figure 51). The most familiar phase is sulphur yellow with wide, dark brown or black crossbands. Females are lighter in color than the males, the male becoming almost black with age. The average length of the snake is from three and one half to five feet, and occasionally as long as six feet.

Rattlesnake Flags and Symbols

Since the fall of 1775, a three-man committee of the Continental Congress had been fitting out and arming vessels for the navy. One of the three was Christopher Gadsden of South Carolina. Feeling it was especially important that Commodore Esek Hopkins, the commander-in-chief, have a distinctive standard for the flagship *Alfred*, Gadsden designed a new flag bearing the rattlesnake symbol. The *Alfred*, with three other ships, sailed from Philadelphia on January 4, 1776, and waited near Liberty Island for the Delaware River to thaw. A fifth ship, the sloop *Providence*, joined the squadron two weeks later; she carried on board Gadsden's rattlesnake flag to be given to Hopkins (Figure 52).

It has been suggested that the flag hoisted by John Paul Jones over the *Alfred* on December 3, 1775, was the Gadsden Standard or rattlesnake flag rather than the Continental Union flag.* This is not possible, however, as more than a month elapsed between the raising of the Grand Union and of the Gadsden Standard. A fragmentary and undated letter to Commodore Hopkins from Timothy Matlack, clerk of the naval committee of Congress, refers to the arrival "last night at 12:00 o'clock" of the king's speech and the address of Parliament. These were received in the Congress on January 13, 1776. The same letter says that the Resolution of the Congress was delivered "last

DON'T TREAD ON ME

Fig. 52 *The Gadsden Flag*

---

* See below, Chapter 6.

evening" to Captain Hazard of the *Providence* and concludes with the statement that Hazard "brings with him also the *Standard*." This is a reference to the Gadsden flag. The log of the *Andrew Doria*, one of the ships of Hopkins's squadron, shows that the fleet sailed from Liberty Island on the morning of January 17 and ran down to Reedy Island that same day. So, the *Providence* could not have delivered the Gadsden Standard before January 13.

Gadsden wrote to Hopkins on January 15, saying that he intended to set out from New Castle, Delaware, on January 18, to get a packet ship for Charleston, South Carolina. The minutes of the South Carolina Provincial Congress record Gadsden's arrival on the night of February 8, 1776. The next day he took a seat as a member of that body. The minutes also state that Gadsden presented the Provincial Congress with "an elegant standard, such as is to be used by the commander in chief of the American navy; being a yellow field, with a lively representation of a rattle-snake in the middle, in the attitude of going to strike, and these words underneath 'DON'T TREAD ON ME'. Ordered, that the said standard be carefully preserved, and suspended in the Congress room."

The use of the rattlesnake symbol continued to spread. North Carolina used it on its twenty-dollar notes issued on April 2, 1776. A unique use of the symbol was that on the flag of Proctor's Independent Battalion, Westmoreland County, Pennsylvania, raised in 1775 (Figure 53). This was number fifty-two of a total of fifty-three battalions of the Associators of Pennsylvania. Colonel John Proctor was the commanding officer. The flag of the battalion is an old English red ensign altered for use by the Associators. In the center of the flag is a large rattlesnake coiled to strike; it faces the English ensign in the canton.

*Fig. 54   Flag of Sullivan's Life Guard
Rhode Island Historical Society.
Photograph by Robert P. Emlen*

The tail of the snake has thirteen rattles. Below the snake in large letters is the motto: "Don't Tread on Me." Above is the monogram *J.P.* and below these initials the letters *I.B.W.C.P.*, which stand for "John Proctor, Independent Brigade, also Battalion Westmoreland County, Pennsylvania." The flag measures seventy-six inches long by seventy inches wide.

Proctor's battalion did not fight in the Revolution as an organization, and it is not known if this flag was ever in battle. The flag was preserved by Colonel Proctor, and on his death passed to the next surviving officer. In 1879, when Benson Lossing was doing research, it was in the possession of Margaret Campbell Craig, the daughter of General Alexander Craig, the last surviving officer of the battalion. By 1907 it belonged to Miss Jane M. Craig of New Alexandria, Pennsylvania; it is now in the possession of the William Penn Memorial Museum at Harrisburg, Pennsylvania. As far as can be ascertained, this is one of the few surviving rattlesnake flags from the Revolution.

Another rattlesnake flag that survives in fragmentary form is the silk, regimental Sullivan flag, associated with the campaign in Rhode Island in 1777. This consists of nine blue and white stripes, with white at the top and bottom. The remnants of the canton show that it was white and had a rattlesnake painted on it, with the words "Dont Tread on Me" on a curved ribbon above the snake. The flag is preserved in the Rhode Island Historical Society in Providence (Figure 54).

Evidence of the continuing popularity of the rattlesnake as a symbol of the United States can be seen in a report of a group of Continental Navy captains dated February 17, 1777. The group suggested that the full dress uniform of a post captain in the Continental Navy should include a gold epaulet on the right shoulder with a rattlesnake embroidered on the strap as well as the motto "Don't tread on me." The buttons would also carry the rattlesnake and motto. The same report indicates that lieutenants would wear epaulets, and that their buttons would carry an anchor instead of the rattlesnake.

Fig. 55

Symbols of the warring nations during the Revolutionary War: the French cock, the Spanish lion, the English leopard, and the American rattlesnake. Tu la voulu *is translated "You wished it" or "You asked for it,"* A qu'el d'Estain *as 'O what a fate!" or "O what a destiny!" The original caption on the print translates as "From tyranny was born independence"* Library of Congress

76

Fig. 56 *Raising the Continental Union Flag over Prospect Hill; painting by Clyde De Land. Smithsonian Institution, courtesy of the Board of Education of Somerville, Mass.*

Still another indication of the use of the symbol appears in a French engraving inspired by the entry of France and Spain into the conflict against Great Britain. The engraving shows a female lion representing Britain being attacked by a male lion representing Spain, a rooster indicating France, and a rattlesnake symbolizing the United States (Figure 55).

The Continental Union Flag at the Siege of Boston

Meanwhile, Washington had been trying to weld the various colonial units before Boston into a disciplined army. In keeping with this effort, on January 1, 1776, he raised the Union flag over his encampment on Prospect Hill as a "compliment to the United Colonies" (Figure 56). On the same day Washington's camp received a copy of the king's speech to Parliament in which he expressed tenderness and compassion for his American subjects. Although Washington had proclaimed the new army and raised the flag before the speech arrived, the British in Boston interpreted the flag-raising as an indication that submission to Parliamentary authority would soon follow. Three days later, when Washington wrote to his secretary Joseph Reed in Philadelphia, he described the incident and added: "By this time, I presume, they begin to think it strange that we have not made a formal surrender of our lines."

MAJ. GEN'L
RICHARD GRIDLEY
HIS limned by HORN
Capt. Sam Gridley for Company E
finished in Feb of '76

AN APPEAL TO HEAVEN

FT. WM HENRY IN '55
FT. EDWARD ½ MOON IN 56
AND OTHERS
DESIGNED AND LAYED
by
GRIDLEY
AT LOVISBOVRG IN 58 AND
QUEBEC IN '59
COMMANDING ARTILLERY

CHARLESTOWN HTS IN '75
GRIDLEY LAYED YE WORKS

RETIRED IN NOV OF 75
NOW
FIELD-GUN FOUNDER
TO THE
CONTINENTAL CONGRESS

LOVISBOVRG IN '45
LT. COL. GRIDLEYS
ARTILLERY WON YE SIEGE

PRESENTED
by the
ASSEMBLY

LIFE IS ALL VNEVEN

Fig. 57 Drawing of the sketch on the powder horn of Major General Richard Gridley, February 1776 Massachusetts Historical Society

But not all the British misread the significance of the event on Prospect Hill. *The Middlesex Journal and Evening Advertiser* published an excerpt from a letter written by a captain of a British transport in Boston harbor, dated January 17, in which he said: "I can see the Rebels' camp very plain, whose colours a little while ago were entirely red; but on receipt of the King's speech (which they burnt) they have hoisted the Union Flag, which is here supposed to intimate the union of the provinces."

The *Annual Register,* published in London, also reported that the Americans "burnt the king's speech, and changed their colors from a plain red ground, which they had hitherto used, to a flag with thirteen stripes, as a symbol of the union and number of the colonies." The red flag may have been the regimental colors of the Second or Third Connecticut Regiment. Both carried mottos,

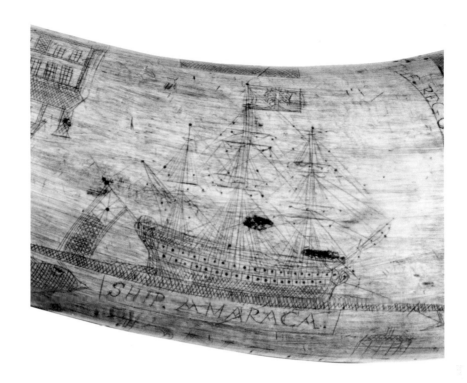

Fig. 58 *The Selden powder horn (detail): note the Pine Tree flag at the mainmast and the Grand Union flag at the stern. Massachusetts Historical Society*

but the lettering probably was not discernible at a distance. Although mistaken about the particular details of the flag on Prospect Hill, the conclusions of the British had a special significance. A plain red flag had long been associated with an act of protest or of defiance. The Americans in arms outside of Boston were surely involved in an act of defiance. But it was not simply a protest by Massachusetts men, for the men in arms had been adopted by the representatives of the thirteen colonies. The action of one colony represented the feelings of all.

The Continental Union flag is depicted on two contemporary powder horns. The first of these, now in the possession of the Bostonian Society, belonged to Major General Richard Gridley. Gridley was an engineer officer during King George's War and at the siege of Louisbourg he demonstrated great ability. After the battle of Lexington he served under General Artemus Ward, preparing a network of defensive positions of the colonial batteries on Dorchester Heights in March 1776. His powder horn was limned by his son in February of that year. It shows the colonial flag under which he served at Louisbourg in 1745, another under which he fought in the French and Indian War, and the third that flew over the American position on Charlestown Heights (Prospect Hill) in 1775 and 1776. This last flag has thirteen stripes and the British union in the canton (Figure 57).

A second powder horn of the period belonged to Major Samuel Selden, and is now preserved by the Massachusetts Historical Society. Selden was a member of the Provincial Assembly of Connecticut and a major in the Connecticut militia serving under Washington. His horn, dated March 9, 1776, shows the American positions only eight days before the British army evacuated Boston. It also shows the ship marked "Amaraca," which has the Continental Union flag at its stern. At the masthead is a flag bearing a broad-branched Liberty tree (Figure 58). The Union flag appears on other powder horns of this period, but

79

less clearly drawn. It also was depicted on some of the colonial currency issued at the time.

In line with preparations for the coming fight, Washington issued a General Order on February 20, 1776, designed to get the men distinctive uniforms and regiments distinctive flags. Unfortunately for Washington, this goal was not to be achieved for most of the war. By February 26, there were sufficient men and ammunition to go ahead with the seizure of Dorchester Heights on the night of March 4. In anticipation of a British attack, a system of flag signals was worked out to coordinate the movements of the three American divisions surrounding Boston. The Continental Union flag flying on a tall mast on Prospect Hill was by now a familiar sight. So too was the flag on the laboratory in Cambridge where cartridges were made and guns and accoutrements repaired. Washington ordered on March 4 that these flags were to be hoisted only in the event of a general alarm. When those flags were raised, "every Officer and Soldier, must repair to his alarm post."

On the evening of March 4, the American batteries opened fire on Boston to cover the advance on Dorchester Heights. The heights were seized and fortifications thrown up. Lord Howe, the British commander, was amazed to discover that the work had been done so rapidly. Continental guns now commanded the city and British shipping. The British were faced with the alternative of retaking the heights or abandoning Boston. At first Howe planned to attack, but bad weather made him change his plans. On March 17, British troops and loyalists boarded vessels and sailed to Halifax. Troops under General Ward, accompanied by an ensign bearing the Continental Union flag, entered the city. The main body of the army joined them there on March 20. Upon receipt of this news the Continental Congress gave a vote of thanks to Washington and his soldiers and ordered that a gold medal be struck and presented to the general.

Other Flags in the Beginning of the Revolution

Three flags are associated with the early period of the American Revolution. The first of these is the Hulbert flag, named for John Hulbert, the captain of a company of Minute Men from Long Island (Figure 59). In August 1775 Hulbert's company was ordered to Fort Ticonderoga to escort a group of British prisoners to Trenton. According to one account, they had a stars and stripes flag made for the company before they left Long Island. This flag consisted of thirteen red and white stripes with the red stripe at the top and bottom. Its thirteen six-pointed stars were arranged in a diamond formation so that the star design was 1-3-5-3-1.

Another version of the story of the Hulbert flag states that it was made from a captured British regimental flag acquired enroute to Ticonderoga. Still another version has the flag being made while the unit was in the Champlain Valley. The flag was supposedly flown at Fort Ticonderoga, but outside the fort. After delivering his prisoners, Hulbert reported to the Continental Congress in Philadelphia, supposedly taking his flag along with him. According to some accounts, Francis Hopkinson observed Hulbert's flag in Philadelphia and was thus inspired to work on designs for a flag that were eventually presented to the Continental Congress. But Hopkinson did not arrive in Philadelphia until June 28, 1776, some seven months after Hulbert had left.

Fig. 59   The Hulbert Flag
Smithsonian Institution, courtesy
Suffolk County Historical Society
Museum, Riverhead, N.Y.

Fig. 60　*The Forster Flag*
Dr. Whitney Smith, Flag Research
Center, Winchester, Mass.

Fig. 61
Canton of the flag of Major Israel
Forster
Essex Institute, Salem, Mass.

Documents relating to Hulbert's service and a flag wrapped in paper were found in the wall of a house in Bridgehampton, New York, in 1926. The documents have been generally accepted as authentic, but when Grace Cooper examined the flag in 1972 she determined that it was stitched with thread and had cotton muslin stars that were not used prior to the nineteenth century. The stars were also attached in a manner that was not typical of flags to be used in the field or flown from a staff. On the basis of this evidence, Mrs. Cooper concluded that the Hulbert flag is not a Revolutionary War flag, and that it could not date to any time prior to the middle of the nineteenth century. The flag found in Bridgehampton may be a copy of an earlier flag that deteriorated, but that is pure speculation.

Another flag that has been linked to the early days of the Revolution is the Forster flag, owned by the Flag Research Foundation of Winchester, Massachusetts. This is a red silk flag with thirteen white bars sewn along the hoist edge. It measures approximately five by seven feet.

According to oral tradition, the Forster flag was made from a captured British flag. The canton containing the Cross of St. George and the Cross of St. Andrew was cut out and replaced with a piece of cloth to match the field of the flag. The white cloth from the removed crosses was used to cut thirteen stripes, each approximately 2¼ inches wide and 6 inches long. Six of these were sewn to one side of the flag and seven to the other. By this method an attempt was made to create the effect of thirteen red and white stripes on each side of the flag (Figure 60). The flag is said to have belonged to Israel Forster and was supposedly used about the time of the seige of Boston. A textile and thread examination of this flag by a Smithsonian curator indicates that the flag could date from the Revolutionary War. It is believed to have been used as a Grand Division Color.*

Mention of the name Forster in connection with this flag led to an examination of another flag associated with Israel Forster that is preserved at the Essex Institute, Salem, Massachusetts (Figure 61). This flag has white and blue

---

* A Grand Division consisted of two companies acting under the command of a single officer.

horizontal stripes of ribbon fabric and measures 20½ inches wide by 21⅛ inches high. There is evidence that the canton originally had stripes of ribbon ⅞ inches wide that were placed equidistant from each other. At some point these were replaced by the present open, plain weave ribbon. The indications are that the piece preserved was the canton of a flag, presumably one with a white fly. A Smithsonian textile expert has also examined this second Forster flag and has indicated that there are no technical aspects which would prevent its being of the Revolutionary War era.

Since both of these flags are associated with the same family, there is speculation that the color schemes and stripe arrangements were used to provide both similarity and diversity after the fashion of company flags of the pre-Revolutionary times.

Flags in the Defense of the Northern Frontier

In the fall of 1775, while Washington's Army was before Boston, a Continental force under General Richard Montgomery invaded Canada. It was hoped that the invasion would encourage the Canadians to join forces with the thirteen American colonies in their struggle against the British. Montreal surrendered to General Montgomery on November 13, 1775. He then joined with a force under General Benedict Arnold for an assault on Quebec. The attack was begun during a snowstorm on the night of December 30. Montgomery was killed, Arnold was wounded, and the attack failed; a large number of Americans were captured. A remnant under Arnold held on until the spring, then retreated. By June it was apparent that the Canadians were not going to join with the colonists and the campaign was abandoned.

The British now implemented a plan to split New England from the middle colonies. From Halifax, Nova Scotia, General Howe sailed with a strong force of troops to attack New York City. It was planned that another army under Sir Guy Carleton would move from Canada via Lake Champlain to Albany, New York, on the Hudson River. Here he would be met by elements of Howe's army advancing upriver from New York City.

The British offensive in the north was not successful, due to the efforts of General Benedict Arnold. Bringing shipwrights and carpenters from New England coastal towns to Lake Champlain, he supervised the building of a fleet of two small schooners, two sloops, four galleys, and eight gondolas to dispute the British passage down the lake. While this fleet was being prepared, General Philip Schuyler, the commander of the Continental troops in northern New York, forwarded to Washington a list of thirty-eight kinds of equipment needed for the flotilla, including "40 small Colours Continental, some red blue for Signals."

About three weeks later General Schuyler's secretary, Richard Varick, sent Washington another request for supplies. The list, which included flags, indicated that such articles "cannot be procured at ALBANY, or at any place between this and NEW YORK." Among the items forwarded to Schuyler by Stephen Moylan, the quartermaster general of the Continental army, were "1 piece Blue Bunting" and "2 Ensign Colours."

The Continental flotilla, now commanded by General Benedict Arnold, had aroused the concern of the British, who constructed a fleet of their own to oppose it. A watercolor sketch of Arnold's fleet was made by one C. Randle,

Fig. 62   *The Continental flotilla on Lake Champlain (detail)*
Public Archives of Canada

Fig. 63   *Contemporary sketch of the Grand Union flag on the* Royal Savage, *1776 (detail). Schuyler Papers, Manuscripts and Archives Division, New York Public Library.*

presumably a spy, and sent to Canada. It shows Arnold's flagship, *Royal Savage*, with the union flag (Figure 62). Instead of the blue background of the British union, the *Royal Savage's* flag embodies an interesting arrangement of red and blue triangles. Also, both crosses are white instead of the St. George's red and the St. Andrew's white.

Another watercolor sketch of the *Royal Savage* turned up in the Schuyler Papers in the New York Public Library (Figure 63). The artist and date are unknown, though it was filed under the date of June 22, 1776. On the back of the sketch in the handwriting of General Schuyler is an endorsement identifying the vessel as "Wynkoop's Schooner." Colonel Cornelius Wynkoop was in command of the *Royal Savage* from May 7 to August 18, 1776, when he was replaced by Arnold.

On October 11, Arnold's flotilla was attacked by the larger British squadron on the lake. After a seven-hour battle during which the Americans lost two ships and many men, the British withdrew to refit. It was their intention to finish Arnold's force off in the morning, but he escaped with what was left of his command. The British moved on to Fort Ticonderoga but decided that it was too strong to take except by siege and there was too little time left for that before winter. Carleton thus withdrew his forces to Canada. Arnold's actions saved the northern frontier and perhaps the Revolution itself.

Following the British evacuation of Boston, Washington moved his army to New York and strengthened the city's defenses. In anticipation of the arrival of the British fleet, he appointed a committee to devise a system of warning signals. The committee recommended the use of large "ensigns with broad stripes of red and white" to signal the alarm, or, at night, a system of fires.

On July 1, 1776, transports bearing 32,000 British and German troops under the command of Sir William Howe arrived off Sandy Hook. The southern phase of the British offensive to split the colonies was about to begin. By the end of the month the troops were encamped on Staten Island and thirty British men-of-war and hundreds of transports were in New York harbor. Ambrose Serle, who was aboard Admiral Lord Howe's flagship *Eagle* when it entered the harbor, described the experience in a letter to the Earl of Dartmouth. On the matter of the flag flown by Continental forces, he wrote: "They have set up their Standard in the Fort upon the Southern Point of the Town. The Colors are thirteen Stripes of Red and White alternately, with the English Union cantoned in the Corner."

The British landed on Long Island on August 22, and forced Washington's army to withdraw to Manhattan Island. A subsequent British attack in September drove the Americans from Manhattan. Washington retreated with his army across New Jersey and into Pennsylvania. British forces occupied New York and New Jersey. The southern phase of the British offensive in New York state was off to a good start.

The American Winter Offensive: Trenton

The loss of New York City and New Jersey was a severe blow to the American cause. Independence had been declared barely six months before, and now hopes of achieving it were quite low. As enlistments expired men left for home. Others deserted. With Washington's army in its retreat across New Jersey was Thomas Paine, whose pamphlet *Common Sense* had done so much to infuse the spirit of independence in the colonists. Paine now wrote a new address, *The American Crisis*, which was read to each regiment. It began: "These are the times that try men's souls: The summer soldier and the sunshine patriot will, in this crisis shrink from the service of his country; but he that stands it now deserves the love and thanks of man and woman." That stirring pamphlet helped to inspire a new spirit of determination in the army.

Leading a portion of his army across the Delaware River, Washington attacked a Hessian camp in Trenton on the morning of December 26, 1776. The attack was a complete surprise. Thirty Hessians were killed and 32 officers and 888 men were captured. Washington lost only two dead and three wounded. The victory gave inspiration to the army and to the people. Later, Lord Germain, speaking before the House of Commons, said: "All our hopes were blasted by that unhappy affair at Trenton."

A century later the victory was commemorated in the painting by Emanuel Leutze, *Washington Crossing the Delaware*. Leutze, who used the Rhine as his model, depicted huge chunks of ice that were totally out of keeping with actual conditions on the Delaware River. But the most serious error was the inclusion of the stars and stripes on the painting. The battle took place six months before the stars and stripes were adopted and many years before such flags were in use by the army.

Notes

For a detailed account of the beginnings of the war see Christopher Ward, *The War of the Revolution*, 2 vols. (New York, 1952), 1:32–305. The British diary entry on Concord is from Lieutenant P. F. Thorne of the 4th Foot, quoted in Isaac J. Greenwood, *Captain John Manley*

(Boston, 1915), p. 77. The Bedford flag is described in Frank Earle Schermerhorn, *American and French Flags of the Revolution* (Philadelphia, 1948). The flag itself is preserved in the Bedford Free Public Library, Bedford, Mass.

Concerning the flags used in the fighting around Boston, the quotation from Benson J. Lossing is from his work, *The Pictorial Field Book of the Revolution*, 2 vols. (New York, 1852), 2:541. The reference to Mrs. Manning is on the same page in footnote 4. Preble's conclusions about the absence of flags at Bunker Hill are in his *History of the Flag of the United States*, pp. 199–201. Trumbull's account is in Colonel Theodore Sizer, ed., *Autobiography of John Trumbull* (New Haven, 1953), p. 19. The account by the Royal Marines officer is John Clarke, *An Impartial and Authentic Narrative of the Battle Fought on the 17th of June 1775 . . .* (London, 1775), p. 31. On regimental colors in use during the Revolution see Gherardi Davis, *Regimental Colors of the War of the Revolution* (New York, 1907), and Schermerhorn, *American and French Flags of the Revolution*. Details on the flag of the Philadelphia Troop of Light Horse are in Joseph Lapsey Wilson, ed., *Book of the First Troop of Philadelphia City Cavalry, 1774–1914* (Philadelphia, 1915), pp. 1–8. Photographs of the original receipts for painting the flag were sent with the letter of Raymond V. Shepherd to William R. Furlong, April 14, 1964.

Events connected with the raising of the Grand Union flag over the American camp are discussed in Preble, pp. 217–19. A more detailed account, aimed in part at correcting portions of Preble's work, is Alfred Morton Cutler, *The Continental "Great Union" Flag* (Somerville, Mass., 1929). Prospect Hill is located in what is now the city of Somerville, and the pamphlet by Cutler was published by the Somerville School Committee. The text of Washington's letter to Joseph Reed of Jan. 4, 1776, is published in John C. Fitzpatrick. ed., *The Writings of George Washington From the Original Manuscript Sources, 1745-1799*, 37 vols. (Washington, 1931–40), 4:210–11. Washington's orders of Feb. 20, 1776, and of March 4, 1776, are published in 4:341 and 368–69. The quotation from a captain of a British transport in Boston harbor is from Preble, p. 218. The full text is printed in Peter Force, ed., *American Archives*, 4th Ser., 11 vols. (Washington, 1837–53), 4:710–11. The quotation from the *Annual Register* for 1776 is from the third edition (London, 1782), p. 147. On the raising of the flag of the Third Connecticut Regiment on Prospect Hill on July 18, 1775, see the diary entry of Paul Lunt of Newburyport, Mass., published in the Massachusetts Historical Society *Proceedings*, 1st Ser. (Boston, 1879–   ), 12:195.

Preble's work contains information on the rattlesnake flags, the outfitting of Esek Hopkins's fleet, and the flag of the *Royal Savage* on Lake Champlain, pp. 212–20. Documents relating to the naval aspects can be conveniently consulted in the multivolume series published by the Naval Historical Center, U.S. Navy Department, *Naval Documents of the American Revolution*, edited by William Bell Clark and William J. Morgan (Washington, 1964–   ), hereafter cited as *Naval Documents*. Timothy Matlack's letter is in the Esek Hopkins Papers in the Rhode Island Historical Society and is printed in *Naval Documents*, 3:671. Christopher Gadsden's letter to Esek Hopkins is printed in the same volume on pages 805–06. The log or journal of the *Andrew Doria* is in the British Public Record Office, Admiralty 1/484, copies of which are in the Library of Congress. The journal is printed in *Naval Documents*, 3:838–39. Gadsden's presentation to the Continental Congress of a flag is in the same volume, p. 1190.

The letter written by a British captain in Boston Harbor on Jan. 17, 1776, is in Force's *American Archives*, 4th Ser., 4:710–11, and is reprinted in *Naval Documents*, 3:835.

The long quotation on the rattlesnake is from Force's *American Archives*, 4th Ser., 4:468–69, and is reprinted in *Naval Documents*, 3:266–68. The work by a modern naturalist is Laurence M. Klauber, *Rattlesnakes: Their Habits, Life Histories, and Influence on Mankind*, 2 vols., (Berkeley, 1956).

For the story of the Hulbert flag see Morton Pennypacker, "Capt. John Hulbert and His Flag of 1775," *New York History*, 14 (1933):356–59. Grace Rogers Cooper's reports on the Hulbert and Forster flags are in the custody of the Division of Naval History, Smithsonian Institution.

General Philip Schuyler's letter to George Washington of July 12, 1776, and its enclosures are in the Washington Papers, as is Richard Varick's letter of Aug. 3, 1776. Varick's letter has been printed in Force's *American Archives*, 5th Ser., 744. Additional data relating to the supply question may be found in *Naval Documents*, 5:1306–07, and 6:33–34. Stephen Moylan's letter to Schuyler is printed in *American Archives*, 5th Ser., 1:919. Ambrose Serle's description of the Continental Union flag is in Benjamin Franklin Stevens, ed., *Facsimiles of Manuscripts in European Archives Relating to America, 1773-1783*, 25 vols. (London, 1889–95), 24:2040. These volumes were reprinted by the Mellifont Press of Wilmington, Del., in 1970.

As this work goes to press information has been received casting doubt on the dating of the rattlesnake flag of the United Train of Artillery Company of Providence, R.I. Research by Carol D. Andrews of Marblehead, Mass., indicates that the flag was painted by John Ritto Penniman, who was not born until 1782. In 1805 Penniman set up his shop in Boston and began his career as an ornamental painter. By 1811 he was recognized as an accomplished painter of military standards. It is believed that the standard of the United Train of Artillery was painted in 1826, on the occasion of the 50th anniversary of the unit. This information is in a letter of Carol D. Andrews to Harold D. Langley, February 12, 1981, in the files of the Division of Naval History, Smithsonian Institution.

*Fig. 64 Contemporary sketch of a floating
battery with a Pine Tree flag (detail)
Library of Congress*

CHAPTER **6**

Flags Used at Sea, *1775–1777*

Fig. 65   The Pine Tree flag design used by Washington's cruisers

The Pine Tree Flag

In September 1775 two strong scows were launched on the Charles River and armed with four swivel guns and at each end a heavy cannon. These scows, known as floating batteries, were pierced near the water line for oars so that some degree of maneuverability could be achieved (Figure 64). As an ensign, they flew a white flag with a pine tree design and the slogan: "An Appeal to Heaven" (Figure 65). The use of a tree on early New England flags has already been mentioned. It was perhaps in keeping with this tradition that some Americans thought the tree flag a fitting symbol to use at sea.

On October 7, 1775, the Continental Congress debated a resolution from Rhode Island that a fleet be created to intercept British supplies coming to Boston by sea. Congress authorized the outfitting of two vessels on October 13. Soon after this, Washington's headquarters received word that a small British squadron was bombarding Falmouth and Portsmouth. Colonel Joseph Reed, Washington's secretary, was concerned about how the American vessels might attack this squadron and wrote to Colonel John Glover and Stephen Moylan, who were supervising the outfitting of the force. "Please to fix upon Some particular Colour for a Flag—," wrote Reed, "& a Signal, by which our Vessels may know one another—What do you think of a Flag with a White Ground, a Tree in the Middle—the Motto (*Appeal to Heaven*)—This is the Flag of our floating Batteries—We are fitting out two Vessels at Plymouth & when I next hear from you on this Subject I will let them know the Flag & the Signal, that we may distinguish our Friends from our Foes."

Glover and Moylan replied that the vessels had sailed that morning, and, "as they had none but their old Colours, we appointed them a signal, that they may Know each other by, & be known to their friends—the ensign up to the Main topping Lift." The old colors referred to evidently meant the British flag that had normally been with the ship in peacetime.

The Continental armed brig *Washington*, captured by the British on December 5, 1775, and taken into Boston, was a subject of some interest to the king's forces. In reporting the capture to Lord Sandwich in England, Sir Hugh Palliser described the colors of the ship as "a white field with a green pine

87

tree in the middle: the motto, Appeal to Heaven." The flag was to be sent to Admiral John Montagu, whose son, Captain George Montagu of H.M.S. *Fowey*, captured the *Washington*. It was, however, first shown to King George III. We know that this flag was made by Lucy Hammett in November 1775 for fourteen shillings.

The Massachusetts Council, or upper house of the legislature, meeting on December 29, 1775, noted that several of the colonies had thought it expedient to fit out armed vessels for the defense of American liberty and the protection of the colony by sea. It therefore resolved to appoint a two-man committee to draw up a plan for fitting out one or more armed vessels. With the appointment of this committee the Massachusetts navy began. On the basis of the committee's report, the General Court passed several resolutions in April 1776 relating to the sea service of Massachusetts. One relating to uniforms and flags said: "*Resolved*, That the Uniform of the Officers be Green and White, and that they furnish themselves accordingly. and the Colors be a White Flagg, with a Green pine-tree and an inscription 'appeal to Heaven'."

The pine tree flag was also used by privateers licensed by Massachusetts. The armed brig *Yankee Hero*, commanded by Captain James Tracy, was captured off Boston in June 1776 by H.M.S. *Milford*. A white flag with a pine tree is mentioned in a news item on the capture published in Halifax, Nova Scotia, on June 10.

The flag of the privateer *Cumberland*, captured by H.M.S. *Pomona* on January 26, 1778, had an unusual combination of symbols. According to the journal of John Greenwood, an eighteen-year-old midshipman on the *Cumberland*, their colors were "a very large white flag, with a green pine tree painted in the middle of it, beneath which was represented a large black snake in thirteen coils and cut into as many pieces, emblematic of the thirteen United States; under the snake, in black letters, was the motto—'Join or Die'."

The Continental Union Flag: The First Flag of the Alfred

Thoroughly alarmed by the British actions in New England, and by Lord Dunmore's hostilities and his attempts to foment a slave insurrection in Virginia and the Chesapeake Bay region, the Continental Congress voted funds on November 2, 1775, to fit out a fleet. Congress hoped to send this fleet under the command of Commodore Esek Hopkins to protect the southern colonies. Four vessels were purchased, armed, and manned; they were named *Alfred, Columbus, Cabot*, and *Andrew Doria*. While the ships were being prepared, the Wharton Ship Yard of Philadelphia was also busy making various pennants, ensigns, and flags. A December 2, 1775, entry in an account book of the Wharton Yard credits Margaret Manny with making an ensign for the ship *Alfred*.

In addition to carrying the Continental Union flag with its red and white stripes, ships of Commodore Hopkins's fleet and others were sometimes supplied Union flags with different colored stripes. This was done to make positive identification of a ship much easier, and was evidently an adaptation of the British practice of using blue, red, or white ensigns to distinguish the three divisions of the fleet. An example of the practice can be seen in the account book of Philadelphia ship chandler James Wharton. On December 6, 1775, the Naval Committee of Congress ordered a flag for Captain Allen Moore that had

Fig. 66   A contemporary painting of Captain Esek Hopkins: note the Pine Tree flag and the Navy Jack with a rattlesnake in the background U.S. Naval Academy Museum

blue and white stripes. Another order, placed by the Committee on December 20, 1775, called for a Union flag with thirteen green and red stripes, as well as three pennants: one green, one white and one red. On January 1, 1776, the Committee was also billed for two blue and white flags, and one red, white, blue and green flag.

On December 2, the same day that Margaret Manny was credited with making the *Alfred's* flag, Commodore Esek Hopkins agreed to take command of the Continental Navy (Figure 66). The next day, Lieutenant John Paul Jones hoisted the Union ensign on the *Alfred*, which had previously been named the *Black Prince*. A description of this event was sent to the Earl of Dartmouth by Bernard Page, a Loyalist clergyman who since Lexington had twice visited eight colonies and observed preparations. Regarding such activities, he said in part:

A Continental and Provincial currencies, to facilitate this great undertaking, are emitted, which circulate freely, and are daily exchanged for silver and gold. Their harbours by the spring will swarm with privateers. An Admiral is ap-

Fig. 67 The Continental or Grand Union Flag

pointed, a court established, and the 3d instant, the Continental Flag on board the *Black Prince*, opposite Philadelphia, was hoisted.

It has been suggested that the flag noted may have been one of the old colonial flags. It seems unlikely that Page would make such an error, however, for he was an educated and well-traveled man. Nor does the context in which the flag is mentioned suggest that it was a familiar colonial color. Another informer reported that the *Alfred* carried "English Colours but more Striped. . . ."

An American account of the sailing of the fleet was sent from Philadephia to New Bern, North Carolina, where its substance was incorporated in another letter. After naming the ships and the number of guns carried, the New Bern letter says: "They sailed from *Philadelphia*, amidst the acclamation of the many thousands assembled on the joyful occasion, under the display of a *Union Flag*, with thirteen stripes in the field, emblematical [*sic*] of the thirteen colonies."

This fleet, under the command of Commodore Esek Hopkins, attacked two British forts on New Providence Island in the Bahamas, capturing a number of cannon and a large quantity of shot. A letter from New Providence, published in the London *Ladies' Magazine*, described the flags of the American fleet that attacked. The colors were "striped under the union, with thirteen strokes, called the thirteen United Colonies and their standard a rattlesnake, motto, 'Don't tread upon me'." This description confirms those given when the fleet sailed from Philadelphia.

Another observer, writing to England to December 6, 1775, spoke to the *Alfred* under its previous name: "The Black Prince, a fine vessel, I believe you know her well, carries a flag, and mounts twenty to thirty twelve and sixteen pounders, beside swivels, and fights them mostly under deck."

Four years later, in a letter to the president of the Continental Congress, John Paul Jones recalled a ceremony he had participated in as the ranking first lieutenant of the *Alfred*. "I hoisted with my own Hands the Flag of Freedom the First time that it was displayed on board the Alfred on the Delaware." But he wrote these words after independence had been declared. On December 3, 1775, he hoisted the Grand Union flag which did not signify freedom, but a united resistance to Parliamentary tyranny while proclaiming loyalty to the king (Figure 67).

The question of how the Continental Union flag came to be purchased for the *Alfred* has intrigued historians of the flag. As a first lieutenant in charge of preparing the *Alfred* for sea, Jones had no authority to purchase or to hoist the Union flag. That authority and initiative apparently came from Joseph Hewes, a delegate to the Continental Congress from North Carolina and a member of the committee of the Congress charged with fitting out its newly acquired ships. The friendship between Jones and Hewes went back to Scotland where, as John Paul, the former joined a masonic fraternity at Kircudbright; his application was attested by James Smith. This James Smith was the brother of Robert Smith, a partner of the mercantile firm of Hewes and Smith of Edenton, North Carolina, whom Jones later met when he came to the colonies. Another fellow townsman from Scotland was David Sproat, who settled in Philadelphia. When Jones went from Virginia to Philadelphia in the fall of 1775 to seek employment in the ships being fitted out by the Continental Congress, letters were addressed to him in care of David Sproat. By late September or early October Jones was in Philadelphia. Joseph Hewes arrived there on October 22. On October 30, Hewes was one of the four members added to the naval committee to hasten the work of outfitting the ships of the Continental

*Fig. 68 The Grand Union Flag on North
Carolina currency of 1776*

Navy. As a member of the committee, Hewes may well have called upon Jones
to help with the job.

Two days after Hewes arrived in Philadelphia, there was a bit of excitement
when Captain Abraham Markoe and a part of the Light Horse Troop took two
loyalists to Lancaster and York for confinement. Hewes, Jones, and others may
have seen or heard talk of the flag of the Troop, perhaps of its thirteen
symbolic stripes. It is likely that there was some talk of the colors the ships
would carry, and presumably Hewes or the committee authorized the making
of the Continental Union flag.

We do know that Hewes himself was interested in the new flag, for he
purchased a large one from Margaret Manny on February 8, 1776. This flag
was sent to his home in Edenton, along with colors, drums, and "sundry
articles" which were distributed to the North Carolina troops. The large
Continental Union flag was raised in Edenton. By this time, according to
Governor Johnston, "All our people are full of the idea of independence . . . ."
A picture of the Continental Union flag was used on a seven and a half dollar
paper note issued by North Carolina on April 2, 1776 (Figure 68). That same
day a twenty dollar note bearing a rattlesnake was also issued. (See above,
p. 91).

While the British were moving against New York, the Continental sloop-of-
war *Reprisal* under Captain Lambert Wickes was on a mission to the French
island of Martinique to obtain muskets and powder. He was also to land there
William Bingham, an agent of the Continental Congress. A few hours before
the *Reprisal* arrived off St. Pierre, the British sloop-of-war *Shark* entered the
harbor and anchored. Her commander, Captain John Chapman, made an
official call on the governor. Captain Chapman was returning to his ship when
he saw the *Reprisal* with her strange flag. In his report he says: "I saw a sail in
the Offing with Colours which I was unacquainted with (being red and white
striped with a Union next the Staff)."

Chapman rightly assumed that the ship was "the property of his Brittanick
Majesty's Rebellious Subjects in North America" and sailed out to speak to it.
The *Reprisal* failed to answer hails in French and English. A hot fight lasting

Fig. 69 The Lexington *and its flag*
National Maritime Museum,
Greenwich, England

about three quarters of an hour ensued, after which the *Shark* broke off the fight to chase a small schooner. The schooner came under the protection of a shore battery which fired two shots, whereupon the *Shark* stood out to sea.

After the fight Captain Wickes came ashore at St. Pierre, where the inhabitants gave him a warm and happy reception. The following morning the *Shark* returned to the harbor and Captain Chapman had a chance to learn the name of his American opponent and the identity of his ship. In a letter to Vice Admiral James Young he noted that the *Reprisal* carried 120 men and 18 six-pounder cannons. "The Colours which the ship hoisted had 13 Red & White stripes in the field, with the Union in the upper part next to the staff." The colors described by Captain Chapman are the same as those used in Esek Hopkins's fleet, the Continental or Union flag, which some historians have called the Grand or Great Union flag.

Another early rendering of the Continental Union flag can be seen in a painting of the ship *Lexington* (Figure 69). In 1777 the *Lexington*, under the command of Captain Henry Johnson, was one of three vessels sent out from France by Benjamin Franklin, then one of the American commissioners there, to raid British shipping. The commanders were instructed to capture ships of the Irish linen fleet. They missed those ships, but captured eighteen others.

Fig. 70   First official salute to the American
flag; painting by Philipps Melville,
1976
The White House

On returning to the French coast the American vessels were chased by a larger British ship into French ports. The British ambassador protested to the French government over its having permitted American ships and prizes to be brought into French ports. Diplomatic pressure forced the ships to sail for America. En route the *Lexington* was captured by the H.M.S. *Alert* and taken to Plymouth, England. A water color painting of the *Lexington*, presumably done in Plymouth, is now preserved in the National Maritime Museum in England. There is no date of the painting, and the name of the artist is unknown; it was among the pages of an old manuscript that was published in 1787, ten years after the scene depicted. The *Lexington*'s flag is hoisted at the masthead under the British flag. The Continental Union flag has the crosses of St. George and St. Andrew in the canton, and thirteen stripes of red, white, and blue in the fly.

First Foreign Salutes to the Continental Union Flag

The first salute by a foreign power to the Continental Union flag of which there is any proof took place at the Danish island of St. Croix on October 25, 1776. A British sympathizer or spy named Kelly sent word of the incident to the British Vice Admiral Young, who forwarded it to Lord George Germain. Kelly mentioned the departure of an unnamed American schooner (merchant vessel) from St. Croix with a small cargo of powder. He added: "But my astonishment was great to find such a Commerce countenanced by Government here. The Vessel went out under American Colours, saluted the Fort and had the compliment returned the same as if she had been an English or Danish ship."

When the Continental brig *Andrew Doria* arrived in the harbor of the island of St. Eustatius on November 16, 1776, she was saluted by the guns of Fort Orange with eleven guns (Figure 70). This was the first foreign salute to the

93

Continental Union flag received by an American man-of-war. Isaiah Robinson, her captain, was pleased to receive this honor a few months after the adoption of the Declaration of Independence. On board the *Andrew Doria* was seventeen-year-old John Trottman, a son of a pro-British merchant at Barbados. Young Trottman had been attending Princeton College when he was seized in Philadelphia and impressed into Continental service on board the *Andrew Doria*. In a subsequent affidavit he swore that the ship was saluted by thirteen guns at St. Eustatius and replied with nine or eleven guns; he also said that the ship had "the flag of the Continental Congress Colours then flying." Trottman escaped and rowed to the British island of St. Christopher, where he gave this story to the authorities.

Another witness of Loyalist persuasion was James Fraser, who was talking to two officers on board a sloop in St. Eustatius harbor when the *Andrew Doria* entered. He quotes himself as saying: "There comes the tender of a man-of-war," meaning a small vessel that sometimes accompanied a man-of-war. But no, he recalled one of his companions, a Captain Dean, replying: "No, by G-d, it is an American privateer,—for do you not see the flag of the Continental Congress with thirteen stripes?"

The Trottman and Fraser affidavits were sent by the governor of St. Christopher to the British ambassador. He forwarded them to the Estates General of the Netherlands with a note informing the Dutch government that the British king demanded a formal disavowal of the salute and the recall of the Dutch governor. The Dutch replied that they disavowed any past or future act that might be construed as recognizing the independence and sovereignty of the North American colonies of Great Britain. Furthermore, orders had been sent to the governors and commanders in the Dutch colonies in the West Indies to observe earlier prohibitions against the exportation of ammunition to the British settlements.

In keeping with this policy, the Dutch government ordered Johannes de Graef, the governor of St. Eustatius, to return to Holland. He asked to be excused because he was severly affected by sea sickness when he traveled on ships, and this was a long journey. Eventually he was required to leave, but by the time he reached the Netherlands in 1778 the independence of the American colonies was so generally recognized there that the case against him was not pressed. He later asked for a promotion, but died before any action was taken.

Notes

The sources for this chapter may be most readily consulted in the volumes published by the U.S. Navy Department, Naval History Division, *Naval Documents of the American Revolution*. For material on the floating batteries see volume 2. The original letter of Colonel Joseph Reed to Colonel John Glover and Stephen Moylan is in vol. 2, p. 538; their reply is on pp. 565–68. Sir Hugh Palliser's letter to Lord Sandwich is in vol. 3, pp. 481–82. The reference to Lucy Hammett's flag is also in vol. 3, p. 321. On the origins of the Massachusetts navy see 3:291, and 4:667–68, 779 and 796. The quotation on uniforms and the pine tree flag is in 4:1302–3. For descriptions of the flag of the *Yankee Hero* see 5:391–92, 507–08, and 725. The reference to the flag of the *Cumberland* is in Isaac J. Greenwood, *The Revolutionary Services of John Greenwood of Boston and New York, 1775–1783* (New York, 1927), p. 50.

Documents on the preparation of the fleet of Esek Hopkins are in *Naval Documents*, 2:441–442 and 1305; 3:207, 215, 607–11, 848, and 1377–91. On Margaret Manny see the Wharton account books in the Historical Society of Pennsylvania, p. 34. Pertinent entries are published in *Naval*

Documents 3:1380. On the hoisting of the flag on the *Alfred* see *Naval Documents* 2:1306–7, and footnote 2. The quotation from Bernard Page is from his letter of Dec. 20, 1775, to the Earl of Dartmouth in the Dartmouth Papers, William Salt Library, Stafford, Staffordshire, England. Permission to reproduce the letter in full was given by the then Earl of Dartmouth to Admiral William R. Furlong, in a letter dated Sept. 31, 1962, from Mr. F. B. Stitt, librarian of the Salt Library, to Admiral William R. Furlong, Furlong Files, Division of Naval History, Smithsonian Institution. For another Page quotation on the raising of the flag on the *Alfred*, see *Naval Documents* 3:186. The letter of the unidentified informer pertaining to the flag of the *Alfred* is dated Philadelphia, Jan. 4, 1776, and enclosed with a letter from Captain Hyde Parker, Jr., to Vice Admiral Molyneux Shuldham; see *Naval Documents* 3:615. The quotation on the sailing of Hopkins's fleet from Philadelphia is in the same volue, pp. 1322–23. The letter from New Providence describing the union and the rattlesnake flags is published in the [London] *Ladies Magazine* 7 (1776):390. For Captain Chapman's letter to Vice Admiral James Young, RN see *Naval Documents* 5:1278.

For the report of the spy, Kelly, to Vice Admiral Young on the salute to the Continental flag, see the letter dated St. Croix, October 27, 1776, in the Public Record Office Transcripts, Colonial Office, class 5, vol. 126, pp. 247–50, in the Library of Congress. On the role of the Dutch on St. Eustatius see J. Franklin Jameson, "St. Eustatius in the American Revolution," *American Historical Review* 8 (1903):638–708.

Fig. 71   Battle of Princeton (detail);
painting by James Peale
Princeton University

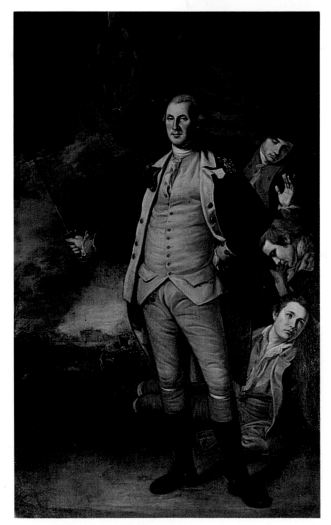

Fig. 72   Washington at the Battle of
Princeton; *painting by Charles*
Willson Peale, c. 1778–81
Princeton University

Fig. 73   Washington at the Battle of
Princeton; *portrait by Charles*
Willson Peale, c. 1778–81
Pennsylvania Academy of Fine Arts

CHAPTER 7

The Evolution of the Stars and Stripes

The American victory at Trenton was followed by another at Princeton on January 3, 1777. Artists Charles Willson Peale and his brother James commemorated the Princeton battle in paintings which include illustrations of flags. James Peale's painting, done some years later, showed a flag with an entirely blue field and no stripes. The six-pointed stars are apparently arranged in three rows (Figure 71). It would appear that if the flag were spread out with the flag pole at the left, the stars would be in the upper left-hand corner of the flag. According to the late Donald D. Egbert, a professor of art and archeology at Princeton University, the painting was done before April 1786, not earlier than 1779, and probably not earlier than November 1783. The use of the stars indicates that Peale could have known that the army quartermaster in Philadelphia was ordering stars to be placed on regimental colors in 1778.

A painting of George Washington after the battle of Princeton, done by Charles Willson Peale, was executed in 1783–84 for Princeton College. This shows the stars and stripes, and in the background a small blue flag with a circle of white stars. The latter is obviously the Washington Headquarters flag. The stars and stripes are anachronistic, for they had not yet been adopted at the time of the battle of Princeton (Figure 72).

Still another painting of Washington after the battle of Princeton, one of a long series done by Charles Willson Peale between 1778 and 1781, shows a blue flag with a circle of thirteen white stars (Figure 73). Although Peale was actually in the battle of Princeton, these paintings, done in his Philadelphia studio, evidence considerable artistic license. Peale depicted a flag that he had obtained in Philadelphia after Congress had adopted the stars and stripes, and after the use of the stars in regimental colors had been ordered in 1778.

After the victory of the Continental forces at the battle of Princeton, Washington led his army into winter quarters at Morristown, New Jersey. In the spring of 1777 Washington and General Howe at New Brunswick sent small forces to probe each other, seeking a favorable opportunity to do battle. By June it was apparent to Washington that the British were going to make

Fig. 74 Francis Hopkinson; *portrait by*
Thomas Sully
National Gallery of Art

another attempt to take Philadelphia. He sent General Mifflin to that city to apprise the Congress and the people of the coming danger.

Congress responded by taking steps to strengthen the defenses on the Delaware River. A three-man board, created by Congress on November 6, 1776, to execute navy business under the direction of the Marine Committee, set about welding the Pennsylvania navy and the Continental armed vessels on the Delaware into a coordinated defense team. The Navy Board, chaired by Francis Hopkinson, sent a letter to Robert Morris, the chairman of the Marine Committee, asking him to sound out the Congress on the question of whether command of the combined units ought to go to a continental Navy captain or a Pennsylvania navy commodore.

That same day a second letter was sent to Morris by the board asking for the views of Congress on the steps to be taken in the event of an extreme emergency. Specifically, it wanted to know whether the ships should be burned, sunk, or surrendered in the event the British were successful.

Immediately after this the Congress passed another resolution: "that the flag of the thirteen united States be 13 stripes alternate red and white, that the union be 13 stars, white in a blue field representing a new constellation." So it was that on June 14, 1777, Congress adopted the new United States flag. No special committee was appointed, and there is no record of any discussion either in the Congress or in contemporary letters.

Members of Congress, acting under pressure, knew the reason for the decision to use stars in the flag, but the rationale was not incorporated into the resolution or minutes. It might have remained unknown had not Francis Hopkinson petitioned Congress three years later for a recognition of his services.

Francis Hopkinson and the Design of the Stars and Stripes

Francis Hopkinson (Figure 74) presented his credentials to Congress as a delegate from New Jersey on June 28, 1776. With the other delegates from New Jersey, he voted for independence on July 2, and signed the Declaration of Independence on July 4. On July 12 he was appointed a member of the Marine Committee, and five days later was also assigned to the committee to publish the *Journals of Congress*. The latter committee did not complete its labors until 1777, when the journals for 1774 through 1776 were published. In the meantime Hopkinson served on various other committees of Congress including the Secret Committee and the Committee of Intelligence. Congress resolved on November 6, 1776, to appoint "three persons well skilled in maritime affairs" to take care of "the business of the navy under the direction of the Maritime Committee." Hopkinson was one of the three men appointed to what was known as the Continental Navy Board. The other two members were John Nixon, a shipping merchant and former owner of the ship *Black Prince*—renamed the *Alfred*—one of the first five vessels that was purchased, manned, and armed by the Continental Congress, and John Wharton, Philadelphia shipyard owner and a member of a distinguished Philadelphia family. The Continental Navy Board administered all the business of the navy except that of appointing the commander-in-chief and directing the movements of the fleet. Hopkinson seems to have served not only as chairman of the Board but also as its secretary, since many letters sent by the Board are in his handwriting.

98

Fig. 75 *Bookplate of Francis Hopkinson
showing his coat of arms with stars*

It was while a member of the Navy Board that Hopkinson turned his
attention to designing the flag of the United States. His use of the stars in that
design is believed by the authors to have been the result of an experience in
the war directly related to his property.

One of the books in Hopkinson's library was a volume by William Smith,
D.D., *Discourses on Public Occasions in America* (London, 1762), which was a
gift from the author while provost of the College and Academy of Philadelphia
(later the University of Pennsylvania). In December 1776 a Hessian soldier took
this volume from Hopkinson's home in Bordentown. The soldier, one I.
Ewald, wrote on the inside cover that he had seen the author near Philadelphia
and that he, Ewald, had taken the book from a fine country seat near
Philadelphia. The book was subsequently given to someone in Philadelphia
who returned it to Hopkinson.

The book, with the Hessian's inscriptions, was a unique souvenir of the
operations near Bordentown in 1776—a dark year of the war. Its safe return
could have symbolized to Hopkinson the revival of the American hopes. The
Hessian soldier had written above and below Hopkinson's bookplate. The
bookplate carried his coat of arms, which had three six-pointed stars, and his
family motto, "Semper Paratus," or "Always Ready" (Figure 75). That senti-

99

ment may well have been in Hopkinson's mind as he tried to make ready for the British advance on Philadelphia. The idea of stars for the flag presumably came from the stars on his bookplate.

In his letter to the Board of Admiralty in 1780 Hopkinson asserted that he had designed "the flag of the United States of America" as well as several ornaments, devices, and checks appearing on bills of exchange, ship papers, the seals of the boards of Admiralty and Treasury, and the Great Seal of the United States. Hopkinson had received nothing for this work, and he now submitted a bill and asked "whether a Quarter Cask of the public wine" would not be a reasonable and proper reward for his labors.

The Board forwarded Hopkinson's letter to the Congress, which referred it to the Board of Treasury. Apparently acting on a request from the Congress, Hopkinson presented a detailed bill on June 6, and asked for the total sum of £2,700. The Continental dollar was then worth ninety cents. The Congress sent this bill to James Milligan, the auditor general, who in turn referred it to the commissioners of the Chamber of Accounts. Six days later, on June 12, the commissioners returned the bill with a report to Milligan stating: "That they have examined the account of Francis Hopkinson, Esqr., for sundry Devices, Drawings, Mottos &c for Public Use, amounting to Seven thousand two hundred dollars and are of the Opinion that the Charge is reasonable and ought to be paid." Milligan gave the report of the Commissioners a favorable endorsement and passed it on to the Board of Treasury. The board now began to raise objections. The account was returned to the auditor general for reconsideration on the grounds that no vouchers were included with the bill.

At this point Hopkinson submitted a new copy of his bill, this time with a charge noted after each item. The flag was now listed as "The Naval Flag of the United States" and the charge for it was £9. These words clearly show that the flag was first designed for the Navy. The new bill was followed by a letter from Hopkinson to the Board of Treasury in which he said that his earlier charges were made on the basis of hard money, not Continental currency. Since one dollar in hard money was equal to sixty in Continental, he assumed that the board might not want the account in hard money. He therefore substituted a new bill giving the cost of each item in Continental currency. The most expensive item on the list was the charge for designing the two sides of the Great Seal, for which he was asking £600. The new total for all services was £2,700 in Continental currency. Hopkinson's bill was again forwarded through the auditor general to the Board of Treasury; the board again rejected the account and the auditor asked once more for its favorable consideration. After another round of referrals through the departments, the board filed the correspondence and did nothing further about it for two and a half months.

By this time Hopkinson was exasperated. He wrote to Charles Lee, the secretary of the Board of Treasury, accusing him of lying about having received a copy of the amended statement and of delaying the settlement of the claim. Hopkinson threatened to send the report to Congress unless Lee gave a satisfactory explanation of his conduct. Lee failed to satisfy Hopkinson, and the latter sent to Congress a list of charges against the board. He accused the board of refusing to cooperate with other government officers, and with the neglect and loss of public papers, carelessness in keeping accounts, obstruction of public business by raising technicalities, and alteration of documents.

Congress appointed a committee to investigate the matter. The various government officers concerned with the claim appeared before the committee at its request. Only the men of the Board of Treasury ignored the summons. In its report to the Congress the committee cited irregularities in its conduct of business, and concluded that the Board had "destroyed all friendly communication of Counsels, and harmony in the Execution of Public Affairs." It recommended that the present board be dismissed.

After hearing this report, the Congress sent it back to the committee for further consideration. Another investigation and another report followed. In its second report the committee noted that this time members of the Board answered the summons, but frequently tried to dictate the way in which the investigation should be made. Much jealousy and animosity prevailed among the Board members. The committee felt that the Treasury should be directed by a single individual responsible to Congress. The committee made no recommendation in regard to Hopkinson's claim, however. That matter remained unsettled until August 23, 1781, when Congress passed a resolution asking that the claim be acted upon. Meanwhile Hopkinson had grown weary of the controversy and on July 23, 1781, he resigned his office as Treasurer of Loans. Robert Morris, the financier-general, wrote to the president of the Congress that Hopkinson's resignation should be accepted because the office was now becoming unnecessary and the dispute tended to delay business. One of Hopkinson's chief opponents on the board of Treasury resigned that same day.

Between the first and second report of the committee the Board of Treasury gave its own report to Congress on the history of the Hopkinson claim. Its reasons for rejecting the claim, aside from the lack of vouchers, were that members of the board knew that "Hopkinson was not the only person consulted" on the matter of designs and therefore could not rightly claim the whole amount; in addition, the board felt that the public was entitled to these extra services from men who drew high salaries.

Hopkinson's enemies blocked all attempts to have him paid for his services, but they never denied that he made the designs. The journals of the Continental Congress clearly show that he designed the flag. In the minds of the authors of this volume, there is no question that he designed the flag of the United States.

Flag of the Ranger

During the winter of 1776–77, the Continental ship *Ranger* was being prepared for sea at Portsmouth, New Hampshire, and the Marine Committee of the Continental Congress was most anxious that those in charge of this work be informed of the new resolutions on the flag. William Whipple and William Ellery, both members of the committee, were about to leave Philadelphia for their homes in New England. Ellery was headed for Rhode Island, but Whipple was going on to Portsmouth. The committee prepared a letter and copies were sent to Whipple, to John Langdon, the governor of New Hampshire and the builder of the *Ranger*, and to John Paul Jones, who was given command of the ship, informing them of the Congressional resolution on the flag.

Whipple and Ellery left Philadelphia on June 19, 1777, and Ellery kept a diary of the journey. Whipple failed to find Jones in Boston. But he did see Ezra Stiles, who noted in his diary on July 10 that: "The Congress have substituted a new Constella of Stars (instead of the Union) in the Continental Colours." As Stiles was an important minister in touch with the city's leading people, it seems likely that he spread any of the news he heard, even the news about the flag. This question is important, for it has a bearing on whether or not such news was known in the region before the battle of Bennington. On July 25, 1777, two weeks after the entry regarding the stars in the flag, Stiles noted in his diary that troops under General John Stark had marched the day before from New Hampshire toward Castletown to defend the frontiers; Stark and William Whipple had been made generals in the New Hampshire militia by Governor Langdon. The march that Stiles recorded was a preliminary to the battle of Bennington, which will be discussed below.

The Burgoyne and St. Leger Campaigns

With the coming of the spring of 1777 the British forces in Canada under General John Burgoyne completed preparations for a new campaign to split the colonies. The main army was to move south toward Albany via Lake Champlain and capture Fort Ticonderoga on the way. A second British army was to advance to Albany by way of Oswego and the Mohawk Valley. Meanwhile General Howe, at New York, would move up the Hudson River and link up at Albany with the other two armies. If successful, such a move would isolate New England from the rest of the colonies and neutralize most of New York state.

Burgoyne's forces assembled at the head of Lake Champlain on June 20. Moving down the lake, they reached Crown Point on June 27. When the British seized Mount Defiance overlooking Fort Ticonderoga, the Americans abandoned the fort and retreated. By July 7, Fort Ann had been lost and the British seemed to be well on their way to reaching Albany. Jealousies and factionalism between General Horatio Gates and General Philip Schuyler created problems on the American side. Finally Congress removed Schuyler and made Gates the commander of the northern army. The British advance had now been slowed by the necessity of cutting a road through the woods. Fort Edward was abandoned by the Americans, and here, some fifteen miles from the Hudson River, Burgoyne had to wait for supplies to catch up with him.

While Burgoyne's advance was slowed, a second British army under Brigadier General Barry St. Leger landed near Oswego on Lake Ontario, and advanced toward Albany via the Mohawk River Valley. Near present-day Rome, New York, stood Fort Schuyler, built in 1777 on the ruins of Fort Stanwix of French and Indian War days. The fort was a key position in the line of communications between Lake Ontario and the Hudson River. Against the position St. Leger now moved with a force of 1,700 British, Tories, and Indians. His advance party reached the fort on August 2 and began to surround it.

Holding the fort was a garrison of about 750 men under Colonel Peter Gansevoort, with Lieutenant Colonel Marinus Willett the second in command. It is from Willett's narrative that we learn of the steps taken to provide a flag for the garrison. He says:

The Fort had never been supplied with a Flagg. The importance of having one on Arrival of the Enemy had set our injenuity to work an a respectable one was formed. The white stripes were cut out of Ammunition Shirts, the blue strips out of the Cloak formerly mentioned taken from the Enemy at Peek-Kill. The red Strips out of different pieces of stuff collected from sundry persons. The Flagg was sufficiently large and a general Exhilartion Spirits appeared on beholding it Wave the Morning after the arrival of the enemy.

It is important to note that Willett mentions white stripes and blue strips. There is no mention of stars or of material used for making anything other than stripes. The blue strips were apparently for the background of the canton carrying the cross of St. George and St. Andrew. The flag was therefore the Grand Union and not the stars and stripes. Given Willett's statement about the importance of having a flag for the fort, it seems likely that if the garrison had heard anything about the action of the Congress in authorizing a new flag, they would have made some effort to make their own colors like the new rather than the old design.

General Nicholas Herkimer of the Tryon County Militia sent word to the fort that he was some eight miles away with a part of his force, and that he intended to relieve the garrison. To assist in this effort, he asked that a sortie be made from the fort to distract the British. The garrison made plans to comply.

On August 6, while Herkimer was advancing with his force of eight hundred men through a deep and narrow ravine near Oriskany, he was attacked by British soldiers, Indians, and Tories. A furious battle followed. Herkimer's horse was killed and his leg was shattered. He sat on his saddle on the ground with his back against a tree and continued to command his force.

A heavy thunderstorm checked the battle for a time, then it resumed with new fury, including hand-to-hand combat. It was at this point that the British force, hearing firing to its rear, withdrew, leaving the Americans in possession of the field. The firing was the sortie from the fort into the encampment of the Tories and Indians. Troops protecting the camp were routed by Willett's men. Provisions were destroyed and much equipment captured, including five stands of colors. Willett later wrote that after they returned to the fort the five flags "were displayed on our flag staff under the Continental flag." It is significant that Willett used the term Continental flag rather than a flag of stars and stripes.

Further evidence of the flag used at Fort Schuyler comes from two powder horns of men who served there. James Thomson's horn is dated Fort Schuyler, October 8, 1777 (Figure 76). On one side is the name Wilhelm Klein and a drawing of the Continental flag. Only the Cross of St. Andrew is shown, probably because of the small space occupied by the Union. The second horn bears the name of J. McGraw and the date December 25, 1777. It shows the St. Andrew's Cross on the Continental Union flag (Figure 77). Both horns are now preserved in the Grider Collection at the Massachusetts Historical Society. The horns, together with Willett's testimony, indicate that the flag flown over Fort Schuyler was not the stars and stripes but the Continental Union flag.*

St. Leger continued to lay siege to the fort. On the evening of August 8, after bombarding the fort during the day, the British sent a flag of truce with the announcement that unless the fort surrendered, the settlers in the Mohawk Valley would be attacked. Willett refused to capitulate. That same evening he sent Lieutenant Stockwell out of the fort to get a relief force.

---

* For a full discussion of the flag over the fort, see the appendix by John Luzader in Luzader, Luis Torres, and Orville W. Carroll, *Fort Stanwix* (Washington, 1978).

Fig. 76 Drawing of a sketch on the powder horn of James Thompson, 1777 Massachusetts Historical Society

Meanwhile General Schuyler at Albany was already taking steps to relieve the fort. When he called for a brigadier general to lead the relief force only Benedict Arnold, a major general, volunteered. Arnold now resorted to a ruse to help the fort. A mentally retarded Tory prisoner under sentence of death was offered his life if he cooperated with the scheme. He agreed. At his request, some shots were fired through his coat, which he then donned and made his way to the British camp. There he told them that he had escaped while en route to the gallows, and though shot at was not hit. He also told them that Arnold was on his way to their camp with a large force. Both the British and the Indians respected Arnold's ability as a fighter. An Oneida Indian, also sent by Arnold, came to the camp and confirmed the story of Arnold's advance with a strong force. The Indian allies of the British promptly decamped. The next day the British retreated to Oswego and thence to Montreal, leaving behind artillery and some camp equipage. The loss of St. Leger's support was to prove one of a series of disasters for Burgoyne.

Arnold reported the retreat of St. Leger and the relief of Fort Schuyler to General Gates, who sent the report on to the Congress but not to Washington. The good news was published by Congress. The copy of Arnold's report that appeared in the *Pennsylvania Gazette* on September 3, 1777, is of special interest, for immediately below it was published the resolution of the Congress of June 14, establishing the flag of thirteen stars and stripes. The same report appeared in the *Pennsylvania Evening Packet*.

Neither of these issues marked the first appearance of the news of the flag in Philadelphia newspapers, however. According to the diary of Dr. James A. Thacher, Philadelphia papers first carried the official announcement of the flag resolution on August 3, 1777. But the first *official* announcement was published in the *Pennsylvania Evening Packet* on August 30, 1777. The various reprintings

104

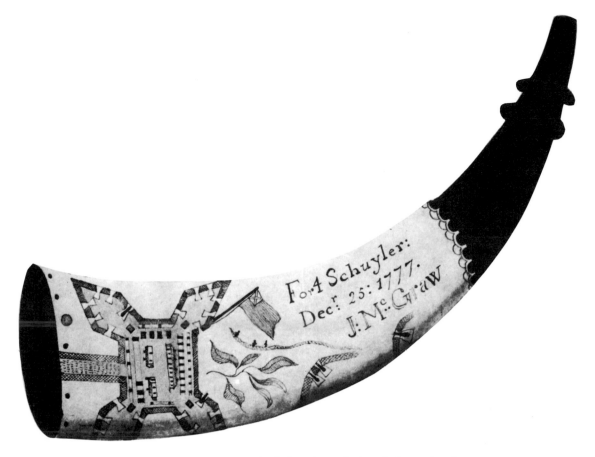

Fig. 77 The flag on the powder horn of J.
McGraw, 1777: note that only the
Cross of St. Andrew was carved,
probably because of the small area
Massachusetts Historical Society

of the resolution were doubtless intended to help make the news widely
known. It is possible that news of the flag resolution may have appeared in
handbill form in New York State prior to the battle of Fort Schuyler, but no
evidence of this has come to light. It therefore seems improbable that the news
of the new design was known in upstate New York prior to St. Leger's attack
on Fort Schuyler.

The Battle of Bennington

Meanwhile, Burgoyne heard that near Bennington, Vermont, the Americans
had large stores of food and ammunition. He sent a mixed force of about five
hundred men to seize the supplies.

On the afternoon of August 16, 1777, a small American force under General
John Stark attacked the British and the battle of Bennington began. After two
hours of fierce fighting, the Americans were the victors and the retreating
British left behind much equipment.

In the Bennington Museum in Vermont, there is preserved a faded blue silk
canton with thirteen five-pointed stars. This and some loose green fragments
are all that remains of a flag which Stark claimed he carried in the battle of
Bennington (Figure 78). The several small pieces were cut from the fly of the
flag as souvenirs; what has become of the other fragments is not known. The
remaining strip of the field is green. Thus the original flag had a green field
and a blue canton with thirteen gold painted stars, arranged in a horizontal
pattern.

This flag was brought to the attention of the public at the time of the
centennial celebration of the battle of Bennington. Five of General Stark's

Fig. 78 Remnant of the canton of the Stark
flag
Smithsonian Institution, courtesy
Bennington Historical Society

105

granddaughters were present. One of them, Miss Abbey Stark, had nursed the general through his last illness and had heard him relate various incidents in his life. The granddaughters had cut pieces from the silk flag the general had preserved, to give to his descendants. One descendant, Miss Eleanor Gamble, carried the remnant of the flag at the dedication of the Bennington battlefield monument in 1891. The general's great-great-granddaughter, Mrs. John L. (Jennie A.) Osborne, bore the flag at the sesquicentennial of the battle in 1927; she also unveiled a marker on the site of Stark's first Bennington camp. It was she who gave John Spargo, a flag historian, the flag remnant that included the canton which she had inherited. Spargo subsequently gave the fragment to the Bennington Museum.

The Bennington Museum also has on exhibit what has become known as the Bennington or Fillmore flag (Figure 79). The red and white stripes have now faded to a light-brown appearance. In the canton there are thirteen seven-pointed stars, eleven arranged in a semicircle and the remaining two in the upper right- and upper left-hand corners of the canton. In the middle of the canton, underneath the semicircle of stars, is the number "76" in white tape. A plaque on the frame states: "Flag used at the Battle of Bennington, August 16, 1777. Oldest stars and stripes in existence. Raised by the Vermonters and others who fought with General Stark." These statements are based on assertions by John Spargo in his book, *The Stars and Stripes of 1777*, published in 1928. It was this book that in large measure was responsible for drawing public attention to the Bennington or Fillmore flag.

According to Spargo, one Nathaniel Fillmore was a participant in the battle of Bennington; after the battle of Saratoga in 1777 he guarded a storehouse at Bennington. At some point he acquired a flag which remained in his possession until 1812, when he gave it to a nephew, Septa Fillmore. Septa, in turn, gave it to his nephew, Philetus P. Fillmore, who had a passion for family history and relics of the War of 1812. Philetus later settled in Aurora, Illinois, where he displayed the flag on his house during the centennial years 1876–77 with a caption saying that it had been carried during the battle of Bennington. "During the last years of his life," says Spargo, "when his mental powers were weakened and the eccentricities that he had long manifested were intensified, Mr. Fillmore insisted that the flag had been carried by his father, Lavius Fillmore, both at Bennington in 1777 and at Lake Champlain in the War of 1812. But Lavius Fillmore was only ten years old when the battle of Bennington took place, and there is no record of his having served in the War of 1812, or any good reason for believing that he did."

Philetus gave the flag to his nephew, Franklin Bosworth Fillmore of Champaign, Illinois, who carried the flag in a parade at the national encampment of the Grand Army of the Republic in Minneapolis, Minnesota, in 1884. Franklin Fillmore left the flag unattended while he was in a restaurant, and a souvenir hunter cut off the top stripe and one of the stars. The mutilated flag passed to Franklin's children upon his death, and his daughter Maude lent it to the Chicago Public Library for display in its Grand Army of the Republic room. In 1926 she gave it to the Bennington Battle Monument and Historical Association where it was displayed for some time before being moved to the Bennington Museum.

For a number of years the Bennington flag has been displayed under glass in a handsome bronze frame. All who wish to study it have to do so through the glass. Unfortunately no textile or thread report was done on the flag before

Fig. 79 *The Bennington or Fillmore Flag*
Smithsonian Institution, courtesy
Bennington Historical Society

it was framed. Only such an analysis could answer positively the questions that have arisen about the age of this flag. Until this is possible, the claims advanced for the Bennington flag must be viewed with skepticism.*

The battle of Bennington was the first of a series of disappointments experienced by General John Burgoyne in August 1777. The second was the retreat of the British forces under St. Leger from the Mohawk Valley back to Canada. Burgoyne kept his disappointment from his troops and determined to press on to Albany. He looked to Sir Henry Clinton in New York to make a move up the Hudson to meet him. Strengthened by artillery and ordnance stores from Lake George and by a month's supply of provisions, Burgoyne moved from Fort Edward on September 13 and crossed to the west side of the Hudson River toward Saratoga. By this time the morale of the Americans was high as a result of the victory at Bennington. Hundreds of volunteers streamed into Schuyler's camp on Van Schaick's Island in the Hudson River. These recruits, plus the brigades of Nixon and Glover and Morgan's Virginia riflemen, brought Schuyler's army up to about 9,000 men. Then, on August 19, Schuyler was relieved by General Horatio Gates. Three weeks later, Gates moved his army from the island toward Bemis Heights near Saratoga. Burgoyne's army was now encamped about two miles north of Bemis Heights.

* A Smithsonian textile expert who studied this flag through the glass concluded that it was made of power woven fabric, and probably dated from the Centennial celebration of 1876.

American Victory at Saratoga

On the 19th of September the British attacked the Americans. The fight that followed was variously known as the battle of Freeman's Farm, or Stillwater, or as the first battle of Bemis Heights. Major General Benedict Arnold gave a splendid account of himself in this action. The battle itself was technically a draw, but British losses were double those of the Americans. Burgoyne did not renew the battle but decided to wait for reinforcements from Sir Henry Clinton's forces in New York. While he waited, Burgoyne's troops began to dig entrenchments toward the Hudson River. Three weeks passed with no sign of help from Clinton. Meanwhile Burgoyne received news that Fort Ticonderoga had been recaptured by the Americans. With it the British lost more than 200 gunboats or batteaux which he needed in the event of a retreat to Canada.

Now that his retreat route was cut, Burgoyne resolved to force his way to Albany. A reconnaisance of the American position on October 7 led to a furious battle. Once again Arnold made a major contribution to victory. The British suffered heavy losses in officers, men, and artillery. That night Burgoyne moved back to some hills overlooking the river and positioned his men to receive an attack on the eighth. But the attack never came. Only brief skirmishing took place that day. Fearful that his army would be trapped between the Hudson River and the American army, Burgoyne retreated to Saratoga. By October 14 his army had rations for only three more days and Burgoyne sent a staff officer to Gates to negotiate for a capitulation. Details were worked out, and on October 17, 1777, the formal surrender ceremony took place.

Gates agreed to very generous terms under which the British surrendered their arms, but not their men. The defeated Britishers were to march to a port, sail for England, and agree not to serve again in North America. As things turned out, the Congress refused to send them home, for this would only release more British soldiers for American service. Instead, they were kept first near Boston and later held in Virginia for the duration of the war. The victory at Saratoga was the turning point of the war. That success led to France's decision to enter into an alliance with the Americans, and French aid eventually led to final victory.

A local historian of Saratoga later claimed that the stars and stripes was first flown over a vanquished enemy at this surrender ceremony. The authority for this statement is unknown, but its source was presumably a George Strover, whose father, John Strover, was a resident in the area and a scout for the Continental Army. According to the local account, when it became apparent that Burgoyne was going to surrender some Americans felt the necessity of a flag for the ceremony. The ladies of Saratoga and some of the wives of American officers allegedly got flannel petticoats of the required red, white, and blue colors and made a flag. It consisted of thirteen red and white stripes with a blue canton or union with thirteen white stars. This homemade flag supposedly was presented to Gates, and as Burgoyne approached Gates's tent the flag was raised to the top of the staff and saluted with the music of fifes and drums and the playing of "Yankee Doodle." George Strover was born in the vicinity of Saratoga in 1791, and perhaps heard the story from his father. When the Schuyler family offered their old home for sale in 1837, George Strover purchased it. It is not known what became of the flag, or if it ever really existed. There is no known record of it nor of the source of the information in

Fig. 80 Surrender of General Burgoyne at Saratoga, New York, October 17, 1777; *painting by John Trumbull Architect of the Capitol*

the local history volume. Therefore, the story must be viewed with a great deal of skepticism. Subsequently, we shall examine the question of a flag that is said to have belonged to the Schuyler family.

The surrender at Saratoga was one of the subjects chosen by John Trumbull for his series of paintings on great moments in the Revolution. The series was planned in 1786 and completed about 1816. Trumbull had hoped to have engravings made of the Saratoga painting and his other great scenes to sell to the public, but he was unsuccessful. The original oil painting of that battle was sold to Yale College in 1831. Meanwhile, Trumbull used the same scene as the basis for a series of huge paintings on historic events that were sold to the government between 1817 and 1824 and used to decorate the United States Capitol building (Figure 80). In both the Yale and the Capitol paintings of the surrender of Burgoyne we see General Gates on the left, standing among his officers. Over the tent the artist shows the stars and stripes with the thirteen stars in the flag arranged in a square pattern. Although Trumbull was familiar with persons and scenes associated with the Revolutionary War, the flag depicted in the surrender of Burgoyne has a star pattern that is more characteristic of the early nineteenth century than of documented designs from the Revolution.

109

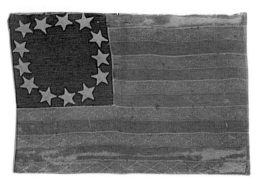

Fig. 81   The Schuyler flag
Smithsonian Institution, courtesy
Fort Ticonderoga Museum

The story of the Saratoga surrender flag illustrates a common trait among Americans of the late nineteenth and the twentieth centuries: a hunger for relics associated with great events of the past. For the most part, the Revolutionary generation tended to see flags as utilitarian objects. There was no particular desire to save them intact as relics. Even had there been such a desire, time and the problems of proper storage would have taken their toll on objects stored in private homes.

For most of the first half of the nineteenth century, Americans were generally indifferent to the history of their flag. One indication of a growth of interest was the establishment of the Annin Flag Company in New York in 1847. The Civil War saw an outburst of flag making, but most of it was focused on the size of the union as it existed during that conflict. With the approach of the centennial of the Declaration of Independence, there was great public interest in the Revolution. The Centennial Exhibition in Philadelphia, and the publicity surrounding the Betsy Ross story, stimulated public interest in the history of the flag. A desire for authentic relics became so great in some quarters that various early flags began to take on a Revolutionary association. There was not necessarily any conscious effort to deceive, for many times the facts surrounding a particular flag were transmitted orally and were confused or forgotten by later generations. It has been the task of flag historians to separate the fact from the wish as best they can.

The Schuyler Flags

Preserved in the museum at Fort Ticonderoga, New York, is a thirteen-star flag identified as General Philip Schuyler's headquarters flag of 1777, and as "probably the earliest surviving Stars and Stripes" (Figure 81). It was a gift of Schuyler Hamilton, a descendant of Major General Schuyler Hamilton, who allegedly got it from its original owner, General Philip Schuyler of Revolutionary War fame. The flag itself is now covered with a fine translucent net and framed behind glass. It has not been possible to submit the flag to a fabric and thread examination, but a Smithsonian textile expert deduced that the red and the white stripes were of a single ply bunting. The blue could not be determined through the glass. The five-pointed stars appear to be of cotton muslin and appliqued by hand to both sides with what looks like linen thread. Presumably the stars were intended to suggest a circle, but the arrangement is somewhat squared at the top and rounded at the bottom.

The flag itself measures 23 inches by 31½ inches plus a 1¼-inch heading. This heading shows signs of having once had two metal grommets. There are several layers of cording laying on the heading and tacked down, the purpose of which is not known. Both the heading and the stripes are machine stitched. Since machine stitching cannot have been done much before the third quarter of the nineteenth century, this flag cannot be earlier than that time.

It happens that Major General Schuyler Hamilton gave an address before the New York Historical Society on June 14, 1877, on the history of the stars and stripes. The address was later published in pamphlet form and the publication carries an illustration of a thirteen-star flag with stars in the 3–2–3–2–3 arrangement. There is no indication in this book that his family owned a flag dating from the Revolution, and it would have been a natural thing to refer to

Fig. 82   Silk flag presented to General
Schuyler
Independence National Historic
Park

such a flag if it existed. We can therefore deduce that Hamilton had no
knowledge of any flag owned by a Revolutionary ancestor, and that the flag in
the Fort Ticonderoga museum was not acquired until after his address in 1877.

Another flag associated with General Philip Schuyler is the silk presentation
flag preserved in the Army-Navy Museum at Independence National Historic
Park, Philadelphia. This Schuyler flag has seven white and six red stripes. A
white stripe is on the top and bottom, but the effect is obscured somewhat by
the dark fringe. The blue canton has an eagle and shield painted on and a
circlet or arch of thirteen five-pointed stars between the wings of the eagle.
Since General Schuyler did not have any troops under his command after
August 1777, it is doubtful that this presentation flag could have originated
prior to 1782. Possibly dating from as early as 1784, the Schuyler flag may well
be the earliest example of a thirteen-star, thirteen-stripe flag in existence
(Figure 82). Flags with the eagle in the canton were frequently found in artistic
renderings made during this early period.

The British Advance on Philadelphia

After failing to find or force a weak point in the American defense of the Jerseys, General Howe retired to New York, where on July 23, 1777, he embarked with his army for Chesapeake Bay. Members of the Continental Congress and the men of Washington's army spent an anxious month wondering where the British would strike. Upon receipt of word from the president of the Congress that the British fleet had been sighted off the Delaware Bay capes, Washington moved his army to Germantown, some five or six miles from Philadelphia, where they camped. The British did not enter Delaware Bay as expected, so Washington moved his camp to an area some twenty miles from Philadelphia, along Neshaning Creek. While there he received the Marquis de Lafayette, the young Frenchman who had come to offer his services to the Americans. News that the British were in the upper Chesapeake Bay led Washington to break camp on August 22, and to head southward.

To raise the spirits of his countrymen, and especially those in Philadelphia who feared British occupation was imminent, Washington marched a part of his army through the city. At the head of the column rode Washington and his staff, including Lafayette, who had been given a major general's commission by the Continental Congress. In keeping with the spirit of the occasion, the men in the ranks wore sprigs of leaves in their hats. Although the new flag had been adopted two months earlier, there is no mention of it in the newspaper accounts of the march. It would seem that if the sprigs of leaves were worthy of comment the new flag would also have been noted.

Among the thousands who viewed the march were members of the Congress, and perhaps they noted the absence of any new flags. At any rate, Charles Thomson, the secretary of the Congress, promptly publicized the action of Congress to establish a new national flag. The *Pennsylvania Evening Post* of Saturday, August 30, 1777, published the first public announcement of the adoption of the stars and stripes resolution. The same announcement appeared in the *Pennsylvania Gazette* on September 3, 1777. The word gradually spread. Editors evidently did not feel it necessary to praise or otherwise to comment on the new flag.

The British army landed at Turkey Point and advanced northward toward Philadelphia by way of present-day Elkton, Maryland. On September 3, 1777, near Cooch's Bridge, Delaware, a skirmish took place. A claim has been made that it was here that the stars and stripes flag first appeared in battle, but there is no documentation for this assertion. There is, however, documentation on the use of a Delaware Militia flag of unique design at this time.

A few days before the battle of Brandywine, September 11, 1777, Captain W.C. Dansey of the British 33rd Infantry Regiment captured the horse, arms, baggage, drums, and color of a colonel in the Delaware Militia, along with the colonel's brother. Captain Dansey kept the horse, arms, and colors as souvenirs. Subsequently the flag was taken to England, where it remained until the Delaware Historical Society purchased it in 1927 (Figure 83).

The Dansey flag, as the color is known, measures 62 inches by 47 inches. It was made of dark olive-green silk. In the upper left-hand corner are seven red horizontal stripes and six white ones. The whole striped canton measures 18 inches long by 16½ inches high. The silk tassels of blue and white, the colors of the Delaware Militia, hang from cords from the upper left-hand corner and are held together with gold mesh. A fringe made from the olive-green silk of the flag is at the right end.

Fig. 83 *The Dansey Flag*
Historical Society of Delaware
Photograph by James Bader

Fig. 84 *The Easton Flag*
Smithsonian Institution, courtesy
Easton Public Library

Similar to the Dansey flag is the silk color preserved in the Easton Public Library, Easton, Pennsylvania. The flag has a blue field with thirteen inset eight-point stars. Twelve of these stars are arranged in a circle, and the thirteenth is in the center of the circle. The canton contains thirteen red and white stripes (Figure 84). According to the Easton librarian, the earliest documentation on the flag is dated 1811. The flag is framed under glass, and no detailed thread or fabric examination could be done by Mrs. Grace Cooper. She believed that the flag could date from the Revolution, but that it could also date from the War of 1812. Thus the exact dating of the Easton flag remains conjectural.

*Fig. 85   The Brandywine Flag
Smithsonian Institution, courtesy
Independence National Historical
Park*

*Fig. 86   Flag over Fort Mifflin, Red Bank,
N.J., in Montressor's map: note
red, white, and blue stripes (detail)
Library of Congress*

Claims have been advanced that the stars and stripes flag was first used in the battle of Brandywine, September 11, 1777, but there is no proof of this. A regimental flag of stars and stripes design, associated with the battle, is now preserved at the Army-Navy Museum at Independence National Historical Park in Philadelphia (Figure 85). According to a family tradition, the "Brandywine Flag" was carried by Captain Robert Wilson's Company, Seventh Pennsylvania Regiment, in the battles of Brandywine and Paoli. The field or canton is of white silk with thirteen eight-point red stars arranged in a 4–5–4 horizontal design. There are seven white stripes inlaid on the red. The first and last stripes are white. At one time the flag was fringed with hand-loomed silk made in England. There is a heavy border of red about the flag. Small, hand-sewn eyelets were used to mount the flag to its staff. This flag was presented to the Independence Hall museum in 1923. It was not possible to examine the fabric or the threads in the flag to ascertain its age, but it is believed to be authentic.

The British advance on Philadelphia was contested unsuccessfully at the battles of Paoli, September 21, 1777, and of Germantown, October 4. The Continental Congress left Philadelphia and took up a temporary residence in Lancaster, Pennsylvania, before moving on to York. According to a later reminiscence, there was an association of the stars and stripes with the land battle of Germantown. An early and unidentified researcher on the American flag made a newspaper appeal to old Philadelphians in February 1844 to share their recollections of flags of the Revolutionary era. Citing one such reminiscence, he said: "And it is remembered, that the flag used by the Americans before and at the battle of Germantown, was that of thirteen stripes and stars. Such a one used to fly daily, before that battle, upon a liberty pole, set up in Germantown, in the middle of Manheim Street, at the present Cox's Tavern." Certainly the inhabitants of Germantown were in an excellent position to know about the decision the Congress had made the previous June concerning the flag. If the flag at Germantown did in fact exist, nothing is known about its subsequent fate. It would also appear that the early flag researcher did not get the additional testimony he sought.

Although Washington's army delayed the capture of Philadelphia nearly four months, ultimately it could not be prevented. The first units of the British army had marched into the city on September 26. The British fleet then attempted to seize the approaches to Philadelphia via the Delaware River so that their communications to the sea would be secure. To stop such plans the Americans manned Fort Mercer at Red Bank, New Jersey, and opposite it Fort Mifflin, on Mud Island (Figure 86). The British attacked Fort Mercer on October 21, with a force of about two thousand men, mostly Hessians, and were repulsed with heavy losses.

While this was taking place, British ships attacked Fort Mifflin. Several ships ran aground and were battered by the fire from the fort and from American row-gallerys and floating batteries. One ship blew up and another was abandoned. The British then mounted five batteries of heavy guns, howitzers, and mortars on Providence Island; they also brought a large twenty-two gun floating battery into the channel between the fort and the mainland and proceeded to bombard Fort Mifflin for five days. With more than half the garrison dead or wounded, the remaining men left the fort at night and crossed the river to Fort Mercer. Five thousand British troops now moved against Fort Mercer, so the garrison abandoned it. The Pennsylvania navy burned its galleys. Having overcome the American defenses on the Delaware,

Fig. 87   Flag over Fort Mercer in Montressor's map: note canton and stripes (detail)
Library of Congress

Fig. 88   Colonel Samuel Smith; portrait by
Charles Willson Peale
Independence National Historical
Park

Fig. 89   Colonel Samuel Smith (detail)
Independence National Historical
Park

the British occupied Philadelphia and secured their access to the sea.

The flag flown at Fort Mercer appears on a British map by John Montressor dated November 15, 1777 (Figure 87). It shows a flag with white and blue stripes. The canton is indistinct, but seems to have a large red cross on it. Possibly there was an eagle on the canton.

The defense of Fort Mifflin was immortalized by Charles Willson Peale in the background of his portrait of Colonel Samuel Smith, the commander of the fort (Figure 88). This portrait, painted sometime between 1778 and 1793, shows a flag with blue and white stripes and an eagle in the canton (Figure 89).

The Legend of Betsy Ross and the First Flag

It seems appropriate at this point to consider the legend that Betsy Ross made the first stars and stripes flag. The story has an enormous popularity. Yet the known facts do not substantiate it.

115

The claims of Betsy Ross were first brought to the attention of the public in 1870 by one of her grandsons, William J. Canby. In a paper he read before a meeting of the Historical Society of Pennsylvania, Canby stated that his maternal grandmother, Mrs. John Ross, was the maker and partial designer of the first flag combining the stars and stripes. George Henry Preble, who wrote one of the most complete histories of the flag of the United States, took notice of Canby's claims in the 1872 and 1880 editions of his book. In the latter edition he quoted from a letter written by Canby on the subject of the Betsy Ross story:

It is not *tradition*, it is *report* from the lips of the principal participator in the transaction, directly told not to one or two, but a dozen or more living witnesses, of which I myself am one, though but a little boy when I heard it. I was eleven years when Mrs. Ross died in our house, and well remember her telling the story. My mother and two of her sisters are living, and in good memory. I have the narrative from the lips of the oldest one of my aunts, now deceased, reduced to writing in 1857. . . . Washington was a frequent visitor at my grandmother's house before receiving command of the army. She embroidered his shirt ruffles, and did many other things for him. He knew her skill with a needle. Colonel Ross with Robert Morris and General Washington, called on Mrs. Ross and told her they were a committee of Congress, and wanted her to make a flag from the drawing, a rough one, which, upon her suggestions, was redrawn by General Washington in pencil in her back parlor. This was prior to the declaration of Independence. I fix the date to be during Washington's visit to Congress from New York in June, 1776 when he came to confer upon the affairs of the Army, the flag being no doubt, one of these affairs.

Although Canby asserted that the stars and stripes were in common if not general use soon after the Declaration of Independence, and nearly a year before the resolution of Congress proclaiming the flag, Preble could not accept this statement, nor can subsequent historians. There is no record of the flag being discussed or of a committee being appointed for the design of the flag in either the *Journals* of the Continental Congress or the diaries and writings of Washington. Meetings with Colonel Ross or Robert Morris on the subject cannot be documented. When Washington came to Philadelphia in 1776 to take up various matters with Congress, we have some records of what was on his mind. The subject of flags occurs in a postscript of a letter that he wrote on May 28 to Major General Putnam in New York. Washington wrote: "I desire you'll speak to the several Colls. & hurry them to get their colours done." Upon receiving this letter, General Putnam had the following entry placed in his orderly book under the date of May 31, 1776: "Genl. Washington has wrote to Genl. Putnam desiring him in the most pressing terms, to give positive orders to all colonels, to have Colours immediately completed for their respective regiments." If Washington had worked with Betsy Ross on the design of the national colors, he made no mention of it in these instructions to General Putnam.

The claims for Betsy Ross that were made by William Canby in his talk before the Historical Society of Pennsylvania were presented in more detail in a book by his brother and a nephew published after Canby's death. The book, *The Evolution of the American Flag*, by George Canby and Lloyd Balderston, appeared in 1909. Among other things, the authors describe the formation of the Betsy Ross Memorial Association and reproduce a painting by Charles H. Weisgerber of the alleged meeting of the committee of Congress with Betsy Ross. The picture of Betsy Ross is a composite portrait made up from pictures of her granddaughters and other descendants. Entitled *Birth of Our Nation's*

Flag, it was first exhibited at the Columbian Exposition in Chicago in 1893 where it stirred a great deal of public interest in the subject. The artist took liberties with history by painting the stars in the flag in a circle. When art and history mingle, alas for history!

Subsequently, money to purchase the Betsy Ross house in Philadelphia was raised by selling ten-cent subscriptions to The American Flag House and Betsy Ross Memorial Association, incorporated in Pennsylvania in 1898. Each contributor received a lithographed certificate of membership in the association that included a picture of the house of Betsy Ross, her grave in Mount Moriah Cemetery in Philadelphia, and a color reproduction of the Weisberger painting. This campaign did a great deal to give the Betsy Ross story wide publicity and the Weisberger painting was reproduced in school history textbooks throughout the United States. The legend that Betsy Ross made the first stars and stripes flag persists despite the fact that there is no foundation for the story. A search was made of the volumes of account books of that period and nothing was found there or elsewhere to substantiate the myth. What could have inspired the story that Canby heard as a boy from Betsy Ross and from his aunts? This germ of truth on which the story is based can be found in the published volumes of the *Pennsylvania Archives*.

The Committee of Safety of Pennsylvania ordered Captain Proctor on February 24, 1776, to "procure a Flag Staff for the Fort with a Flagg of the United Colonies." But the design of a flag for the state galleys had not been approved as of late October 1776. The correspondence does not disclose the design of the flag finally ordered for the galleys, although the union flag had been ordered for the fort. The anxiety of the captains to obtain colors for the galleys is shown by the letters of Captain William Richards to the committee. On August 19, 1776, he wrote:

I hope you have agreed what sorts of Colours I am to have made for the Galleys, & c. as they are much wanted.

You will please to order how you will have the Goods paid for, that are bought for the Provincial Store, I am in want of a Sum of money for that and the Signals.

Two months went by with no action taken by the state. On October 15, Richards again wrote to the Council:

The Commodore was with me this morning, and says the Fleet has not any Colours to hoist if they would be called on Duty, it is not in my power to get them done, until there is a design fix'd on to make the Colours by."

Seven months more passed before Captain Richards and others got their colors. The minutes of the State Navy Board show that William Richards finally got his colors in May 1777. The minutes for May 29, 1777, say in part: "An order on William Webb to Elizabeth Ross for fourteen pounds twelve shillings, and two pence, for making ship's colours, &c, put into William Richards store. £ 14.12.2"

The minutes show that Elizabeth Ross made ship's colors for the Pennsylvania state ships. They were made after much clamoring for colors by the galley officers and after repeated letter writing by the storekeeper for a design for them.

It is illogical to assume that Washington was present at the alleged meeting with Betsy Ross on the design of the flag when it is known that he wanted a national standard made for the use of the army in 1779. On May 10, 1779, the War Board wrote to Washington as follows:

. . . The Board have been frequently applied to on the Subject of Drums and Colours for the several Regiments. It is impossible to comply with all the Requisitions for these Articles, as we have not materials to make either in sufficient numbers. . . .

As to Colours we have refused them for another Reason. The Baron Steuben mentioned when he was here that he would settle with your Excellency some Plan as to the Colours. It was intended that every Regiment should have two Colours one the Standard of the United States which should be the same throughout the Army and the other a Regimental Colour which should very [vary] according to the [uniform] facings of the Regiments. But it is not yet settled what is the Standard of the U. States. If your Excellency will therefore favour us with your Opinion on the Subject we will report to Congress and request them to establish a Standard and so soon as this is done we will endeavour to get Materials and order a Number made sufficient for the Army. Neither can we tell what should be the Regimental Colours as Uniforms were by a late Resolution of Congress to be settled by your Excellency.

Thus the board states that the design of the United States flag for use by the army was not yet established in May 1779, or nearly two years after the passage of the flag resolution by the Continental Congress.

It was not until September 3 that Richard Peters of the War Board wrote to Washington as follows:

The enclosed Drafts of a Standard for the Army are sent for your Approbation, Rejection or Alteration. The Officers will be by and by pressing for Colours and if Materials can be procured they shall be made when you send us your Ideas of the Plan of the Standard. The one with the Union and Emblems in the middle is preferred by us as being [a] variant for the Marine [Navy] Flag.

Unfortunately these sketches of a standard have not been preserved. All that we know about them comes from Washington's reply to Peters on September 14, 1779:

I agree with you in opinion, that the standard, with the Union and Emblems in the centre, is to be preferred, with this addition the Number of the State to which it belongs inserted within the curve of the Serpent, in such place, as the painter or designer shall judge most proper. . . .

Peters's statement that the proposed flag was a variant of the Marine or Navy flag suggests thirteen red and white stripes. Washington's reference to the serpent suggests the rattlesnake stretched out as in Esek Hopkins's Navy Jack and in the South Carolina navy flag. His reference to placing a regimental number and the state name "within the curve of the Serpent" suggests that the snake was in a circular or semi-circular arrangement in the middle of the flag. But Washington and Peters both refer to a design that placed "the Union and Emblems" in the middle of the flag. One emblem was the rattlesnake. What was the other? Perhaps a pine tree. Were there other emblems, such as the use of the "U.S." for United States, which was used on Continental Army buttons? We do not know. The term Union could mean the thirteen stripes, but this long after the flag resolution one would assume that there would be a reference to stars. Therefore, it seems logical to assume that Union meant the stripes and emblems meant the stars and the rattlesnake.

This conclusion leads to the thought that the red and white stripes might have been in a rectangular or square arrangement in the middle of the flag and surrounded by thirteen white stars, possibly following the outline of the stripes. If a rectangle was used we might expect four stars at the top and five at the bottom with two stars on each side. If a square was used we might expect three stars on three sides and four stars at the bottom. The snake presumably formed a circle or semicircle around these emblems. To keep from crowding the center of the flag we might assume that the snake made a smaller loop above or below the center design to accommodate the regimental number and the state designation. The background of the flag would be the same color as the facings of the uniforms of the specific states.

So much for speculation on the design of the regimental flags. It seems clear from the correspondence quoted above that the main concern of the War Board was to try to design regimental flags that would allow for both uniformity and differences. The board apparently had not yet been able to address itself to Washington's question concerning the design of "the Standard of the United States." That matter had still not been decided more than two years after the passage of the flag resolution and more than three years after Betsy Ross allegedly created a design that pleased Washington.

The War in 1778

Although the news of the action of the Continental Congress in approving the stars and stripes design for the flag was disseminated in newspapers for several months, it does not appear to have prompted any outburst of flag making. The shortage of suitable material may have been one of the reasons. Even in the case of the Fort Schuyler flag or of that supposedly used at the surrender of Burgoyne, the flags were improvised from whatever cloth was available. Such improvised colors would not have lasted very long in regular use. There was also the matter of the pattern of the war for two or three years after the French alliance. The lack of any decisive victory on a par with Saratoga, and the tendency of the war to drag on, probably had an adverse effect on patriotic feelings. Finally, there is the fact that from the very beginning Washington's army had recognized the utility of regimental colors, but had no particular interest in or need for a national flag. If flown at all it would have been used over forts, hospitals, supply depots, and headquarters. It would not have been carried into battle. The story of the use of the stars and stripes for the remainder of the war is therefore rather brief and episodic.

With the discouraging lack of progress in the war, General George Washington was concerned about keeping his army intact in the face of mounting problems. During the bitter winter of 1777–78 Washington's army was encamped at Valley Forge, Pennsylvania, virtually destitute of supplies. By February 5, 1778, Washington had four thousand men who were unfit for duty because they lacked clothing. Soldiers died at the rate of four hundred a month. Hundreds deserted. Associated with these trying times is the commander-in-chief's flag, now preserved at Valley Forge. This flag was originally a medium-blue, plain-weave light weight silk. It has since faded to a baby blue color. Thirteen white six-pointed stars made of the same weight silk are set into the flag in a horizontal design (Figure 90). The effect is striking. Questions about the authenticity of this flag have been raised from time to time. The authors of this volume concluded that the flag was authentic.*

---

* Subsequently a Smithsonian textile expert made an examination of this flag. It was found that the original flag had been cut on all four sides to make it fit a frame. It now measures 27½ inches by 34½ inches. The conclusion was that the flag was really a canton from a late eighteenth century flag of stars and stripes.

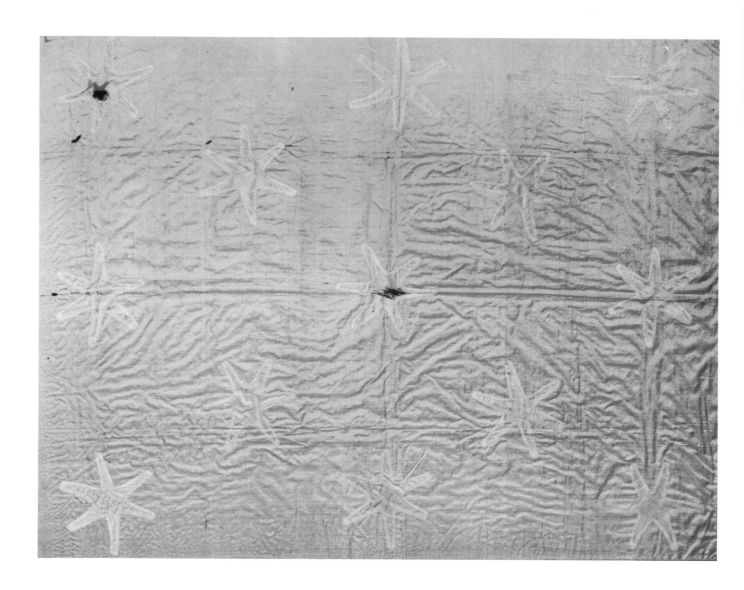

Fig. 90 *The Commander-in-Chief's Flag*
The Valley Forge Historical Society

To Washington's camp at Valley Forge during the winter of 1777–78 came foreign officer volunteers, among them the Marquis de Lafayette and Baron von Steuben. Both helped to inspire American troops. It was von Steuben who devised a drill system for the troops and who began the formal training of the soldiery at Valley Forge. By spring Washington had a stronger, better trained and more resolute force. Recruiting built up its numbers.

On May 5, 1778, Washington's army celebrated the news of the ratification by the Continental Congress of the treaties of commerce and alliance with France. French aid would now be forthcoming in abundance.

On the British side, Sir William Howe resigned and Sir Henry Clinton succeeded to the command of the British army in the United States. King George III ordered Clinton to abandon Philadelphia and possibly New York, so that the troops could be moved to Newport, Rhode Island, in preparation for a campaign against the French island of St. Lucia in the West Indies. Some of the troops were also to be sent to Florida. A three-man group, known as the Carlisle Commission, was sent out by the British government to offer the Americans home rule, but not independence or the withdrawal of troops. The

Fig. 91 First Salute to the Stars and
Stripes; *painting by Edward
Moran, 1898*
U.S. Naval Academy Museum

Ford et al., eds., *Defenses of Philadelphia in 1777* (Brooklyn, 1897); Samuel Adams Drake, *Burgoyne Invasion of 1777* (Boston, 1889); Herbert Darling Foster, *Stark's Independent Command at Bennington* (Manchester, N.H., 1908); Caleb Stark, *Memoir and Official Correspondence of General John Stark* (Concord, 1860); John Spargo, *The Stars and Stripes in 1777, An Account of the Birth of the Flag and its First Baptism of Victorious Fire* (Bennington, 1928); and John F. Luzader, Luis Torres, and Orville W. Carroll, *Fort Stanwix* (Washington, 1976).

The life and contributions of the designer of the stars and stripes are described in George E. Hastings, *The Life and Works of Francis Hopkinson* (Chicago, 1926). Hopkinson's letters and claims can be consulted in the Papers of the Continental Congress in the National Archives, item no. 136, vol. 4, folios 665, 671, 673–75, 677, 681, 683, and 685; item no. 37, vol. 4, folio 243; item no. 19, vol. 3, folios 177–78; item no. 78, vol. 12, folio 171; item no. 133, vol. 1, folio 89; and the *Journals* of the Continental Congress, 18: 983–84; 21: 783–84, 899. A copy of Hopkinson's letter to Charles Lee, secretary of the Board of Treasury, of June 26, 1780, was in the possession of Edward Hopkinson, a descendant, when Admiral Furlong did his research. The book containing Francis Hopkinson's book plate is in the hands of a direct descendant.

The case for Betsy Ross is set forth in George Canby and Lloyd Balderston, *The Evolution of the American Flag* (Philadelphia, 1909). A summary of the case against the claim that she made the first stars and stripes flag can be found in Milo M. Quaife, Melvin J. Weig, and Roy E. Appleman, *The History of the United States Flag* (New York, 1961), pp. 94–98. Documents relating to the procurement of flags for the state galleys are in Samuel Hazard et al., eds., *Pennsylvania Archives*, 1st Ser., vol. 5, pp. 13, 46, 51. The letter of the War Board to George Washington of May 10, 1779, and the one of Richard Peters to Washington of Sept. 3, 1779, are in the Papers of George Washington at the Library of Congress. Washington's letter to Richard Peters of Sept. 14, 1779, is printed in John C. Fitzpatrick, ed., *The Writings of George Washington From the Original Manuscript Sources, 1775–1799*, 35 vols. (Washington, 1931–44).

Information on the Brandywine, Dansey, and Easton flags was supplied by the respective owners to H.D. Langley, and is in the files of the Division of Naval History, Smithsonian Institution. Grace R. Cooper's report on the Easton flag is also in the Division of Naval History. The history of the Dansey flag was furnished to Admiral Furlong by the director of the Delaware Historical Society and is in the Furlong Flag Files. See also J. H. L., "The 33rd Regiment of Foot, 1771–1785," *The Journal of the Society For Army Historical Research* 7 (1928): 243–47.

The quotations from the diary of Ezra Stiles are from Franklin Bowditch Dexter, ed., *The Literary Diary of Ezra Stiles, D.D., L.L.D., President of Yale College*, 3 vols. (New York, 1901), 2: 181, 186.

The Thompson and McGraw powder horns are in the custody of the Massachusetts Historical Society. Information about them was supplied to Admiral Furlong by the Society, and is in the Furlong Flag Files.

The manuscript of the Narrative of Marinus Willett was studied by Commodore McCandless while it was in the custody of the New-York Historical Society. This manuscript was sold to Robert R. Johnson at an auction in 1947, and its whereabouts are not known to the editor. For related information see William M. W. Willet, *A Narrative of the Military Actions of Colonel Marinus Willett* (New York, 1831), and John F. Luzader, Luis Torres, and Orville W. Carroll, *Fort Stanwix*, pp. 30–69.

On the surrender at Saratoga, the local history reference to a flag allegedly furnished by John Strover is in Evelyn Barrett Britten, *Chronicles of Saratoga* (Saratoga Springs, N.Y., 1959), p. 16. Corrections on this story were supplied by Violet Dunn, Saratoga historian, in a letter to H.D. Langley of April 7, 1977, in the files of the Division of Naval History, Smithsonian Institution.

Circumstances surrounding the creation of the painting by John Trumbull of the surrender at Saratoga are described in Colonel Theodore Sizer, ed., *Autobiography of John Trumbull* (New Haven, 1953), pp. 257–60, 309–10, 314; and in Colonel Theodore Sizer, ed., *Works of Colonel John Trumbull, Artist of the American Revolution* (New Haven, 1950), pp. 74–75, 146–47. See also the chapter, "Trumbull's Variations of the American Flag," pp. 106–108.

Schuyler Hamilton's views on the flag that was present at the surrender at Saratoga are set forth in his book, *Our National Flag, the Star Spangled Banner. The History of it* (New York, 1887). It is interesting to compare this account with one written earlier, before he knew about the Betsy Ross story, *The History of the Flag of the United States of America* (Philadelphia, 1852).

An early attempt to write the history of the American flag, and one which requested the recollections of Philadelphians, is the article by P. F., "Historical Notes: The American Flag," *Army and Navy Chronicle*, 3 (1844): 82–89, 239, 832.

The ordeal of Washington's army at Valley Forge is described in Christopher Ward, *The War of the Revolution*, 2:543–55; and in Willard M. Wallace, *Appeal to Arms*, pp. 169–79, but neither has any mention of the the Washington Headquarters Flag nor the commander-in-chief's flag. The latter is described in Frank E. Schermerhorn, *American and French Flags of the Revolution, 1775–1783*, pp. 32–34, but is identified there as the Washington Headquarters flag. The commander-in-chief's flag is briefly described in the booklet published by the Valley Forge Historical Society, Ronald E. Heaton, *Valley Forge, Yesterday and Today* (Norristown, Pa., 1968), p. 65.

Circumstances surrounding the departure of John Paul Jones in the *Ranger*, and the first foreign salute to the stars and stripes are described in Samuel Eliot Morison, *John Paul Jones: A Sailor's Biography* (Boston, 1959), pp. 100–114, 128–30, 423–25.

The letter of Arthur Lee to Henry Laurens of Sept. 20, 1778 is printed in Richard Henry Lee, *Life of Arthur Lee*, 2 vols. (Boston, 1829), 2:149–50.

The letter of Franklin and Adams to the ambassador of Naples is printed in Francis Wharton, ed., *The Revolutionary Diplomatic Correspondence of the United States*, 6 vols. (Washington, 1889), 2: 759–60.

CHAPTER 8

Flags and the Winning of Independence

The stalemated condition in the war prompted some bloody fighting in frontier areas. Coming from Canada, a combined force of Loyalists and Iroquois Indians massacred settlers in Pennsylvania's Wyoming Valley and New York state's Cherry Valley in the summer and late fall of 1778. The following summer the Americans avenged these deeds by sending a force of four thousand men under General John Sullivan from Easton, Pennsylvania, to western New York State where they destroyed the Indian villages and broke their power.

On the northwestern frontier General George Rogers Clark led a small force of Americans from a camp near present-day Louisville to capture British garrisons at Kaskaskia, Cahokia, and Vincennes between July and August 1778.

The campaign added some intriguing lore to the history of the flag. According to the accounts of a French merchant at Vincennes, Captain Leonard Helm, the American commander there, was billed in November 1778 for the cost of red and green serge cloth and for a flag. Also included was the cost of having a local French woman, Madame Goderre, make a pavilion, or a company flag, rather than a drapeau, or a national flag. The account says that 3¾ ells of green cloth was purchased along with 5 elles of red serge.*

As soon as General Henry Hamilton, the British commander at Detroit, learned of the fall of Vincennes, he made preparations to retake it. More than half of the force that Hamilton assembled was of Indians. They traveled the six-hundred-mile distance in seventy-one days. As they approached Vincennes, Hamilton noted that "the American flag" was "displayed on the Fort." The stars and stripes had been adopted almost eighteen months earlier, but there is no reason to assume that Hamilton knew that, or would expect to find one on the frontier. The only American flag that Hamilton would surely have known about was one of thirteen red and white stripes.

Whatever the case was, General Hamilton recaptured Vincennes on December 17, 1778, and took Captain Helm prisoner. Six weeks later General George Rogers Clark heard of the fall of Vincennes, and made plans to win it back.

---

* In pre-revolutionary France an ell or *aune* was variously given as 43.9 inches or 44 or 46.8947 French inches. A French foot equalled 12.78933 English inches.

Frenchmen were enlisted for the expedition. The French women or girls of Cahokia made one stand of colors, and the women of Kaskaskia made ten or twelve stands. These were company or regimental colors.

When Clark and his men arrived before Vincennes, he engaged in a bit of deception to make Hamilton think that the American force was larger than it actually was. Clark paraded his colors so that they could be seen but not his men. Hamilton was taken in by the ruse, and was persuaded to surrender on February 25, 1779. According to the journal of Captain Bowman, one of Clark's officers, "the American colors" were hoisted over the fort after the surrender. In his journal General Hamilton also noted that the Americans raised a flag "with their 13 Stripes over them."

But this was not the only flag seen. Isador Chêne, Hamilton's interpreter, who was in the village of Vincennes when the Americans entered, said that "the Rebels entered at the lower end of the Village with a drum beating and a white Colour flying. . . ." This was not a flag of truce, but most likely a French flag as France was the ally of the United States. At that time the flag for the French Navy was a white field with yellow or gold fleurs-de-lis. This would have been a comparatively easy flag for Frenchwomen to make. Since Clark's force included Frenchmen, the use of French colors doubtless had an important psychological impact on both the troops and the citizens being liberated.

The victories in the west made American control of the region secure. But elsewhere the American cause received a severe setback at the end of the year 1778, when Sir Henry Clinton shifted the scene of British operations to the south. Anticipating help from a larger number of Loyalists in the region, Clinton sent Lieutenant Colonel Archibald Campbell with a large force to capture Savannah. Campbell succeeded in defeating the defending force of Americans and captured the city on December 29.

Writing to Clinton about the resources of Savannah and its environs, Campbell added: "I need not inform your Excellency, how much I prize the hope of being the first British Officer under your auspices, to rent a stripe, from the Rebel Flag of Congress. In that event it will rest with your Excellency to decide its merit and consequences."*

Apparently Campbell was never able to realize his hope, due in part perhaps to the small number of flags around. Indeed, on the same day that he wrote the above boast, he forwarded a report on the campaign that resulted in the capture of Savannah. Among the items taken were "one stand of colours, forty eight pieces of Cannon, twenty-three mortars," and other objects. The stand of colors mentioned was probably a regimental color.

The British followed up their gains at Savannah by capturing Augusta. The Americans successfully defended Port Royal and defeated a Loyalist brigade at the battle of Kettle Creek, both in South Carolina. Two American attempts to recapture Augusta failed.

The Flag at Stony Point

In the north, Clinton moved British troops up the Hudson River and seized two unfinished American forts at Stony Point and Verplanck's Point. But on the night of July 15, 1779, General Anthony Wayne led 1,200 men in a bayonet

---

* Campbell may have been using a metaphor to indicate his hope of capturing all of Georgia.

Fig. 92   The Robinson Flag

attack that recaptured Stony Point. Wayne's men dismantled the fort before evacuating the site on July 18.

According to a later account, a stars and stripes flag was carried in the battle and raised over the fort. After the war this flag was brought to Illinois by Major Thomas Posey, a former aide to Washington and a participant in the Stony Point battle. Posey settled in Shawneetown, Illinois, in 1802 and remained there until his death in 1818. At that time the flag passed through the major's sons to Lloyd T. Posey, who gave it to Judge William Bowman. The judge had his offices in a building in Shawneetown that was owned by Michael Robinson. In the drug store Robinson had a collection of antiques and Indian curios that had been dug up in the region. Judge Bowman decided to give Robinson the old flag for his collection. The flag was displayed in the drug store for a number of years, and ownership passed through various members of the Robinson family. Sometime in the early years of the twentieth century the flag was lent to a chapter of a local genealogical group for one of their meetings. While in the custody of this group the flag was mutilated. Several stripes were cut off or shortened by persons seeking souvenirs. The flag was further damaged in the 1930s by flood waters that ravaged Shawneetown. After the flood, the remaining portions of the flag were pinned on a piece of white sheeting and framed under glass. When the last Robinson in Shawneetown died in 1967, the flag became the property of Fred Robinson of Tulsa, Oklahoma, who moved the flag to his Oklahoma home. There it was photographed and studied by a representative of the Smithsonian Institution in November 1972 (Figure 92).

The report that resulted from that study showed that the flag now measured 38 inches by 59 inches, and that the field measured 27½ inches by 32⅝ inches. The red and white stripes and the heading are made of a single ply cotton yarn. Only portions of ten stripes remain. The field is made of a plain weave wool bunting. Single ply cotton muslin was used to make the five-

127

Fig. 93 The Storming of Stony Point, 1779; *painting by Constantino Brumidi, 1871*
Architect of the Capitol

pointed stars, which are inlaid in the field in a 3–2–3–2–3 horizontal pattern. All of the stitching in the flag has been done by hand. The types of cotton thread used to sew this flag indicates that the flag was not in use before the middle of the nineteenth century. The single ply warp bunting is also of a later type than that associated with the eighteenth century and the cotton cloth appears to be power woven. Therefore, this cannot be a Revolutionary War flag.

It is possible, of course, that there was such a flag raised at Stony Point and that Posey took it with him to Illinois. If there were such a flag it may have worn or rotted out and have been replaced in the nineteenth century by a flag of similar design. It may also be possible that at some point this flag was substituted for another—perhaps when it was loaned. The Posey story is plausible enough, but the existing flag is not the flag that flew at Stony Point.

Over the east wall of the Senate Appropriations Committee room in the United States Capitol building in Washington, D.C., there is a lunette painted by Constantino Brumidi in 1871 on the *Storming of Stony Point, 1779* (Figure 93). The picture shows American soldiers holding a British flag. One points to a flag pole without colors. General Wayne, sword in hand, is being carried toward the group by two soldiers. Behind Wayne and his bearers are two more soldiers, one of whom carries a stars and stripes flag with five-pointed stars in a horizontal arrangement. It is not known what information Brumidi may have had when he painted the picture, or whether the presence of the flag was only the artist's device for producing a dramatic scene.

A contemporary illustration of the stars and stripes appears on the Harmon Stebens powder horn, dated 1779. Made for Captain John Graham, the horn names the battles in which Captain Graham took part and uses the flag as decoration (Figure 94).

Flags of John Paul Jones's Squadron

In France in February 1779, Captain John Paul Jones secured a twelve year-old merchant vessel that was a veteran of the East India trade and converted it for

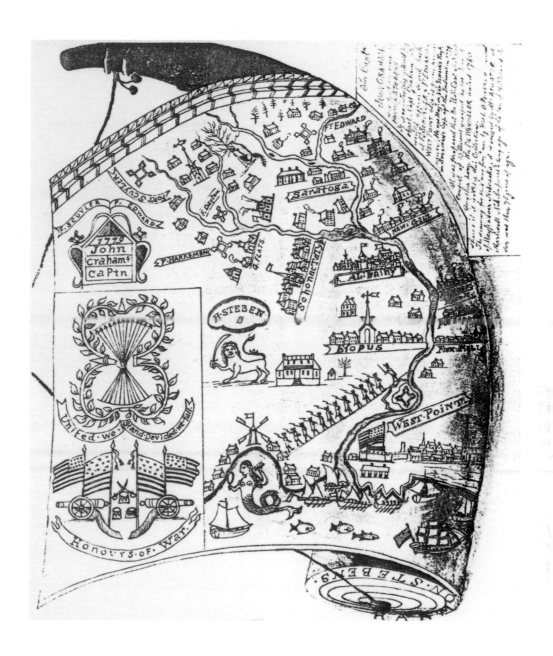

Fig. 94 Drawing of the sketch on the Harmon Stebens powder horn, 1779: note the stars and stripes flag

war purposes. He renamed it the *Bonhomme Richard* in honor of Benjamin Franklin's publication, *Poor Richard's Almanac*. The French government assigned Jones a frigate, a brig, a cutter, and two privateers. Franklin placed the new American-built frigate, the *Alliance*, under Jones's jurisdiction. With this squadron Jones went in search of prizes off the British Isles. In a remarkable battle off Flamborough Head on the eastern coast of Great Britain on September 23, 1779, the *Bonhomme Richard* forced the British frigate *Serapis* to surrender. Another ship of Jones's squadron, the *Pallas*, captured the British sloop of war *Countess of Scarborough* at the same time. The *Bonhomme Richard* was in such a battered condition that it had to be abandoned; it sank soon after the last man got off. Jones transferred his flag to the *Serapis* and took his prizes to the Dutch port of Texel.

Thanks to a Dutch artist at that port we have a vivid record of two types of American flags used by Jones's squadron. The *Serapis* carried a stars and

129

Fig. 95   *The flag of the* Serapis
Chicago Historical Society

Fig. 96   *The flag of the* Alliance
Chicago Historical Society

stripes flag of unusual design. On this flag, the seven-pointed stars are arranged on a blue canton in a 4–5–4 design. The thirteen stripes begin with a blue stripe at the top followed by one of red and one of white. The red and white repeat again before another blue stripe comes in adjacent to the bottom of the blue canton. Next come a red and white stripe followed by a red, a blue, and a white. A blue and red stripe then finish out the stripe design. We thus have a flag with five red stripes, four white stripes, and four blue ones (Figure 95).

A second flag used by the squadron is identified as flying from the frigate *Alliance,* which arrived in France from the United States in May 1779, and which presumably was aware of the most up-to-date information on the flag. The thirteen stars in its blue canton are seven- and eight-pointed, and were arranged horizontally in a 3–2–3–2–3 design. It has thirteen white and red stripes, with a white stripe at the top and bottom. There are seven white and six red stripes (Figure 96). It is therefore apparent that there was a considerable difference of design even in Jones's small squadron; the differences in the colors made it possible to identify each ship. The victories of John Paul Jones's squadron gave a great lift to American and French morale. Unfortunately, his services did not keep the British Navy away from American shores.

The War in the Carolinas

Early in September 1779 Admiral d'Estaing returned to the United States with his fleet of thirty-five ships and with four thousand French troops. He moved to attack the British garrison at Savannah. Joining him in this venture were some fourteen hundred American troops under General Benjamin Lincoln. In the meantime the British garrison had been reinforced by troops from Port

Royal and had refused offers to surrender. A siege now became necessary. The siege began on October 4; four days later it had become apparent that it was largely ineffective.

Admiral d'Estaing became worried. It was taking too long to capture Savannah. Knowing that October was the season for hurricanes in that region, he was fearful that his fleet might be driven off. There was also the possibility that a British fleet might catch his ships in a disadvantageous position. So, to hurry things along, d'Estaing urged that the British fort be stormed. On October 9, the French and Americans attacked but were driven back, suffering heavy casualties. Among those killed was Count Casimir Pulaski, a Polish volunteer serving with the Americans. The siege was abandoned on the evening of October 18. D'Estaing withdrew his troops and ships. General Lincoln led his troops back to Charleston.

Sir Henry Clinton now decided to take the offensive in the south. It had long been customary to suspend campaigning in the north during the winter months, but it would be an ideal time in the south. His plan was to capture Charleston and use it as a base for operations inland. Clinton arrived off the Carolina coast on February 1, but in the leisurely fashion that characterized many British operations during the Revolution he did not begin his siege until March 29.

A British surgeon at Charleston made the following reference to the American flag in his diary entry of April 3, 1780:

In the evening I walked across James Island to the mouth of Wapoo Creek in Ashley River; saw the American thirteen-striped flag displayed on the works opposite the shore redoubts commanded by Major Mackleroth, the two other flags displayed in their works opposite our forces on Charleston Neck—while they were cannonaded our working party on the Neck—their great battery fronting Charleston harbor had the American flag of thirteen stripes displayed. *This, up to this day, had been a blue flag with field and thirteen stars. The other flag never hoisted until today.*

This curious entry suggests that a blue flag with thirteen stars, perhaps similar to the Washington Headquarters flag, was in use as well as the red and white striped flag, and that the two designs had not yet been incorporated in a single flag.

Clinton's force of ten thousand troops and five thousand seamen closed in on the Americans and forced them to surrender on May 12. The British captured Lincoln's fifty-four hundred soldiers—the whole American army in South Carolina—plus four ships. Lincoln's force was the largest body of American soldiers ever captured down to the fall of Bataan in World War II. The loss of Charleston was the greatest American defeat of the war.

Two comments about the American flag at Charleston were made by Tories in private letters written at the time. One letter, dated May 19, 1780, says of the Americans at Fort Moultrie that on "May 7, they marched out, and Captain Hudson of the navy marched in, took possession, levelled the thirteen stripes with the dust, and the triumphant English flag was raised on the staff."

Another letter, written on May 22 from Charleston states: "On the memorable 12th of this month I had the pleasure to see the thirteen stripes with several white pendants levelled to the ground, and the gates of Charlestown opened to receive our conquering heroes, General Sir Henry Clinton and Admiral Arbuthnot." With a base on the coast now secure, Clinton sent out a series of detachments composed mainly of Tories to subdue the interior of the

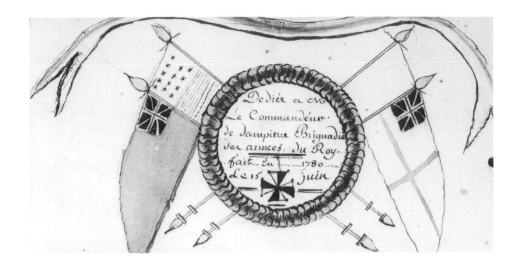

Fig. 97 *Cartouche on a Frenchman's map of Savannah in 1780 The Edward E. Ayer Collection, The Newberry Library*

country. The result was a civil war marked with much violence, bitterness, and malevolence.

In June 1780 an unknown Frenchman drew a map of British-occupied Savannah, probably in anticipation of a renewed campaign to retake it. He was evidently skilled in drawing, but was not familiar with the cartographic practices of his time. Given the circumstances in Savannah and the date of the map, June 15, 1780, he might have been a spy. Whatever the case, the map is of particular interest because of the cartouche showing a grouping of British, American, and French flags (Figure 97). The British red ensign is in the foreground in full color and hides much of the stars and stripes flag behind it. It is possible, however, to see several red and white stripes—more than twenty. The canton is white, probably to provide a contrast to the red, white, and blue British flag in front of it. On the canton are black marks to suggest thirteen stars of six- and eight-points. The star arrangement is horizontal and unique, 5–4–4.

After the capture of Charleston, Sir Henry Clinton's forces soon brought the rest of South Carolina and Georgia under British control. The task of subduing the south was now well begun. Clinton returned to New York with a third of his troops, leaving his second in command, Lord Charles Cornwallis, the task of completing the conquest. In August 1780 Cornwallis routed an American army of more than three thousand men at the battle of Camden. The way was now open for the British invasion of North Carolina. Washington sent one of his best officers, General Nathanael Greene, to see what could be done to retrieve the situation in the south.

Before Greene arrived, southern militiamen captured a portion of Cornwallis's army at King's Mountain, North Carolina. Under the leadership of Greene and Daniel Morgan, the Americans defeated elements of the British forces at the battle of Cowpens and at Guilford Court House in January and March 1781. Cornwallis then withdrew to Wilmington, on the coast, to get supplies. This movement left the rest of North Carolina unprotected, so Greene moved his forces southward to capture British garrisons in South Carolina. Greene's troops captured Fort Watson, thirty miles south of Camden, but met defeat at the battle of Hobkirk's Hill, failed to take Ninety-Six, and lost the battle of Eutaw Springs. Nevertheless, the British evacuated Camden on May 10, 1781. Between May 11 and June 6, the Americans captured five other British outposts in South Carolina. By July the British were holding only Savannah and Charleston in strength.

*Fig. 98 The flag of the Third Maryland
regiment
Smithsonian Institution, courtesy
Maryland State House*

The Stars and Stripes: the Batchelor Flag

It may be useful here to discuss a few flags of Continental units that had stars and stripes designs and were supposedly in use late in the war. The first is the flag of the Third Maryland Regiment that allegedly was carried in the battle of Cowpens, South Carolina, in January 1781. William Batchelor, the color bearer, supposedly was wounded in that battle, and sent home with the flag to Baltimore, where he died. The flag remained in the Batchelor family, and when the British invaded Maryland in the War of 1812 a relative of William Batchelor's carried it in the battle of North Point. In 1894 the Batchelor flag became the property of the Society of the War of 1812, and in 1907 the Society gave it to the state of Maryland. It is now preserved in the Old Statehouse at Annapolis (Figure 98).

That flag contains thirteen red and white stripes and thirteen white stars in a blue canton. Twelve of the five-pointed stars are arranged in a crude circle, or ellipse, on one side; the thirteenth star is in the center. The flag is made of wool bunting and measures 33½ inches at the hoist, 72 inches at the top of the whole flag, and 67 inches at the bottom. The vertical measurement at the middle is 29½ inches.

The authenticity of this flag was challenged by William N. Batchelor in a letter to the Baltimore *American* in February 1908. As a result, the Baltimore Society of the War of 1812 appointed J. Appleton Wilson, a member, to investigate the charges. After consulting the records of the War Department and the Archives of Maryland, Wilson stated that William Batchelor was a member of the Third Maryland Regiment at the time of the battle of Cowpens, thus supporting the statement that Batchelor carried the flag in that battle. Wilson also found in the minutes of the Old Defenders' Association for August 1843 the following entry:

William Batchelor [with Joshua F. written in front of it] ensign of the 27th Regiment [Maryland], presented to the Society the battle flag of the Regiment, which was also the battle flag of the 3rd Regiment [Smallwood's], which was carried by his father, William Batchelor, color sargeant in that regiment, who carried it through the fight at Cowpens, in which engagement he was wounded, returned home, and died December 10, 1781. The flag was left in his custody and to be carried by him in the celebrations of this Association.

Wilson found that Joshua F. Batchelor was an ensign in Captain Schwartzauer's company of the 27th Regiment at the battle of North Point during the War of 1812. He believed that Joshua Batchelor carried the flag at that battle and that it was cut in many places by British bullets. The flag was carried in the procession for Lafayette when the Frenchman visited Baltimore in 1824. While it was in the custody of the Society of the War of 1812 it was carried at the dedication of the society's monument to the heroes of the American Revolution. On September 12, the anniversary of the battle of North Point, the flag was placed over the back of the president's chair. On all other occasions it was given a place of honor at all proceedings. There is no record of when or by whom it was made.

When a textile expert of the Smithsonian Institution examined this flag in the early 1970s she found that the red, white, and blue bunting was of single-ply worsted yarns. The stars were of cotton and were appliqued to both sides. A two-ply linen thread was used to stitch the bunting and plied cotton thread to stitch the stars. The use of cotton stars and thread dates this flag from the

*Fig. 99 The Guilford Court House Flag
North Carolina State Department
of Archives and History*

nineteenth century, not the Revolutionary War. There may have been an original Revolutionary War flag deposited with the Old Defender's Association in 1843, but the flag turned over to the State of Maryland in 1907 was not that flag.

A subsequent investigation into the Revolutionary War service of William Batchelor revealed that he served as a private, not a color sergeant, from April 23, 1778, until his death in September 1780, three months before the battle of Cowpens. In his letter to the Baltimore *American* in 1908, William N. Batchelor claimed that his family knew nothing about his namesake who served in the Revolution, and that he himself had carried the so-called Cowpens flag at the battle of North Point in the War of 1812!

The North Carolina Militia Flags

The next flag of note is the Guilford or North Carolina militia flag, now preserved at the Guilford Court House National Military Park. This flag is made of heavy cotton with six hand-sewn blue and red stripes. The canton has thirteen blue stars, each with eight points, on a white field. Its white field has a distinctive shape, measuring twenty-five inches wide by seventy-eight inches long. There is no record of when or by whom it was made (Figure 99).

This flag was first brought to public attention in 1909 when it was presented to the Grand Lodge of Ancient, Free and Accepted Masons of North Carolina. According to the speech of presentation, the flag was carried on the battlefields of North and South Carolina during the Revolution, and was brought to North Carolina at the end of that war. It remained in the possession of Micajah Bullock of Granville County until 1854. In that year Bullock's son Edward, then eighty-one, presented the flag to the Mount Energy Lodge of Ancient, Free and Accepted Masons. From 1854 to 1904 the flag remained at the Mount Energy Lodge. In 1904 it was presumably moved with other lodge property to Creedmore, where it remained until the two oldest male descendants of Micajah Bullock made the presentation to the Grand Lodge. In 1914 the Grand Lodge presented it to the North Carolina Museum of History at Raleigh.

The documentary record on Micajah Bullock and his war service is of some interest. A 1776 list of Captain James Yancey's Company of Granville County Militia contains the name of Micajah Bullock. The name also appears in a list of people in the Dutch District of Granville County who took the oath of allegiance, presumably in late May of 1778. As of 1979 there were twenty-seven living members of the Daughters of the American Revolution who are descendants of Micajah Bullock and who have cited his war service as a part of their proof for membership. Also supporting the claim is the fact that Micajah's son Edward, born in 1773, would have been old enough to remember when his father returned from the war. The story of the flag could have been a fabrication of Edward's, but William P. Brandon, the superintendent of the Guilford Court House National Military Park was inclined to regard the story as true. Brandon tracked down all the information he could about this flag. Over the years various researchers have accepted this Guilford flag as a genuine relic of the American Revolution. The authors of this volume agreed with this conclusion.*

* A Smithsonian textile expert who examined this flag wrote that the union was made of white cotton with blue cotton stars. There are six blue cotton stripes and six are made of a small warp-patterned red woolen fabric. The flag is sewn by hand with a two-ply linen sewing thread. There is no heading. All the edges were

Fig. 100 A Rhode Island regimental flag

The stars in the Guilford flag are in a 4–3–4 design, but with two stars offset to the right of the field it is almost a 5–3–5 arrangement. The colors of the canton and the stars and stripes, as well as the dimensions, all give this flag a distinctive quality. There is evidence that at one time it had at least fourteen stripes, and perhaps even sixteen. It was a custom until 1818 for many persons to add stripes to their flags unofficially as new states came into the union.

Flags of the Rhode Island Regiments

The last starred flags that should be noted are those associated with the Rhode Island regiments. Some earlier writers have suggested that the star arrangement in the flags of these regiments may have influenced the design of the stars and stripes. In 1775 a unit was formed that was designated as the Rhode Island Regiment. Later, on January 1, 1777, another unit was formed and designated as the Second Rhode Island Regiment. Both regiments had similar flags. Each had a blue canton with thirteen five pointed stars arranged in a 3–2–3–2–3 pattern. On the field of one is a blue scroll and the inscription in white letters: "R. ISLAND REGT." This inscription made flag historian Howard Chapin conclude that this was the flag of the First Rhode Island Regiment. But another flag historian, Frank E. Schermerhorn, has identified it as the flag of the Second Rhode Island Regiment. Other flag scholars have agreed with Schermerhorn.

The second Rhode Island flag had displayed on its white field a light blue foul anchor with a dark blue rope. Above the anchor in dark blue letters is the word HOPE (Figure 100). At the Rhode Island State House in Providence this flag carries a label that identifies it as the flag of the First Rhode Island Regiment. Both flags were presented to the General Assembly of Rhode Island on February 28, 1784, by line officers associated with the regiments. It is not known when or by whom the flags were labeled. There is always the possibility that the flags were mislabeled, or that labels were switched at some point after they were presented to the State House.

Above and beyond the identification problem is the question of whether the star designs on these flags influenced the design of the stars and stripes. It is not known when either regiment received its colors, but it is believed that they did not have them until late in the war. If this is true, then the stars and stripes may have influenced these flags rather than vice versa. The authors do not believe that there was any connection between the Rhode Island regimental flags and the design of the stars and stripes.

Early Flag Makers

No record has been found of the makers of the flags flown in the Continental Army's camps around Boston, nor of the maker of the Union flag flown at Washington's headquarters at the fort on the lower end of Manhattan. No

cut on the staff side. The flag was once nailed to a staff. The conclusion was that the flag was made after 1791. She conjectured that the flag may have been made as a fifteen-star, fifteen-stripe flag, in the period 1795–1800; and that, since Edward Bullock was eighty-one when the flag was presented to the Mount Energy Lodge, some confusion could have developed about when and where the flag was used. See Grace R. Cooper, *Thirteen-Star Flags* (Washington, 1973), pp. 26–28.

135

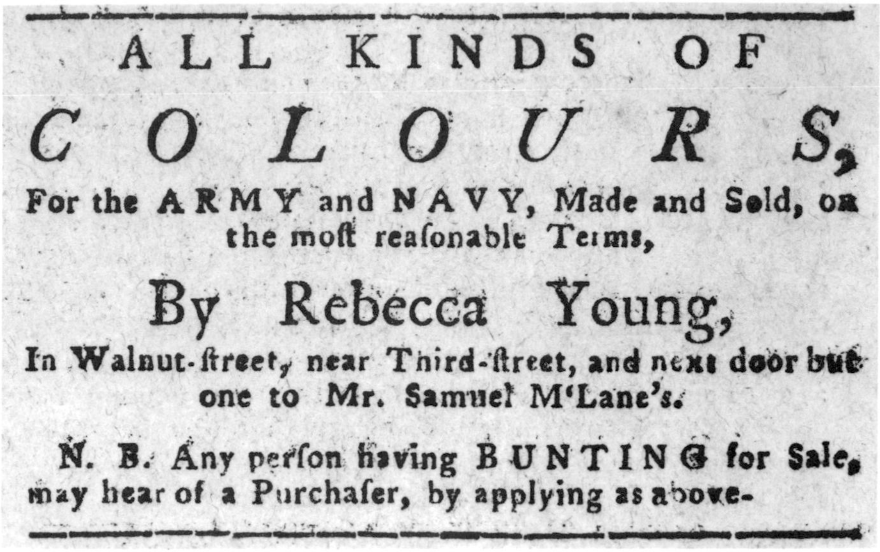

Fig. 101   Rebecca Young's advertisement in the Pennsylvania Packet, *1781 Library of Congress*

mention has been found of the maker of the flags used by Commodore Wynkoop, who in the spring of 1776 was ordered by Washington to command vessels on the Lakes. But the record made by the acting quartermaster general of items "Received at Saratoga" from Wynkoop on July 26, 1777, seems to indicate that the colors flown by him were owned by the government.

When General Schuyler wrote from northern New York to General Washington on Manhattan Island on July 12, 1776, he enclosed a long list of items wanted by the Naval Department on Lake Champlain. The list contained an item for "40 Small Colours . . . Continental; some red blue for signals." This request for colors was repeated in August. Unfortunately for history, neither the returns of Hugh Hughes, who was the acting quartermaster general for the state of New York, nor the records of Major General Thomas Mifflin, who became the quartermaster general of the army in 1776, give the names of flag makers.

An interesting document entitled "Return of ye New Standards and Division Colours for the Use of the United States of America in Possession of Major Jonathan Gostolowe . . ." for July and August 1778 gives the colors of the regimental standards and division colors and indicates the very elaborate designs and mottos used on them. This document is a prime source for information on the richness and diversity of the colors authorized for Continental units. But it too tells nothing about who made these fine flags.

It is only in a return of stores purchased by the commissary general of military stores of June 8, 1781, to June 30, 1782, that we have our first clues to a Revolutionary War army flag maker—Rebecca Young. The entries are:

From	Date	Item
Rebecca Young	July 14, 1781	1 Continental Standard
Sundry Persons	August 7, 1781	34 Bayonets, 24 Pincers
		1 Continental Standard
Rebecca Young	September 7, 1781	1 Continental Standard

Rebecca Young's name also appears in the receipts for money paid by Samuel Hodgdon, assistant commissary general of military stores at Philadelphia, on

136

November 10, 1780, for cutting out and making sixty-eight blankets. She appears in the records on November 29, 1782, when she was paid for forty-seven drum cases, and on February 19, 1785, for supplying one thousand brushes and wires. Her advertisement for making "All Kinds of Colors for the Army and Navy" appeared in the *Pennsylvania Packet* of May 26, 1781, and later (Figure 101).

In the history of flagmaking, therefore, Rebecca Young is an important person. The returns of the Army quartermasters show that she made flags for the Army during the American Revolution. Her family were staunch patriots. Her friends in Philadelphia were among the important leaders of the American cause. One of these was Dr. Benjamin Rush, the noted physician of the Revolution, under whose instruction Young's son Benjamin became a physician. Her brother, Colonel Benjamin Flower, was at one time commissary general of military stores. When the British advanced on Philadelphia in September 1777, Flower worked diligently to remove vast quantities of military stores and clothing from the city to prevent them from being captured. Among other things, he helped to save the Liberty Bell. Later Washington sent him a letter of commendation for his efforts.

The British threat to Philadelphia forced Rebecca and her husband, William Young, and their six children to flee to Lebanon, Pennsylvania. While they were there, Rebecca's husband died while visiting Allentown, Pennsylvania, on February 19, 1778.

Immediately after the British evacuation of Philadelphia on June 18, 1778, Colonel Flower went to the city in the performance of his duties as commissary general of military stores. He procured a house for his widowed sister and asked Major Gostolowe to send her furniture. Later Colonel Flower, his second wife, Delia, and his daughter were to share the house with Rebecca Young and her family. Flower died three years later, in April 1781, and left his sister the sum of one thousand dollars. It seems clear that Rebecca Young's work in making flags was prompted by the need to make a living after the death of her brother. Less than a month after his death her first advertisement appeared in the *Pennsylvania Packet*.

By an interesting coincidence, Rebecca Young's daughter, Mary Pickersgill, was selected to make the flag for Fort McHenry in the War of 1812. Rebecca's granddaughter ascribed this commission to the family connection with Commodore Joshua Barney and Brigadier General John Stricker, who were active in the defense of Baltimore. It was the flag made by Mary Pickersgill that Francis Scott Key observed still flying after a night of British bombardment and that inspired him to write "The Star Spangled Banner."

Mutiny and Conflict, 1780–81

The years 1780 and 1781 brought several events that were most disturbing for the American cause. Aside from the problems of the battlefields, there were mutinies in Washington's army. Disturbed by the drop in value in Continental money and a cut in their rations, two Connecticut regiments paraded under arms on May 25, 1780, and demanded a full ration and an immediate payment of their back wages. Order was restored by the Pennsylvania regiments, but the problem continued to fester.

September brought news of the treason of General Benedict Arnold. While

137

Fig. 102   Flag of Castle William, later Fort Independence
Smithsonian Institution, courtesy Massachusetts State House

Fig. 103   Flag in Abraham Weatherwise's almanac, 1782
Library of Congress

in command of the garrison at West Point, he gave to a British officer the plans of the fort and information on its weak points. The British officer was captured by the Americans, and Arnold was forced to seek refuge aboard a British warship in the Hudson River. Arnold now turned his military talents to helping the British.

In January 1781 the soldiers of the Pennsylvania Line rose up in mutiny and marched off with arms and artillery toward Philadelphia to make their demands to the officials of their state. Concessions were made which ended the mutiny, but over half the Pennsylvania Line left the Continental Army. Later in January, troops of the New Jersey Line mutinied and the outbreak was put down by force. Force was also used against another uprising among Pennsylvania troops in May. Congress struggled with the problems of finance and states ratified the form of government set forth in the Articles of Confederation.

Despite this unrest, elsewhere there was evidence of some confidence in the future. In 1781, Jonathan Fowle of Boston, father of a member of the garrison in Castle William in Boston harbor, arranged to have a flag made and presented to the fort. The flag was made of bunting and consisted of thirteen red and white stripes and a red stripe on the top and bottom. Its blue canton contained thirteen white five-pointed stars arranged horizontally in a 4–5–4 pattern. The flag is now preserved in the State House in Boston* (Figure 102).

Another individual apparently confident about the future of his country was David Rittenhouse, also of Boston. Under the pseudonym Abraham Weatherwise, he began to publish a series of almanacs beginning in 1781. In *Weatherwise's Town and Country Almanack,* published in 1782, there is an illustration of the stars and stripes flag (Figure 103) showing five-pointed stars in a horizontal 3–5–5 arrangement.

In the Congress, two committees had submitted designs for the Great Seal of the United States in 1776 and 1780, but neither was considered suitable. It was not until May 1782 that Congress appointed a third committee. The committee did little serious work. Instead it asked a young Philadelphia lawyer named William Barton to use his knowledge of heraldry and his skill as an artist to produce a design.

Barton's first design no longer exists,** but from a description we know that there were two elements in it of special interest to flag historians. The first was a shield in the center that was decorated with thirteen red and white stripes in a horizontal arrangement. In the upper left hand corner of the shield was a blue canton with thirteen stars in a circle. The shield was supported on the right by a knight in armor holding a lance with a flag on it. This flag had a green field and was decorated with two crossed swords, two fleurs-de-lis, a harp, and a star. Supporting the shield on the left was a maiden dressed in a long white gown and wearing a crown. Across her dress from her right shoulder to her left side was a scarf or sash decorated with stars. In her right hand she held a flag on a pole. This flag is the second item of interest because it consisted of thirteen stripes and had a canton containing thirteen stars. Barton's notes describe the flag simply as "the proper Standard of the United States". The stars on the shield and on the flag represent "a new Constellation. . . . Their Disposition, in the form of a Circle, denotes the Perpetuity of it's Continuance, the Ring being the Symbol of Eternity."

---

* As far as is known, this flag has never been subjected to a textile and thread examination.
** A modern version of this design, drawn by Paul J. Connor of the Insitute of Heraldry, United States Army, is reproduced in Richard S. Patterson and Richardson Dougall, *The Eagle and the Shield: A History of the Great Seal of the United States* (Washington, 1978), p. 58.

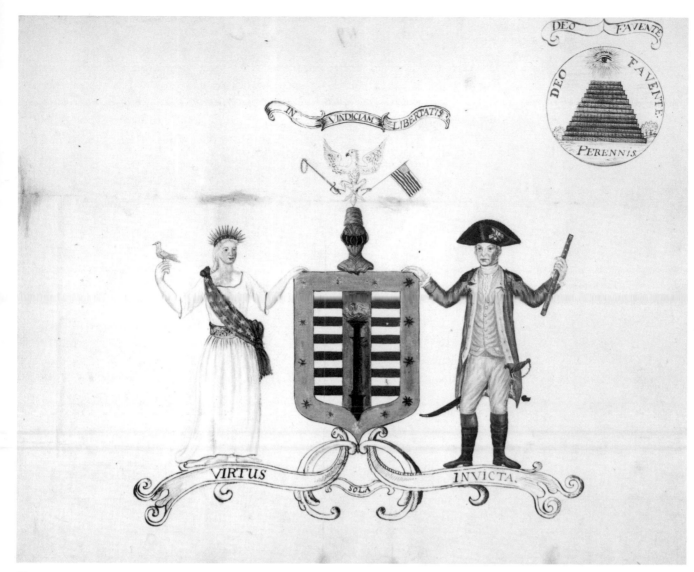

*Fig. 104   Barton's design for the Great Seal
National Archives*

*Fig. 105   Barton's design for the Great Seal
(detail)
National Archives*

139

Barton's first design was too complex to make a good seal, and he was asked to do another drawing. His second design is of interest because it depicted an eagle holding a small stars and stripes flag in one of its claws (Figure 104). This flag had thirteen red and white stripes, beginning and ending with a white stripe, and a blue canton containing thirteen five-pointed stars arranged in a circle (Figure 105). Although Congress also rejected Barton's second design it remains of interest because it is one of the earliest known illustrations of a United States flag with a circle of stars. Perhaps reports of this design stimulated the making of flags in that pattern.

The Siege of Yorktown

Meanwhile, the gains made by the American soldiers under Greene and Morgan in January and March 1781 convinced Cornwallis that the war in the Carolinas could not be won as long as Virginia continued to be a source of supplies and troops. Cornwallis went so far as to propose to Clinton that New York be abandoned, and that all the British forces there be concentrated in the Chesapeake region. Clinton could not agree to anything so drastic, but he did send a large force under Brigadier General Benedict Arnold who joined forces with Cornwallis and the British began to raid deep into Virginia. American troops under Lafayette, von Steuben, and Anthony Wayne moved against Cornwallis, who turned to the coast to establish a base from which he could maintain communication with Clinton in New York. Cornwallis chose Yorktown, and his army began occupying it on August 1.

Two weeks later Washington received a letter from Admiral De Grasse, commanding the French West Indian fleet, saying that he was leaving the West Indies for Chesapeake Bay, and his fleet and his troops would be available for operations until mid-October. Washington seized the opportunity to take the offensive. Washington began moving his army and a French force in Rhode Island under Lieutenant General de Rochambeau toward Virginia.

By the end of August, De Grasse had set up a naval blockade of Yorktown and had sent his troops to join with those of Lafayette in hemming in the British by land. A British fleet under Admiral Thomas Graves appeared and De Grasse moved out of his blockade position to fight it. A naval battle, followed by three days of maneuvering and the arrival of a French squadron to reinforce De Grasse, induced Admiral Graves to head for New York for repairs. De Grasse then sent ships up Chesapeake Bay to bring the bulk of Washington's and Rochambeau's troops to the Yorktown area. With De Grasse in command of the seas, and with a large Franco-American army in position, the siege of Yorktown began on September 28. Cornwallis was forced to surrender on October 18. The following day eight thousand British troops laid down their arms.

A map drawn by Major Sebastian Bauman, Second New York Artillery Regiment, in October 1781, shows the disposition of the forces around Yorktown. Entitled, "Plan of the Investment of York and Gloucester," it contains a cartouche with a panoply of arms and flags in the background. One of the flags is a stars and stripes that has a white stripe at the top and six-pointed white stars arranged in a 3–2–3–2–3 pattern. The canton is a rather pale blue. It is believed that Bauman would not have included this flag in the design if it was not in use at Yorktown. Bauman sent a copy of his plan to Major General

Fig. 106 *Detail of flag in Bauman's Map of Yorktown*
John Carter Brown Library, Brown University

Fig. 107 *Simcoe's view of the American position at Yorktown (detail)*
Colonial Williamsburg

Alexander McDougall with an accompanying letter dated October 24, 1782. This letter calls the plan "accurate in design" but makes no reference to the flag in the decorative motif. The plan was engraved in Philadelphia in 1782 and published in color (Figure 106).

Another indication that the stars and stripes flag was displayed at Yorktown is based on a watercolor drawing by Lieutenant Colonel John Graves Simcoe, who commanded the Queen's Rangers. Looking across the water from the British position at Gloucester Point, Simcoe's drawing shows a stars and stripes flag waving over a distant bluff (Figure 107). It is clear that the flag has a blue canton and thirteen red and white stripes. The size of the painting, 5¼ by 21

Fig. 108 The Surrender at Yorktown;
painting by John Trumbull
Architect of the Capitol

inches, makes it difficult to determine the design on the small canton. The marks on it may have been intended to represent dark blue stars arranged in a horizontal design. It may also be that Simcoe intended to paint in white stars but decided against working on so small a scale.

Another British officer, St. George Tucker, recorded in his journal on October 9, 1781, that the "continental Standard" was hoisted over an American battery. Of course, the term "continental Standard" could mean a flag other than stars and stripes. On the day of Cornwallis's surrender, two officers of the Pennsylvania Line recorded that a detachment of American soldiers took possession of the British batteries and unfurled "the American Flag." A German soldier who witnessed the event wrote that the Americans had hoisted a large flag "which had 13 stripes, which signified the 13 provinces of the United North American free states."

Several years later, in 1797, John Trumbull painted *The Surrender of Lord Cornwallis at Yorktown, Virginia, October 19th, 1781,* which shows a stars and stripes flag (Figure 108). The blue canton contains stars arranged in a square design with the thirteenth star in the center of the square. This is the same design that Trumbull used in his painting of the surrender of General Burgoyne at Saratoga. Both the *Surrender of Cornwallis* and the *Surrender of Burgoyne* were purchased by the government between 1817 and 1824 for the rotunda of the United States Capitol. A different, but more contemporary

commemoration of the victory is Charles Willson Peale's 1784 painting of Washington, Lafayette, and Tench Tilgman, the aide-de-camp at Yorktown (Figure 109).

The Coming of Peace

The news of the surrender of Cornwallis, and of the defeat of the British by the French in the West Indies in 1781 and the early part of 1782, led the House

Fig. 110   Sketch of a flag in the diary of Ezra Stiles (detail) Yale University Library

of Commons to repudiate the policies of the ministry of Lord North. First came the House vote on February 27, 1782, against the continued prosecution of the war in America. This was followed on March 5 by the passage of a bill authorizing the king to make peace with the Americans. Lord North resigned on March 20 and was replaced by Lord Rockingham, who had been responsible for the repeal of the Stamp Act. The British opened direct negotiations with the American peace commissioners in Paris on April 12. Formal negotiations began on September 27, and the preliminary articles of peace were signed on November 30, 1782. They would not take effect until after the British reached an agreement with France. Articles of peace between Great Britain and France were signed on January 20, and on the same day with Britain and Spain. The British announced the end of hostilities on February 4, 1783.

The coming of peace induced the *Pennsylvania Gazette* to reprint the 1777 resolution of the Congress on the flag in its issue of April 23, 1783. It asked that other papers reprint the resolution in order that it be generally known. This request is a striking admission of how slowly the stars and stripes came into use. That same issue carried an account of a meeting of the inhabitants of Pittsgrove, Salem County, New Jersey, and an adjoining town to celebrate the peace. They began the day by raising "a monument of great height, on which was displayed the ensign of peace with thirteen stripes."

The peace celebration in New Haven, Connecticut, was described in the diary of Ezra Stiles, the president of Yale College:

April 24, 1783. Public Rejoicing for the Peace in New Haven. At sunrise, 23 cannons discharged in the Green, and the Continental flag displayed, being a grand silk flag presented by the ladies, cost 120 dollars. The stripes red and white, with azure field in the upper part charged with 13 stars. On the same field and among the stars was the arms of the United States, the field of which contained a ship, a plough, and three sheaves of wheat; the crest, an eagle volant; the supporters, two white horses. The arms were put on with paint and gliding. It took   yards. When displayed, it appeared well.

Stiles made a somewhat rough sketch of the flag he observed, using *x*'s and an extra line to depict six-pointed stars (Figure 110). His sketch also shows the motto "Virtue, Liberty, Independence," which is not mentioned in the description. Stiles was in error about the arms of the United States, but it was an honest error. The ladies who made the flag copied the arms displayed on the title page of a family bible published in Philadelphia. It happened that the arms and motto were those of Pennsylvania, not the United States. It was not until Roger Sherman returned to New Haven from the Congress that information on the real arms of the United States was obtained.

During the long interval between the surrender of Cornwallis and the proclamations ending the war, the British and American armies remained intact pending the outcome of the peace negotiations. Sir Guy Carleton succeeded Sir Henry Clinton as the British commander-in-chief, and he proceeded to concentrate all the British troops in New York City and vicinity. Washington's army was encamped in the Hudson River Highlands. On May 26, 1783, forty-one days after it ratified the peace treaty, Congress furloughed most of Washington's army. The final articles of peace were signed in Paris on September 3, 1783, and in November Congress discharged all but a small force of soldiers under Washington. When the last British troops evacuated New York City on November 25, Washington entered the city accompanied by the governor of New York.

The last days of the British occupation of New York are associated with several references to the flag. The *Pennsylvania Gazette* of May 28, 1783, charged that:

It is positively asserted that the flag of the thirteen United States of America has been grossly insulted in New York, and not permitted to be hoisted on board any American vessel in that port. Congress should demand immediate reparation for the indignity wantonly offered to all America, and, unless satisfactory concessions are instantly made, the British flag, which now streams without interruption in our harbor, Philadelphia, should be torn down, and treated with every mark of indignation and contempt.

On the day of the evacuation of New York, the British claimed the right of possession of Fort George until noon. At the lower end of Murray Street was a tavern whose owner, a Mr. Day, decided to raise the American flag over his tavern on the morning of evacuation day. It was thus the first American flag flown in the city. The British provost-marshal ordered Day to take down his flag, but the owner refused. The provost-marshal attempted to take it down himself, but was attacked by Day's stout wife who beat the officer over the head with a broomstick. Amid the jeers and laughter of a few bystanders, the provost-marshal abandoned his effort and the flag remained flying.

This flag was acquired by the American Museum of New York in 1810 and exhibited in front of the museum on anniversaries of the evacuation and on the 4th of July. The flag was described as being made of bunting and measuring nine or ten feet wide by twelve or fifteen feet long. It had thirteen stars and stripes, but the star arrangement was apparently not recorded or remembered. The flag was destroyed in the fire that burned the museum in 1865.

When the British troops departed from New York City they left their flag behind, nailed to a flagstaff in the Battery. They had removed the halyards and greased the pole, thus making the task of removing the flag very difficult for the Americans. A ladder was secured, and the British flag was torn down. When the stars and stripes were raised, the artillery fired a thirteen gun salute.

Later, on December 4, 1783, Washington met with his officers at Faunces' Tavern and bade them farewell. He then set out for the south. On December 23, he came before the Congress at Annapolis and resigned his commission. His great mission was completed.

Notes

The general pattern of the war is set forth in Christopher Ward, *The War of the Revolution*, vol. 2. Vivid descriptions of the first foreign salute to the stars and stripes and of the battle between the *Bonhomme Richard* and the *Serapis* may be found in Samuel Eliot Morison, *John Paul Jones: A Sailor's Biography*, pp. 128–30 and 226–42. Documents relating to the incidents are in the John Paul Jones Papers in the Library of Congress. The Texel flag illustrations are in the custody of the Chicago Historical Society.

Grace Cooper's reports on the Washington headquarters flag and the Posey or Robinson flag are in the custody of the Division of Naval History, Smithsonian Institution. She discusses the flag of the Third Maryland Regiment or the Cowpens flag and the Guilford Court House flag in her book, *Thirteen-Star Flags*, pp. 26–29. Background information on regimental flags may be found in the works of Gherardi Davis and Frank Earle Schermerhorn. The Castle William flag is described in David Eggenberger, *Flags of the U.S.A.* (New York, 1964), p. 79. Abraham Weatherwise's almanac is in the Library of Congress and in the Brown University Library.

Lieutenant Colonel Archibald Campbell's letter to Sir Henry Clinton of January 16, 1779, is in the Clinton Papers in the William L. Clements Library, University of Michigan.

Background information on the Posey flag is in the custody of the Division of Naval History, Smithsonian Institution. Details on the Constantino Brumidi painting of the *Storming of Stony Point, 1779* are from the book by the Architect of the Capitol, *Compilation of Works of Art and*

Other Objects in the United States Capitol, H.R. *362*, 88th Cong., 2d sess., 1965, p. 304, and from the office of the Architect of the Capitol.

The British surgeon's description of the flag at Charleston is from the diary of Dr. John Jeffries, cited in Preble, p. 284. Comments about the American flag by Tories living in Charleston at the time of its surrender to the British are published in Franklin Benjamin Hough, *The Siege of Charleston by the British Fleet Under the Command of Admiral Arbuthnot and Sir Henry Clinton, which terminated with the Surrender of that Place on the 12th of May 1780* (Albany, 1867), pp. 104–107. A map of British-occupied Savannah, drawn by an unknown Frenchman, is described in Robert W. Karrow, Jr., comp., *Mapping the American Revolutionary War* (Chicago, 1974), p. 7, item 12.

Sources on the early flag makers are scattered. The list of items received by the acting quartermaster general at Saratoga on July 26, 1777, is in the War Department Collection of Revolutionary War Records, Record Group 93, National Archives and Records Service. The long list of items desired by the Naval Department on Lake Champlain and sent by General Schuyler to Washington on July 12, 1776, is in the Washington Papers in the Library of Congress. The return of Major Jonathan Gastolowe on "New Standards and Division Colors" for July and August 1778 is in the War Department Collection of Revolutionary War Records, Book 115. For a discussion and the identification of these flags see Donald W. Holst and Marko Zlatich, "A Return of Some Continental Army Regimental Colors of 1776," *Military Collector and Historian*, 19 (1967): 109–115. See also Donald W. Holst, "Regimental Colors of the Continental Army," in *Military Collector and Historian*, 20 (1968): 69–73. For the return of stores purchased by the commissary general of military stores for June 1781 to June 1782 see the War Department Collection of Revolutionary War Records, Book 115. Samuel Hodgdon's receipts for money paid to Rebecca Young are in the voluminous account books of the period in the National Archives, Book 77 and Book 105. Details on the Young family are from the Young family bible preserved at the Flag House in Baltimore.

Charles Willson Peale painted a portrait of Colonel Benjamin Flower that shows him holding the letter that Washington gave him. The portrait is preserved at the Flag House in Baltimore. On the rescue of the Liberty Bell see the *Journal* of the Pennsylvania House of Representatives, Nov. 28, 1776, to Oct. 2, 1781, p. 144; *Journals of the Continental Congress*, 8: 741; *Pennsylvania Colonial Records*, 11: 306; the *Pennsylvania Packet* of Aug. 22, 1778; the *Pennsylvania Evening Post* of Aug. 22, 1778; and Joseph Mortimer Levering, *A History of Bethlehem, Pennsylvania, 1741–1892* (Bethlehem, 1903), p. 463.

For Mary Pickersgill's work on the Fort McHenry flag see Mrs. Arthur B. Bibbins, *Star-Spangled Banner Flag House Guide to Historic Landmarks of Baltimore* (Baltimore, 1929). A popular account of her role in the Fort McHenry story is in Neil H. Swanson, *The Perilous Fight* (New York, 1945), pp. 255–68. A more recent account is Mary-Paulding Martin, *The Flag House Story* (Baltimore, 1970).

On the role of William Barton in developing designs for the Great Seal, see Richard S. Patterson and Richardson Dougall, *The Eagle and the Shield: A History of the Great Seal of the United States* (Washington, 1978), pp. 48–70.

An engraved copy of Major Sebastian Bauman's map of the siege of Yorktown is preserved in the Phelps Stokes Collection at the New York Public Library. It is reproduced in color in *The American Heritage Book of the Revolution* (New York, 1958), p. 370. For an earlier account of Bauman and his work see "Bauman's Map of the Siege of Yorktown," in *The Magazine of American History*, 6 (1881): 54–55.

The watercolor by Lieutenant John Graves Simcoe is preserved at Colonial Williamsburg, Inc., and is reproduced in color in Quaife, Weig and Appleman, *The History of the United States Flag*, plate 32.

On the observations of St. George Tucker, two officers of the Pennsylvania Line, and a German soldier of the flags at Yorktown, see the unpublished typescript report dated April 4, 1952, by Hugh F. Rankin, "The Genesis of the American Flag, Its Growth, Design, and Triumph at Yorktown, 1776–1781," in the custody of the National Park Service, U.S. Department of the Interior, Washington, D. C., pp. 59–65; this is cited in Quaife, Weig and Appleman, and in Edward M. Riley, ed., "St. George Tucker's Journal of the Siege of Yorktown, 1781," *William and Mary Quarterly*, 3rd Ser., 5 (1948): 375–95.

Information on John Trumbull's painting of the surrender of Lord Cornwallis is in Colonel Theodore Sizer, ed., *Works of Colonel John Trumbull, Artist of the American Revolution* (New Haven, 1950).

The quotation from Ezra Stiles is printed in Franklin Bowditch Dexter, ed., *The Literary Diary of Ezra Stiles, D.D., LL.D., President of Yale College*, 3 vols. (New York, 1901), 3: 69–70. It is also quoted in Preble, p. 289. Preble's work also contains information on the celebration of the peace in Pittsgrove, New Jersey, pp. 284–85. On the British occupation of New York see also Charles Ira Bushnell, *Narrative of the Life and Adventures of Levi Hanford, a Soldier of the Revolution* (New York, 1863), p. 72. Douglas Southall Freeman describes the events of evacuation day in his volume, *George Washington: A Biography*, 5: 458–77. A detailed account is Henry P. Johnson, "Evacuation of New York by the British, 1783," *Harper's Magazine*, 67 (1883): 902–3.

CHAPTER 9

Flags of the New Nation 1783–1818

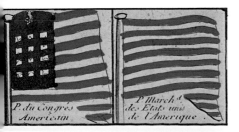

Fig. 111 The stars and stripes on the Mond-hare flag sheet
John Carter Brown Library, Brown University

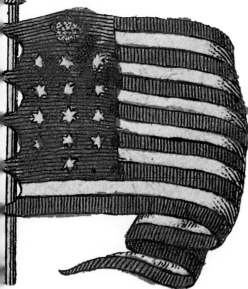

Fig. 112 The American flag on the Lotter flag sheet, 1782
John Carter Brown Library, Brown University

In the closing years of the Revolution, illustrations of the stars and stripes flag began appearing in Europe. The first of these seems to have been the Mondhare flag sheet, published in Paris in 1781 (Figure 111), which shows four flags associated with the United States. The first of these, called the flag of the American Congress, shows thirteen red and white stripes with the red stripe at the top and bottom. Twelve stars were drawn in four horizontal lines in a 3–3–3–3 arrangement, but when the sheet was colored the artist depicted them as white rectangles. He also painted a fleur-de-lis over the top of the arrangement.

The second flag depicted is one of thirteen red and white stripes; it is identified as the merchant flag of the United States. The third flag is a red and white striped pennant, or, as the sheet calls it, the pennant ('flamme') of the United States of America. The fourth illustration shows another pennant with thirteen stars on a blue field arranged in a 5–4–4 horizontal pattern. The stars are depicted as white rectangles. Next to the canton, six red and white vertical stripes can be observed before the flag bends out of sight. The tail of the pennant shows red and white horizontal stripes with red on top, as in the other pennant.

Not long after this, probably in 1782, Tobias Conrad Lotter published in Germany another flag sheet. This showed an American flag with thirteen red and white stripes, and with red stripes at both top and bottom. The blue canton had a long and somewhat narrow shape and extended from the first stripe to the eleventh. It had thirteen six-pointed white stars arranged in 3–3–3–3–1 design. The single star as the bottom is balanced by a fleur-de-lis at the top (Figure 112).

An American flag was added to the background of a portrait painted by John Singleton Copley on the day that King George III formally recognized the independence of the United States. It thus became the first representation of the stars and stripes to be seen in England after the royal declaration. The portrait was of Elkanah Watson of Rhode Island, who had been earlier engaged in private business in France. When it seemed likely that a peace would soon be signed, he made a trip to England to see about opening a branch of his firm there. Soon after his arrival in London in September 1782, Watson won a large sum of money on a bet and decided to use it to have his portrait painted.

147

Copley soon finished the portrait except for background detail. Watson wanted a ship, illuminated by the rising sun, to symbolize the news of the acknowledgment of independence being brought to the United States and thereby heralding a new day in the life of the nation. The ship was to carry the stars and stripes flag and to be very visible in the sunlight. Since his studio was frequently visited by members of the royal family and the nobility, Copley thought it would be imprudent to paint in the flag while Britain was still technically at war. Then, on December 5, 1782, in a speech to the House of Lords, King George III declared the former colonies to be free and independent states. Watson and Copley were present for the historic announcement. Immediately afterward, Copley went to his studio, painted in the stars and stripes, and mounted the unfinished portrait in his studio for visitors to see (Figure 113).

Although a few Londoners may have seen Copley's picture of the stars and stripes, most were not prepared to see that flag flying on a ship in their own waters. British officials were thrown into consternation by the arrival of the American ship *Bedford*, under Captain William Mooers, off Gravesend on February 3, 1783. This was a day before the formal announcement of the end of the hostilities and twelve days before the news was published. When the Nantucket-based ship was reported to the customs house on February 6, she was not allowed to enter the port of London until some consultation took place between the Commissioners of the Customs and the Lords of the Council. Many acts of Parliament were still in effect against the Americans. The *Bedford* anchored at Horsledown, a little below the Tower of London, to await the decision of the British officials. As the first American vessel to display the stars and stripes in a British port, she was the object of much attention in the House of Commons, as well as in the London papers. Only after the king's proclamation ending hostilities was published on February 15 was the *Bedford* permitted to discharge her cargo of whale oil.

While a decision was pending in the case of the *Bedford,* two other American ships arrived on the Thames. Eventually, claims were made that one of four other ships first displayed the stars and stripes in the Thames. Rear Admiral George H. Preble was able to establish proof of the *Bedford's* claim, but unfortunately no description remains of the flag she wore.

One of the vessels that arrived on the Thames not long after the *Bedford* was the *William Penn* under Captain Josiah of Philadelphia. The captain had his wife with him, and her account of those days is mainly of interest for what she says about the attitude of the people of London. According to Mrs. Josiah, the populace was very excited and indignant over the display of the stars and stripes on the ship. Fearing that a mob might board his ship and tear down the flag, Captain Josiah ordered a vigilant watch to be kept, especially at night. When Mrs. Josiah was being entertained ashore, one of the ladies in the company expressed her annoyance at seeing the flag and at the alleged presumption of the captain in displaying it in London. Mrs. Josiah responded somewhat cryptically: "We win gold and we wear it!" It seems likely that these hostile feelings toward Americans were due to the frustrations of a long and indecisive war, and that they were only gradually dispelled as people returned to the patterns of peacetime commerce.

On April 3, 1783, an enterprising London publisher named John Wallis issued a map of "The United States of America" drawn from the best authorities and in accordance with the terms of the preliminary peace treaty.

Fig. 113 Elkanah Watson; *a portrait by John Singleton Copley*
Princeton University Art Museum

149

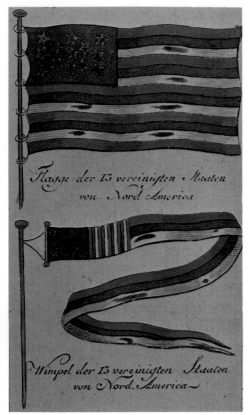

Fig. 115 The stars and stripes in the Haude and Spener Calendar
Anne S. K. Brown Military Collection, Brown University

Fig. 116 The American flag in Bowles's book of flags, 1783
Anne S. K. Brown Military Collection, Brown University

Fig. 114 Cartouche on John Wallis's map of the United States: note the four-pointed stars
Henry F. DuPont Winterthur Museum

The cartouche on the map shows the stars and stripes flag with a white stripe at the top and bottom. The canton shows thirteen four-pointed stars arranged horizontally in a 3–2–3–2–3 arrangement (Figure 114).

The first appearance of the stars and stripes in book form was in Berlin in 1783. That year the firm of Haude and Spener published a *Historic Geneological Calendar, or Year Book of the Most Curious New Events in the World for 1784.* It contained twelve copper plates of incidents of the American Revolution illustrating an account by Professor Matthias Sprengel of the University of Halle. One of three hand-colored copper plates showed the flag of the United States with thirteen red, blue, and white stripes in sequence, so that the first and last stripes are red. The stars are five-pointed and are painted in black on the blue canton. The stars are horizontally arranged in a 3–2–3–2–3 pattern. A similar design appears in the pennant (Figure 115).

Soon after the war, probably in 1783, a British publisher, Carrington Bowles, brought out a book on naval flags of the world. Near the back of the book is an illustration of the United States flag. This shows a thirteen-star flag with stars arranged horizontally in a 3–2–3–2–3 design, and with thirteen red and white stripes beginning with a red stripe on the top (Figure 116). Owners of this book were provided with blank spaces to record any flags that appeared between various editions of the book. Two pages beyond where the American flag appeared, the owner of one copy drew in ink the design of the flag of Revolutionary France and the French Convention flag. In the 1801 edition of this book, the United States flag is again shown as is the "French New Flag, the Tricolor."

150

A beautiful representation of the stars and stripes, based on the Mondhare flag chart, appears in a Beauvais tapestry. Commissioned in 1783 by King Louis XVI of France, and intended as a gift for Washington, the tapestry was begun at the end of the American Revolution. Before it could be delivered, a revolution swept through France, toppling King Louis from his throne and subsequently taking his life. The tapestry shows a female figure holding a flag on a pole surmounted by a Liberty cap. In the illustration the flag is folded so that the top stripe cannot be seen, but evidently it was intended to depict the flag with a white stripe at the top and bottom. A long, narrow canton, stretching from the top of the flag to the tenth stripe, contains twelve five-pointed stars arranged in four horizontal lines. The thirteenth star is on a line below the others, and is offset on the top of the canton by a gold fleur-de-lis. This magnificent item is preserved by the National Trust of Great Britain (Figure 117).

In the United States, a group of former officers of the Continental Army organized themselves into a patriotic and fraternal organization, the Society of the Cincinnati, and asked Major Pierre Charles L'Enfant, a French engineer officer, to make a design for their membership diploma. L'Enfant produced an allegorical scene dominated by an armor-clad person holding a sword in his right hand and a flag in his left. The flag has thirteen stripes, the first and last of which are red. In the canton are thirteen five-pointed stars arranged in an oval (Figure 118). The society adopted this drawing on June 10, 1783. In the final engraved diploma, however, the design was changed. The flag lacks stripes and has only the thirteen stars arranged in an oval design that is reminiscent of Washington's Headquarters flag.

151

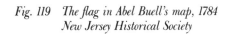

Fig. 120   The flag in Bailey's Almanac *for 1784*
Library of Congress

Fig. 119   The flag in Abel Buell's map, 1784
New Jersey Historical Society

In New Haven, Connecticut, Abel Buell published "A New and Correct Map of the United States," in 1784. This shows a stars and stripes flag with thirteen five-pointed stars in a 3–2–3–2–3 arrangement (Figure 119). Francis Bailey's *Pocket Almanac of 1784,* published in Boston by T. and J. Flett in 1783, shows the stars in a 4–5–4 arrangement (Figure 120).

The year 1784 was also notable for the appearance of flags that had an eagle in the canton as well as thirteen stars. This may have been as a result of the adoption of the Great Seal of the United States in 1782. One early example of this design is the silk Schuyler flag. The eagle is painted in the canton, and above the eagle's outstretched wings are thirteen five-pointed stars in an arc. The stripes are arranged so that a white stripe appears at the top and bottom. It is believed that this flag may be the earliest surviving example of a thirteen stars and stripes flag (see Figure 82).

Thirteen-star flags were a popular design feature used in a number of commemorative fabrics that were printed in France and sold in the United States. One such design, first produced in 1786, entitled "L'Hommage de l'Amerique a la France," was etched on a copperplate that was used to print on cotton. The scene shows a seated female figure wearing a crown representing France. Her right hand is extended and her left hand rests on a shield decorated with fleurs-de-lis. Behind her stands a male figure in armor holding a flag decorated with fleurs-de-lis in his right hand. Facing the two French figures are three Americans: one clad like an Indian, one a woman in a long gown holding a Liberty cap on a pole, and one wearing a beaver hat and hunting shirt and carrying a stars and stripes flag on a pole over his shoulder. This flag has a white canton and thirteen dark colored stars, arranged in rows in a 4–5–4 design. There are thirteen red and white stripes. An adaptation of this design, used for the block printing of cotton furniture covers in 1790, shows the stars arranged in a square, with the thirteenth star in the center. The stripes in this version are in two shades of red and in white. A drape in

Fig. 121 The flag on a French fabric design

the field makes it difficult to count the stripes, but there appear to be seventeen (Figure 121).

Between 1787 and 1790, Captain John Kendrick of Boston, in the ship *Columbia*, and Captain Robert Gray, in the ship *Lady Washington*, first carried the stars and stripes in a voyage around the world. At one point, Gray entered a large river in the Pacific Northwest which he named Columbia in honor of the ship. Gray's discovery later gave the United States an important claim to the Oregon country. Unfortunately, no description exists of the flag that he carried on his voyages. A medal was struck commemorating the first voyage, but the flag on it is too small to be helpful. Later, in 1798, commanding the brig *Alert*, Gray entered the La Plata River in South America, the first American merchant ship to do so.

While the United States flag was being carried to distant regions, it was also the witness to a curious breach of the peace in Londonderry, Ireland, in 1790. It seems that an American named Lemuel Cox was hired to build a bridge across the Foyle River at Londonderry. Bridges built by Cox in Boston and Charlestown brought him contracts in England and then Ireland. With twenty

153

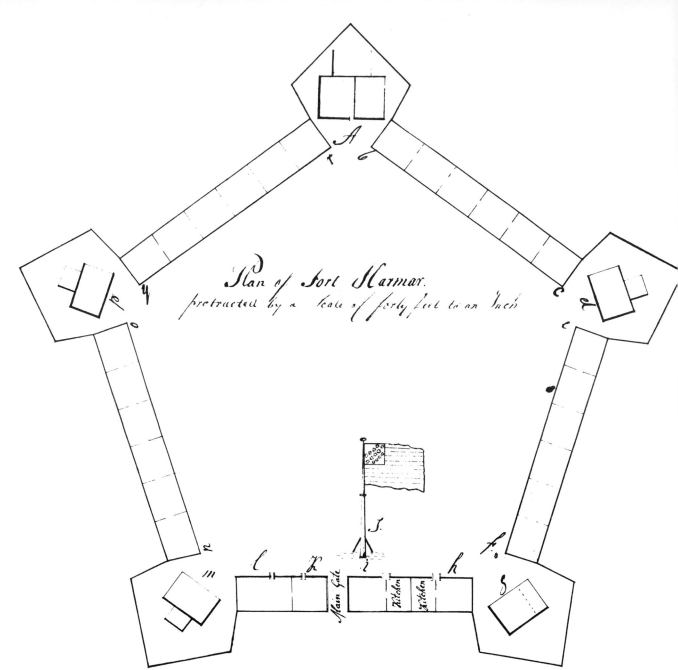

Plan of Fort Harmar.
protracted by a scale of forty feet to an inch

Main Gate

Kitchen Kitchen

Fig. 122 The plan of Fort Harmar: note the flag design
Harmar Papers, Maps, William L. Clements Library, Ann Arbor, Michigan

Boston workmen, a few local laborers, and a supply of American oak, Cox's men built a bridge 1,068 feet long and 40 feet wide in four months time. On the day of its opening, the stars and stripes was raised over the structure. For the first week, the people were allowed to pass over the bridge free. When toll booths were erected the following week, people refused to pay. A disturbance developed and the mayor sent a detachment of British troops to restore order. The Boston workmen took their axes and cut an entrance for the people to use. The Irish people fought the soldiers and three men were killed and several wounded before the crowd was dispersed. The whole affray took place under the stars and stripes.

Meanwhile Americans were concerned about the display of British flags over territory that belonged to the United States. The treaty of peace with Great Britain provided for the evacuation of British posts in the northwest. Britain delayed in complying with this provision on the grounds that the Americans had not made it possible for the loyalists to return to their homes and recover their property.

To the Americans, the British presence in the northwest meant that the British controlled the lucrative fur trade and channeled it through Canada; they also saw it as the cause of Indian unrest. The protection of settlers in the frontier areas led the government under the Articles of Confederation to raise a small regular army and to build several forts. Two of these early forts were Fort Harmar, on the west side of the Muskingham River, and Fort Washington, near present-day Cincinnati. Both of these forts have early flag designs associated with them.

A manuscript plan for Fort Harmar, c. 1786, contains a striking flag (Figure 122). The artist drew the flag stripes in a general way with a series of parallel lines. In the canton, thirteen five-pointed stars are shown in three parallel lines that run from the lower left-hand corner of the canton to the upper right-hand corner. The star pattern thus becomes 4–5–4. A sketch of Fort Washington, drawn in 1790 by Jonathan Heart, shows a thirteen-star flag with the top and bottom stripes of red (Figure 123). The thirteen stars in this sketch appear to be arranged horizontally. While it is not known whether the flag design shown on the Fort Harmer plan was ever actually produced, the one on Fort Washington most certainly was.

Fig. 123   Fort Washington *in 1790; sketch by Jonathan Heart* Chicago Historical Society

Drawn by Capt. Jon.ᵗ Heart U.S.A. 1790.   Oncken's Lithography, Cincinnati, O.

FORT WASHINGTON.

The Adoption of the Constitution

Dissatisfaction over the weaknesses of the government under the Articles of Confederation led all of the states but Rhode Island to send representatives to Philadelphia for what was to become known as the Constitutional Convention. The plan of government that these representatives evolved between May and September 1787 was submitted to the states and approved by eleven of them.

Philadelphia celebrated the adoption of the Constitution and the anniversary of the Declaration of Independence on July 4, 1788. Numerous flags were said to have been carried in the parade, including a white silk one with three fleurs-de-lis, thirteen stars, and the words "Sixth of Feb. 1778" in honor of the French alliance that made independence a reality. Also in the parade was a flag of the calico printers. This had thirteen stars on a blue field and thirteen red stripes on a white field. Surrounding the flag were thirty-seven calico prints of various colors and the words: "May the Union government protect the manufacturers of America!" There was also a flag carried by merchants and traders that had ten stars painted in silver in honor of the ten states that had ratified the Constitution, and three whose outlines were traced in silver to represent those states that were out of the union. The flag had other devices, the descriptions of which have not come down to us.

Upon notification in April 1789 that he had been chosen as the first president, George Washington promptly set out from Mount Vernon for the temporary capital at New York City. As he made his way northward, Washington was the object of much adulation and patriotic sentiment. The major cities on his route all sought to honor him in some fashion. At Gray's Ferry, enroute to Philadelphia, Washington passed over an elaborately decorated bridge. Midway across, the flag of the United States waved over everything in sight. The ferry boat and barge anchored in the river and all the approaches were draped with flags and slogans. The Liberty cap and "Don't tred on me" flag were also in evidence.

When Washington was rowed from Elizabethtown into New York harbor, flags were flown by small craft and by the New Haven and Rhode Island packet boats. Flags also adorned the barge carrying Henry Knox, the secretary of war, and John Jay, the secretary for foreign affairs under the Articles of Confederation, when they met Washington's barge at the Battery. The first shot of a thirteen-gun salute from cannons on the shore was a signal for various small craft to raise flags to their mastheads. Washington landed at Murray's Wharf at the bottom of Wall Street. After receiving and thanking the officers who had conducted the triumphal procession, he went with Governor Clinton for a dinner at the governor's mansion. Indications are that the abundance of flags displayed at this time included many stars and stripes as well as other flags. The welcome in New York was probably the greatest single display of the stars and stripes up to that time.

After Washington took his oath of office on the balcony of Federal Hall, the United States flag was raised to the cupola of the building. This was the signal for a thirteen-gun salute. So began the government of the United States under the Constitution.

The Whiskey Rebellion

As part of its program to raise revenue for the new government, the Washington administration imposed an excise tax on the manufacture of distilled

*Fig. 124   Washington reviewing troops;
            painting by Frederick Kemmel-
            meyer
            Henry F. DuPont Winterthur Mu-
            seum*

*Fig. 125   Flag of the Whiskey Rebels
            Smithsonian Institution, courtesy
            Mrs. G. F. Harrington, Scenery
            Hill, Pa.*

liquor. To backwoods farmers, distilling liquor from grain was an important activity. Liquor was easy to store and transport, and it served as a common medium of exchange. For these reasons, the farmers protested the tax as a burden. In western Pennsylvania, farmers refused to cooperate with the tax collectors and even attacked them. In August 1794, Washington issued a proclamation calling on the rebellious farmers to return to their homes. When they refused, he called out fifteen thousand militia men from Virginia, Maryland, New Jersey, and Pennsylvania, who successfully put down the rebellion.

As commander-in-chief of the armed forces, Washington went to Carlisle, Pennsylvania, to review the troops enroute to suppress the Whiskey Rebellion. An eyewitness, Frederick Kemmelmeyer, recorded the scene on canvas. He showed Washington in uniform and astride a white horse approaching troops lined up in front of a camp. A stars and stripes flag is blowing in the wind, and the artist has painted only nine five-pointed stars in the canton. The stars are arranged in a square with a single star in the middle of the canton (Figure 124).

An unusual flag, believed to have been used by the Whiskey Rebels, has been preserved by a family in western Pennsylvania. The flag consists of a blue silk rectangle approximately two feet by three feet. Though apparently hastily designed, it was painted by a rebel with an artistic flair (Figure 125). In the center is a white eagle with a red and white ribbon in its beak. Surrounding the eagle on three sides are thirteen white six-pointed stars. If one considers the stars in a horizontal design interrupted by the eagle, then the star pattern is 6–2–2–3. The flag is painted only on one side.

157

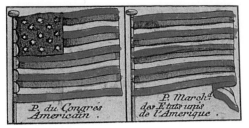

Fig. 126 *American flags on the Lotter flag sheet, 1793*
The Mariners' Museum, Newport News, Va.

The Second Flag Law, 1794

After some delay following the admission to the Union of Vermont on March 4, 1791, and Kentucky on June 1, 1792, the question of their representation in the flag of the United States finally was taken up by the Congress. On December 26, 1793, Senator Stephen Bradley of Vermont introduced a bill for altering the flag of the United States. It passed the Senate without opposition. The House resolved itself into a committee of the whole and debated the bill on January 7, 1794. The essence of that debate, printed in the *Annals of Congress,* provides a most useful insight into the way the flag question was considered by these representatives.

Representatives Benjamin Goodhue and George Thatcher of Massachusetts thought the subject was too trifling a matter to take the attention of the House. Goodhue expressed the view that the flag ought to be permanent and not altered every time a new state entered the Union.

Representatives William Lyman of Massachusetts and Christopher Greenup of Kentucky did not agree. Lyman thought it was important not to offend the new states. Greenup thought it "of very great consequence" that we inform the world that we had two more states. Mr. Nathaniel Niles of Vermont did not think that the subject was important, but suggested that the shortest way to be rid of it was to pass it. The committee passed it and the whole House now took up the bill.

Elias Boudinot of New Jersey, James Madison of Virginia, and William Giles of Virginia spoke in favor of the measure. Representative Israel Smith of Vermont said that the change would cost him five hundred dollars and every vessel in the Union, sixty dollars. He thought that the Senate must have nothing better to do than to send such bills. Smith agreed to approve of the change, but he argued that thereafter the flag should be permanent. The bill passed the House on January 13, 1794.

Another attempt to refer the bill to a select committee where it could be amended to establish a flag of the United States failed by a vote of forty-nine to thirty-nine. Another attempt to recommit the bill to the committee of the whole, so that a clause could be added fixing the flag forever, was also lost by a vote of fifty to forty-two.

President Washington approved the bill on January 13, 1794. In its final form the law stipulated that after May 1, 1795, "the flag of the United States be fifteen stripes, alternate red and white; and that the union be fifteen stars, white in a blue field."

From the time of the first consideration of the flag bill through its final approval, there is no record of any remarks on the subject by Washington. Nor does anything in the debates suggest that Washington had anything to do with the design of the original stars and stripes.

Variations on the Stars and Stripes

Meanwhile some striking examples of variations on the stars and stripes had made their appearances in print and in a flag. The first was the publication in 1793 in Augsburg, Germany, of a flag sheet in French by George Frederic Lotter. It will be recalled that in his flag sheet of 1782 he had shown a fleur-de-lis at the top of the canton. This time his flag sheet showed thirteen six-

Fig. 127   *Flag presented by General Wayne to an Indian chief, 1795 Smithsonian Institution, courtesy Indiana Historical Bureau*

pointed stars in a 3–2–3–2–3 arrangement. The thirteen stripes were depicted in a sequence of red, blue, and white stripes (Figure 126). The Lotter sheet also had a thirteen stripe flag with the same tricolor arrangement identified as the merchant color of the United States.

In addition, the Lotter sheet carried an illustration of a pennant with a blue canton and thirteen stars, arranged as in the aforementioned flag. Beside the canton the pennant had thirteen tricolor stripes in a *vertical* arrangement, followed by a long tail made up of three horizontal stripes: a red on top, a blue in the middle, and a white on the bottom. Since the flag and the pennant are identical with those shown in the German almanac of 1783 that carried Professor Matthias Sprengel's account of the American Revolution, there could be no doubt about the source of Lotter's illustrations. What is interesting is the fact that in ten years time no additional information on the American flag had reached Lotter, whose business it was to supply flag identification charts to his European customers.

Another example of the tricolor arrangement of the stripes in a flag was made in the United States under official auspices. An army under the command of Major General Anthony Wayne was trying to end Indian problems in the Old Northwest. The power of the Indians was broken at the battle of Fallen Timbers on August 20, 1794. The following summer the Indians agreed to the Treaty of Greenville whereby they gave up two-thirds of Ohio and a part of Indiana. In his effort to bind the Indians to the United States government, Wayne presented them with flags to replace those given them earlier by the British. One of these flags still survives, and is in the custody of the state of Indiana. It is a flag without stars or a canton, and with stripes in a tricolor pattern (Figure 127).

According to a story passed down with it, Wayne ordered his soldiers to make the flag. Probably there was not enough blue cloth to make a canton, but as the story goes, Wayne was told that there were no stars. He is supposed to have told them to put his name on the flag in place of the stars, and that his

159

name would mean more to the Indians than the stars. Whatever the truth of the story is, a flag of blue, white, and red stripes was made, and at the top, a piece of white cloth was sewn on bearing Wayne's name in ink.

A note on the flag in the May 1927 issue of the *Indiana History Bulletin* says that President Washington ordered Wayne to have the flag made, and that after the Treaty of Greenville Wayne signed it to present it to She-Moc-E-Nish, the chief of the Miami Indians. This information came from Dr. P. G. Moore, the president of the Wabash County Historical Society, who became acquainted with descendants of the Miami Indians while he was practicing medicine in the Wabash area. In 1868 the doctor discovered the flag in the possession of an Indian woman, and then and several times later tried to purchase it. Eventually he was successful, but another twenty years passed before he got the story of Wayne's presentation of it from Kil-S-Quah, a granddaughter of Se-Moc-E-Nish. Both the soldier story and the tale of the Indian woman suggest Wayne's strong and resolute nature. But the Indian story shows him as a sensitive and considerate person. That is not the way we usually think of Wayne, yet it may be closer to the truth than the soldier story would have us believe.

A textile examination of the Wayne flag revealed that it is made of 2/2 worsted twill wool bunting with a single ply warp and weft. The fifteen stripes are sewn with two-ply linen thread. There was nothing in the analysis that indicated that this flag could not date from about 1795.

Problems with France

Less than three months after Washington's inauguration, France was in the throes of a revolution that soon brought down the monarchy. In September 1792, France was declared a republic. Meanwhile Austria and Prussia formed an alliance against France that led to the outbreak of war in April 1792. Sardinia joined against France in July. After the execution of King Louis XVI in January 1793, England, Holland, and Spain joined the alliance against France.

Five days after the news of the French declaration of war against Great Britain reached the United States, Edmond Charles Genêt, the first minister from the French Republic to the United States, arrived in Charleston, South Carolina. On April 22, four days after Genêt's arrival, and before he had presented his credentials, the Washington administration issued a proclamation of neutrality toward all the belligerent powers. France regarded the alliance of 1778 as still in force, and was offended by the proclamation. In discussions with his cabinet, Washington accepted the interpretation of Secretary of the Treasury Alexander Hamilton that the alliance had been made with a government of France that was no longer in existence. When Genêt arrived at the seat of government in Philadelphia, he received a cool reception from Washington.

Meanwhile, before leaving Charleston, Genêt issued letters of marque to Americans to engage in privateering under the French flag against British shipping in the West Indies. The sympathetic attitude of Charlestonians, and of state officials and local customs officers, led to a great deal of privateering out of Charleston between January 1794 and the end of 1795. Genêt's activities forced Washington to ask for his recall in August 1794, but the pro-French attitude of much of the populace continued.

Fig. 128 French and United States flags on a Liverpool-type pitcher

One manifestation of this sympathy for France can be seen in the production of Liverpool-type creamware pitchers with transfer printed designs. One shows crossed French and American flags. The stars and stripes has far too many stripes, but depicts fifteen dark colored stars in a light colored canton with stars arranged horizontally in three rows of five (Figure 128).

The Washington administration established diplomatic relations with the French Republic by sending James Monroe as minister in 1794. The National Convention, the longest-lived of the French revolutionary assemblies, received Monroe in public. His remarks on the occasion of presenting his credentials were so pleasing to the convention that its president embraced Monroe with emotion. It was decreed that the American and French flags should be entwined and hung in the convention hall as a sign of the union and friendship of the two republics. Monroe shared these sentiments, and he presented an American flag. It was received with great enthusiasm, and a decree was passed that the national flag of France was to be transmitted in return to the United States government.

When the flag of the French Republic was received by President Washington, he was not filled with warm feelings toward that nation. The flag was not hung in the Senate or the House of Representatives—a fact that caused considerable dissatisfaction in the French Convention—but was deposited in the archives of the State Department. Many years later it was transferred to West Point.

The French government under the National Convention was followed by that of the Directory in 1795, and by that of the Consulate in 1799. Napoleon Bonaparte, the First Consul, had himself proclaimed Emperor of the French in 1804, and remained in power until 1814. Throughout most of this period, the various French governments were at war with Great Britain and other powers. During the same long interval, the United States had continual problems with both France and Great Britain over the right of a neutral nation to pursue peaceful commercial activity without interference from the belligerents. It was not a position that commanded much respect from either England or France. Their attitude eventually forced the United States into hostilities with both at different times.

Later Variations

The same Congress that authorized the changing of the flag to fifteen stars and stripes also passed a law calling for the construction of six frigates to protect American commerce in the Mediterranean. The signing of a treaty with Algiers in November 1795 made the frigates unnecessary, but Congress decided to complete three of them anyway. These frigates, the *United States,* the *Constellation,* and the *Constitution,* were launched in 1797 and became the foundation of the United States Navy.

As the first of the new vessels to be launched, the *United States* had a newsworthy quality that appealed to Samuel Harrison Smith, the Philadelphia publisher of the *American Universal Magazine.* The magazine had a policy of giving its readers a plate with each number of the periodical. Smith therefore hired Thomas Clarke to make an engraving of the ship. Clark's engraving appeared in the issue of July 24, 1797. It depicted the ship, launched ten

Fig. 129 Frigate United States; *engraving by Thomas Clarke, 1797* Library of Congress

weeks earlier, under sail and flying the stars and stripes flag. The flag has sixteen stripes and fifteen stars arranged in a 4–4–4–3 pattern (Figure 129).

There were no official sixteen-star flags, but there is a unique rendering of the sixteen-star flag on the overmantel in the northwest parlor of the Chittenden-Martin House in Jerico, Vermont. It is believed to have been painted by a carpenter named Sprague in 1796–97 when the house was being completed by Thomas Chittenden, Vermont's first governor, as a wedding present for his son. The artist painted a single pine tree in the center of the picture. Over the tree is the federal eagle, holding an olive branch and arrows in its talons, and a ribbon with "E Pluribus Unum" in its beak. A red, white, and blue shield is over the eagle's breast. Beside the pine tree and to the right of the viewer is a flag pole and the flag. Its five-pointed stars are arranged horizontally in a 4–4–4–4 design. The flag has sixteen stripes, with a white one on the top and a red one at the bottom (Figure 130).

One of the most curious collections of illustrations of the American flag was published in Leghorn, Italy, by Scotti in 1796 (Figure 131). This shows seven flags and one pennant associated with the United States. One has an oak tree with a banner over the top reading, "I appeal to Heaven." There is also a flag of thirteen red and white stripes and another similar to this but with a narrow vertical row of thirteen stars along the hoist. Each star is set in a field of blue

162

Fig. 130 *A sixteen-star flag painted on an*
overmantel in Vermont
The Countryman Press, Taftsville,
Vermont. Photograph by John
Miller

Fig. 131 *American flags on the Scotti flag*
sheet, 1796
John Carter Brown Library,
Brown University

or white so as to contrast with the adjacent red or white stripe; the back-grounds of the stars at the top and bottom of the flag are white. Another version of the flag also uses the field of red and white stripes, but with a vertical blue band—nearly twice as wide as the band on the flag cited previously—which runs the width of the flag adjacent to the hoist. The blue band contains two parallel rows of six stars each, with the thirteenth star set above and equidistant between the two vertical rows. The sheet also shows a flag similar to the Grand Union flag. The thirteen stripes begin and end with a red stripe. The blue canton contains a red cross edged with white. Thirteen stars are used to form the St. Andrew's Cross so that the thirteenth star appears in the center of the red cross.

Another of the American flags on the Scotti sheet is reminiscent of the illustrations published in Augsburg, Germany, in 1793. This shows thirteen red, white, and blue stripes, beginning with a red, and followed by a blue, a white, and a red, a blue, a white and a red, and ending on a red. The blue canton contains thirteen stars in a vertical arrangement forming a 4–2–1–2–4 pattern that is quite distinctive. In the thirteen-stripe flag with a red stripe on the top and bottom the stars are arranged horizontally in a 4–5–4 pattern. For some reason, the artist did not place his stars very carefully. There is too wide a gap between the first and second star on each of the lines so that the fifth star on the second line appears crowded and smaller than the rest. All the stars in the flags on the Scotti sheet are four-pointed.

The diversity of designs shown on the Scotti sheet must have resulted in a certain amount of confusion if, in fact, all of those flags were actually used. Adding to the confusion was the practice of some American captains of flying a state flag rather than the national flag. While writing to Secretary of State Thomas Jefferson on October 12, 1798, on how American vessels operating in the Mediterranean might avoid capture and condemnation by the corsairs of Algiers, Tunis, and Tripoli, Richard O'Brien, the United States Consul General at Algiers, took up the subject of flags. After discussing passes, proper credentials, and other precautions, O'Brien concluded: "I hope that those that might frequent the Mediterranean will have the real American Colours—if the[y] have those State flags, the[y] will not do, even with a good pass. The Algerines will not beli[e]ve or know them to be Americans. Why because the[y] have not American Colours & the[y] know nothing about yr. State Colours—The[y] will declare the[y] made a peace with one nation & one flag, not with 16 nations &c. 16 flags—look out, O'Brien will give you true Soundings." It is almost unbelievable that such confused conditions existed nearly a quarter-century after the formal adoption by Congress of the stars and stripes as a national emblem.

The Naval War with France

Continuing difficulties with France over the American interpretation of the alliance of 1777, the negotiation and ratification of the Jay Treaty with Great Britain in 1794 and 1795, and other factors prompted the French to seize American merchant vessels. This, in turn, led to an undeclared naval war with France, continuing from 1798 to 1801, and to the establishment of the United States Navy Department.

The first American victory of the war took place on July 7, 1798, when the United States ship of war *Delaware* captured a French privateer schooner, *La Croyable*, off Egg Harbor, New Jersey. The captain of the *Delaware*, Stephen Decatur, Sr., commemorated the event by having a punch bowl made to order with a decoration of the two ships. The *Delaware* flies a flag with thirteen stripes and fifteen stars arranged horizontally in a 5–5–5 pattern. Most intriguing of all is the middle star on the middle line, which is larger than the rest of the five-pointed stars. This may be the earliest known naval example of the practice of making one star larger than the others (Figure 132).

One of the highlights of the undeclared naval war with France was the capture of the frigate *L'Insurgente* by the U.S.S. *Constellation* after a battle on February 9, 1799. The victory inspired Edward Savage to make the first historical aquatints executed in the United States by a native born artist.

Fig. 132 *The United States frigate* Delaware *capturing the French privateer* La Croyable, *1798; a china bowl decoration*
U.S. Navy Department, courtesy Decatur House, National Trust for Historic Preservation

Savage's two prints, *The chase* and *The action*, show the *Constellation* flying a thirteen-star flag with the stars arranged in a 4–4–5 and a 3–3–3–4 pattern (Figure 133 and 134).

The *Constellation's* victory also inspired Gilbert Fox, a British-born engraver working in Philadelphia, to produce a small vignette of the battle for use on the sheet music of a new song, "Huzza for the *Constellation*," printed by B. Carr's Musical Repository. The talented Mr. Fox also sang the song at a performance at the Chestnut Street Theatre. The vignette shows a flag, partly obscured by smoke, and a number of stripes. There is a canton but no star pattern is discernible.

The conflict with France made the United States consider the possibility of enlarging its army. As early as May 1797, Congress authorized President John Adams to enlist ten thousand men as a provisional army to be called into service in case of hostilities. Adams chose not to avail himself of this power nor to ask for a declaration of war. Instead, he hoped to limit the conflict and to work out a peace settlement at the earliest date possible. Adams did nominate George Washington as the commander-in-chief of all the armies raised or to be raised.

Washington's commmission as lieutenant general and commander-in-chief is dated July 4, 1798, and offers a most interesting combination of symbols. The federal eagle is shown with fifteen arrows in its talons. The eagle is facing toward its own right, and in its right claw is a single olive branch. At the bottom of the commission is a panoply of arms dominated by two flags in the

165

Fig. 133 Constellation and L'Insurgent, the Chase; *aquatint by Edward Savage*
Worcester Art Museum

right and left foreground. To the left is a squared flag, presumably light blue in color, with fourteen six-pointed stars in a circle and the fifteenth star in the middle of the circle. This is similar to the Washington Headquarters flag introduced late in the Revolution; it is also similar to the design on the certificates of the Society of the Cincinnati (Figure 135).

To the right of the commission is a draped stars and stripes with fourteen six-pointed stars in a circle and the fifteenth in the center of the circle. It is believed that these renderings of the two flags were inspired by Charles Willson Peale's painting of Washington at Princeton done in 1779.

Louisiana Purchase

Louisiana was initially claimed and settled by the French. During the closing months of the Seven Years War, King Louis XV was fearful of losing Louisiana to the British along with the rest of French colonial possessions in North America. So, on November 3, 1762, he ceded it and the city of New Orleans to Spain. Louisiana remained under Spanish rule until the Treaty of Luneville on February 9, 1801, when Napoleon forced Spain to cede it back to France. By this time the flag of France was the red, white, and blue tricolor adopted during the Revolution. The tricolor replaced the Spanish flag.

166

Fig. 134 Action between the Constellation
and L'Insurgent; *aquatint by Ed-*
ward Savage
Worcester Art Museum

Fig. 135 *Washington's commission as lieu-*
tenant general (detail)
Library of Congress

Napoleon had hopes of reviving the French Empire in America, but he was
forced to abandon these plans. On April 30, 1803, Napoleon sold Louisiana to
the United States for $15 million. This acquisition more than doubled the
original area of the United States. In a ceremony on December 20, 1803, in the
public square, the stars and stripes replaced the tricolor (Figure 136).

Apparently, all the details of the transfer of the territory were not attended to
promptly, for on January 9, 1804, the merchants of New Orleans petitioned
Congress to do something about their plight. Among other things, the merchants said that: "For want of proper Documents to navigate with, the Ships

Fig. 136 The Transfer of Louisiana to the United States; *painting by Thure de Thulstrup, 1906* Louisiana Historical Society

and Vessels of your Memorialists are now laid up, in a perishing State, unauthorized to hoist any Flag whatever; Their Capitals are unemployed; and their merchandise has no Vent." The merchants asked that the necessary arrangements be made that "will place us on the equal footing of Citizens of the United States from the Moment their Flag was hoisted in this City." These problems were resolved and the French and Spanish inhabitants of the city soon proceeded to carry on business under the American flag.

Western Exploration

The acquisition of Louisiana stimulated the interest of the United States government in regions to the west. Between 1804 and 1806, Meriwether Lewis and Captain William Clark made the famous overland expedition that brought them to the Pacific Coast. Recent examinations of the records of the expedition reveal that Lewis and Clark carried a number of flags with them. A large one was regularly hoisted over their camp but the details of this flag are not known. In the course of their journey westward, Lewis and Clark gave flags to various Indian tribes that they met; there is some indication that the stars and stripes flags which they presented to the Indians were not of a customary design. A forthcoming study on this subject is eagerly awaited as this book goes to press.

168

Other important developments for flag history are the explorations of Zebulon M. Pike. In 1805, Lieutenant Pike and twenty-one men left St. Louis to explore the upper Mississippi River. His orders were also to select suitable sites for trading posts with the Indians, to induce them to make alliances with the United States, and to learn all that he could about British traders in the region. On the bow of his keel boat, Pike carried the American flag. So far as is known, this was the first appearance of the stars and stripes on the upper Mississippi and in what is now Wisconsin.

As Pike moved up the Mississippi, he was met at the Rock River by four chiefs of the Sac tribe, fifteen Indians, a Frenchman, and an American. One of their canoes bore an American flag. Pike visited the Indian village, where he met a young warrior named Black Hawk, who was destined to become a famous chief. Pike gave the Indians an American flag, and asked them to lower the British flags that they displayed in their camp. He promised that their new American father would treat them well. The Indians declined: the British king was their father and they did not wish to have two fathers. On this and other occasions, Pike told the Indians of the exclusive claim by the United States to the Northwest Territory.

In the summer of 1806 Pike was on a more important mission, to explore the sources of the Red River in the southern Rocky Mountains. In September, at a Pawnee village, Pike (now a captain) discovered several Spanish flags. One of these was unfurled in front of the chief's door on the day of Pike's council with the Pawnees. Pike demanded that the Spanish flag be given to him in exchange for an American flag and he argued that the Indians could not have two fathers. After a period of silence, an old man took down the Spanish flag and laid it at Pike's feet. Pike gave the chief an American flag for his staff. Other members of the council looked worried, and Pike guessed that they were fearful of offending the Spanish troops that patroled the region. Pike gave them back their Spanish flag with the injunction that it should not be hoisted again during his stay. His action brought forth a shout of approval from the Indians.

On November 27, Pike and his party climbed the mountain that now bears his name, up to a height of nine thousand feet. While encamped in the Rocky Mountains, they suffered from cold and a lack of food. From the mountains, they marched to the Rio Grande. There they were taken into custody by a detachment of Spanish cavalry and escorted to Santa Fe and later to Chihuahua in Mexico. Pike was well treated, but had his papers confiscated. He was sent home by way of Texas and arrived at Natchitoches, on the Red River, in July 1807. Three years later he published the account of his expedition that established his fame as an explorer.

Notes

For the Mondhare flag sheet see *Tableau de tous les pavillons que lon arbore sur les vaisseaux dans quatre parties du monde avec une explication de tous les agrès et manoeuvres des vaisseaux* (Paris, 1781), in the John Carter Brown Library, Brown University, Providence, R. I.

The title of the Lotter flag sheet is *Flaggen aller Seefahrenden Potensen und Nationen in der gantzen Welt . . . (vorgestellt von Mattheaus Seutter in Augspurg [sic])*; it is also in the John Carter Brown Library. According to Philip Lee Phillips, the first edition of this sheet was published by Tobias C. Lotter in Nuremberg in 1778. See Phillips, *A List of Geographical Atlases in the Library of Congress with Bibliographical Notes*, 7 vols. (Washington, 1914), 3: 371, 376. Tobias Lotter died in 1777 and the edition of 1781 or 1782 was published by his sons, Mathieu Alber Lotter and George Frederic Lotter, who also issued a subsequent edition in Augsburg in 1793.

On the flag displayed by the *Bedford* in London, see Preble, *History of the Flag of the United States of America*, pp. 291–94. The story of John Singleton Copley's painting of the stars and stripes in the background of a portrait of Elkanah Watson is told in Preble, pp. 296–97, and in a different form in Jane Carson, "The First American Flag Hoisted in Old England," *William and Mary Quarterly*, 3rd Ser. 11: 434–39. The incident relating to the *William Penn* is in John F. Watson, *Annals of Philadelphia and Pennsylvania*, 2 vols. (Philadelphia, 1857), 2: 333.

The John Wallis map of the United States is in the John Carter Brown Library. The stars are somewhat blurred on this map. Another copy is in the Henry Francis DuPont Winterthur Museum, Wilmington, Del.

A copy of Carrington Bowles's book, *Bowles's Universal Display of Naval Flags of all Nations in the World* (London, 1783), is in the John Carter Brown Library. The 1801 edition is in the Anne S. K. Brown Military Collection, Brown University. The 1760 edition, with a penciled sketch of the American flag in the blank space, is in the Newberry Library in Chicago.

The first German book referred to is M. C. Sprengel, *Allgemeines historisches Taschenbuch, oder Abriss der mertwürdigsten neuen Welt-Begebenheiten, enthaltend für 1784 die Geschichte der Revolution von Nord America von M.C. Sprengel Professor der Geschichte auf der Universatät zu Halle* (Berlin, 1783), also in the Newberry Library.

Pierre Charles L'Enfant's design of a flag for the diploma of the Society of Cincinnati is in the custody of that organization. The almanacs of Abraham Weatherwise for 1782 are in Brown University and the Library of Congress. The frontispiece showing the flag is incomplete in the Library of Congress copy. The almanac of Francis Bailey for 1784 is in the Library of Congress.

Abel Buell's map of the United States in 1783 is in the New Jersey Historical Society, Newark, N. J. The silk flag presented to General Philip Schuyler is in the Army-Navy Museum at Independence National Historical Park in Philadelphia. French decorative fabrics showing the flag are preserved in the Textile Division of the National Museum of American History, Smithsonian Institution. For a note on them, see Grace R. Cooper, *Thirteen-Star Flags*, p. 2.

Information on the first display of the stars and stripes in various parts of the world is in Preble, pp. 299–306. See also George S. Wycoff, "The Stars and Stripes First Voyage Around the World," *The Nautical Gazette*, May 1940, 13–14, 32–33.

The illustrations of the flags at Fort Harmar and Fort Washington are in William H. Guthman, *March to Massacre: A History of the First Seven Years of the United States Army, 1784–1791* (New York, 1975), plates 23 and 24.

The description of the parade in Philadelphia on July 4, 1788, is in Preble, p. 297. Descriptions of the decorations in the locales through which Washington traveled to New York City for his inaugural are in Clarence Winthrop-Bowen, ed., *The History of the Centennial Celebration of the Inauguration of George Washington as First President of the United States* (New York, 1892), pp. 21–50, and in Douglas Southall Freeman, *George Washington: A Biography*, 7 vols. (New York, 1948–57), 7: 167–84.

Frederick Kemmelmeyer's painting of Washington inspecting the troops enroute to suppress the Whiskey Rebellion is in the Henry Francis DuPont Winterthur Museum. Debates on the second flag law are printed in the *Annals of Congress*.

The activities of Edmond Charles Genêt and the privateers he authorized are in Melvin H. Jackson, *Privateers in Charleston, 1793–1796* (Washington, 1969). James Monroe's activities in France are described in his *Autobiography*, edited by Stuart Gerry Brown (Syracuse, 1959); also in Preble, pp. 308–14, and Harry Ammon, *James Monroe: The Quest for National Identity* (New York, 1971), pp. 120–21. On the founding of the U.S. Navy see Marshall Smelser, *Congress Founds the Navy, 1787–1798* (South Bend, Ind., 1959).

The engraving of the *United States* by Thomas Clarke is in Donald M. Mugridge, ed., *An Album of American Battle Art, 1755–1918* (Washington, 1947), pp. 70, 76. Information on the sixteen-star flag illustration is in Peter S. Jennison, ed., *The 1976–77 Official Vermont Bicentennial Guide* (Taftsville, Vt., 1975), p. 2. The Scotti Flag Sheet is in the John Carter Brown Library. For the report of Consul General Richard O'Brien to Secretary of State Jefferson, see U.S. Navy Department, *Naval Documents Related to the United States Wars with the Barbary Powers*, 7 vols. (Washington, 1939–44), 1: 261–62. For a depiction of the victory of the *Delaware* over *La Croyable* see U.S. Navy Department, *Naval Documents Related to the Quasi-War Between the United States and France*, 7 vols. (Washington, 1934–38), 1: frontispiece. The illustration of the *Constellation* and *L'Insurgente* is reproduced in Wendy J. Shadwell, *American Printmaking: The First 150 Years* (Washington, 1969), p. 46 and plates 86 and 87. The cover of "Huzza for the Constellation," is in Mugridge, *An Album of American Battle Art*, pp. 71–72, 77. Washington's commission as a lieutenant general is in the Washington Papers at the Library of Congress.

A comprehensive discussion of Princeton portraits is in Charles Coleman Sellers, *Portraits and Miniatures by Charles Willson Peale* (Philadelphia, 1952), pp. 225–26.

Documents on Louisiana are in Clarence Carter, ed., *Territorial Papers of the United States: The Territory of Orleans, 1803–1812* (Washington, 1940), vol. 9, pp. 157–58.

Information on the flag research in progress on the Lewis and Clark manuscripts is from a letter of Dorothy Claibourne of the Pius XII Library, St. Louis University, to Harold D. Langley, September 15, 1980, in the files of the Division of Naval History, Smithsonian Institution.

Zebulon Pike's explorations are discussed in Donald M. Jackson, ed., *Journals With Letters and Related Documents of Zebulon Pike*, 2 vols. (Norman, Okla., 1966).

CHAPTER 10

Flags of War and Peace

In 1812 a series of grievances resulted in the United States declaring war on Great Britain. The war was notable for the inability of the Americans to capture and retain territory in Canada, and for the British, Canadians', and Indians' inability to seize and hold territory in the United States. While the land campaigns resulted in a stalemate, Americans derived a great deal of satisfaction from victories over British warships. Important as such duels were for public morale, however, they did not affect the supremacy of the British Navy or the effectiveness of the British blockade of the American coast.

Flags of the War of 1812

The patriotic fervor of those who supported the war was manifest in an interest in flags. Several flags connected with incidents in the war are worthy of special attention. On August 19, 1812, the United States frigate *Constitution* captured the British frigate *Guerriere* after a hard fight. The *Guerriere* was too badly damaged to be taken to port as a prize, so it was burned. This engagement was the first victory of the war, and coming soon after the news of the capture of Detroit by the British it was an occasion for great popular exultation. Thomas Birch painted four scenes of the battle, now preserved at the Naval Academy in Annapolis (Figure 137). One of these scenes was chosen by Cornelius Tiebout as the subject for a stipple engraving that was published in Philadelphia by James Webster in 1813. This shows the *Constitution* wearing a flag of thirteen stripes, with a white stripe at the top and bottom. The stars are five-pointed and appear to be arranged in four horizontal rows of four stars each, or possibly with one row having only three stars. The latter arrangement would produce a fifteen-star flag, which was the official version and the most likely type for the ship to have carried. Because the flag is slightly furled, it is not possible to determine the precise number of stars.

Sometime between 1812 and 1814, H.M.S. *Borer* captured an American brig of four hundred tons laden with coal in Long Island Sound. The name of this ship is not recorded, but its flag was taken to Great Britain where it is now preserved in the National Maritime Museum. This flag has fifteen five-pointed

Fig. 137 Constitution and the Guerriere;
painting by Thomas Birch
U.S. Naval Academy Museum

Fig. 138 *Flag captured by H.M.S.* Borer
The National Maritime Museum,
Greenwich, England

Fig. 139 *The flag of the* Chesapeake
The National Maritime Museum,
Greenwich, England

Fig. 141 *The Fort Hill flag*

stars in a vertical arrangement of 3–2–3–2–3–2. It has fifteen stripes, with the red at the top and bottom (Figure 138).

Another early American flag that survived as a result of a defeat at sea is that of the United States frigate *Chesapeake*. On June 1, 1813, Captain P.B.V. Broke of H.M.S. *Shannon* sent a challenge to Captain James Lawrence of the *Chesapeake*. Lawrence had assumed command only eleven days before, he had an untried and inexperienced crew, and his mission was to destroy commerce. But pride induced him to accept the challenge to a fight. In twenty-five minutes it was all over. Lawrence was mortally wounded and most of his officers were dead. Despite his plea, "Don't give up the ship!", the *Chesapeake* was forced to surrender. The flag of the *Chesapeake* is also preserved in the National Maritime Museum. Only the canton and parts of the red and white stripes remain. The five-pointed stars are arranged in the canton in a vertical 3–2–3–2–3–2 pattern (Figure 139).

This British victory inspired Robert Dodd of London to paint two scenes of the battle and to publish aquatints of them in 1813. These show the *Chesapeake* flying three American flags: one at the stern at the top of the spanker sail, one at the top of the mizzen mast, and a third on the main mast between the deck and the crows nest (Figure 140). On these flags the star pattern appears to be horizontal. If there were three flags on the *Chesapeake*, there is no indication which one was preserved or what happened to the other two.

A curious flag associated with a fort is preserved in the Smithsonian Institution's National Museum of American History. This is the Fort Hill flag, which apparently flew from a house used as the garrison headquarters of the Biddeford Militia near or on Fort Hill or Parker's Neck, Biddeford, Maine (Figure 141). In 1814, the British began to raid the coastal settlements of the United States, and in this area they burned some ships. The local militia threw

Fig. 142   *The Stonington flag in 1876*
Smithsonian Institution, courtesy
Stonington Historical Society

Fig. 140   *The U.S. Frigate* Chesapeake *and*
the British Frigate Shannon;
aquatint by Robert Dodd, 1813
Library of Congress

up some breastworks near the home of Captain Waldo Hill near Fort Hill. A company of militia manned these defenses until the late fall of 1814, but was never attacked.

The Fort Hill flag is now about seven feet square, or 88½ inches on the fly and 84½ inches on the hoist. It bears in the union fifteen stars arranged in an unusual manner. There is a row of three stars at the top and bottom, a circle of seven stars in the center with a single star in the center of the circle, and a single star below the third star in the upper right-hand corner of the union. The field has fifteen alternate red and white stripes varying in width from 4½ inches to 7½ inches.

During the British bombardment of Stonington, Connecticut, on August 9–10, 1814, a flag was carried by the local militia company; it is preserved today in the Stonington branch of the Hartford National Bank. The flag was made in 1796 by the ladies of the local Congregational church. Its thirteen stripes do not follow the pattern laid down in the flag act of 1795; the star pattern is four rows of four stars (Figure 142).

Without a doubt, the most famous flag associated with the War of 1812 is that which flew over Baltimore's Fort McHenry, and which inspired Francis Scott Key to write the "Star Spangled Banner." The commandant of the fort, Colonel George Armistead, asked General Sam Smith, who was in charge of the defense of Baltimore, to supply the fort with a flag. The flag was made by Mrs. Mary Pickersgill and her daughter Caroline. According to the latter, the flag was so large that Mrs. Pickersgill had to get permission from the proprietor of Claggett's Brewery, a neighborhood establishment, to spread out the flag on the floor of the malt house. After the flag was completed, Mrs. Pickersgill superintended the work of having the heading fastened in the most secure manner so that it would not be carried away by shots. The wisdom of these

Fig. 143   The Fort McHenry flag

precautions was borne out in the battle, for although the flag was allegedly pierced by many shots it was not torn down.* The receipt for the finished flag gives its dimensions as 30 feet by 42¾ feet.

The British fleet bombarded Fort McHenry on September 13, 1814. Francis Scott Key watched the assault from the deck of a British ship. When the bombardment ceased at 7:00 A.M. on September 14, Key turned his telescope toward the fort. At the sight of the stars and stripes still flying over the fort, he was filled with emotion. He pulled a letter out of his pocket and began jotting down a rhyme. On the way back to Baltimore on a cartel ship, Key finished the rough draft of his poem. That afternoon he took a room at a Baltimore tavern and wrote the final text.

The next morning Key called on a friend, Judge Joseph H. Nicholson, and showed him his poem. Judge Nicholson was pleased with the work and thought that it would help to inspire patriotic feelings in people. The poem could be sung to the tune of an old and popular song, "The Anacreon in Heaven," that had been written by John Stafford Smith for the Anacreontic Society of London. Key's poem was printed for the first time on September 20, in the *Baltimore Patriot*. Thomas Carr, who kept a music establishment in Baltimore and was also the organist at St. Paul's Episcopal Church, put the music and the poem in song form for the first time on September 21. The song was well received and gradually attained the status of a national anthem, but it was not officially proclaimed as such until 1931.

The flag that inspired Francis Scott Key is preserved in the National Museum of American History. Prior to its acquisition by the Smithsonian in 1912, the flag had lost portions of its fifteen stripes. Only 34 feet of the original 42¾ foot field still remain. The fifteen five-pointed stars are arranged horizontally in a 3–3–3–3–3 pattern, but with lines of stars staggered in alternate rows (Figure 143).

In view of the fact that the flag was made between July and August 1813, when there were officially eighteen states in the Union (Louisiana was admitted in 1812), the question has been raised as to why the Fort McHenry flag had only fifteen stars. As noted earlier, there were no offical fourteen-, sixteen-, or seventeen-star flags. There were also no official eighteen-star flags, nor one for nineteen stars when Indiana was admitted to the Union in 1816. Some have argued that the flag should not have been changed in the midst of war, but this situation prevailed before the war as well. It seems likely that the indifference to the subject that was evident in the debates preceding the adoption of the Flag Act of 1794 continued to prevail. But whatever the reason, the fifteen-star flag remained the official flag until 1818.

The design of the national colors carried by the Army in the War of 1812 featured an eagle prominently in the middle of the flag. This was a continuation of the idea proposed during the Revolution of having a national flag for the Army differing from the flag of the stars and stripes.

Six Army flags captured by the British in the War of 1812 and taken to England were originally displayed in the Chapel Royal at Whitehall (Figures 144 and 145). In 1835, King William IV ordered them transferred to the Royal Hospital at Chelsea. Here a Captain Ford, an officer on the staff of the

---

* According to an account by a British midshipman, the big flag was hoisted over the fort when the British were withdrawing. During the battle a smaller storm flag flew over the fort. See Walter Lord, *The Dawn's Early Light* (New York, 1972), p. 365.

174

*Fig. 144   Drawings of United States Army
flags captured during the War of
1812
Manuscripts Division, Windsor
Castle Library*

hospital, made a color record of the flags in 1847. Later, H. F. Barry made colored drawings of them. These drawings are a valuable record of flags actually used by the Army in the War of 1812. Particularly deserving of attention are the designs in the regimental flags and especially that of the stars and stripes flag (Figure 145) supposedly taken from an American ship.

Preserved in the West Point Museum are a number of flags of the War of 1812, some designated as national colors of different regiments and others described as regimental colors only. These flags generally have an eagle in the middle, usually with six-pointed stars above the eagle, the United States shield on the eagle, and the name of the regiment on a scroll beneath it. The national color is usually designated by the letters *U.S.* on the chief of the shield (Figure 146). The infantry, artillery, and cavalry carried flags similar to this.

Army regulations issued in 1834 described the garrison flag as the stars and stripes, and also prescribed the stars and stripes for the artillery. But it was not

*Fig. 146 Colors of the Eleventh Infantry
          Regiment, War of 1812
          West Point Museum*

*Fig. 147 Flag of the Nashville Battalion,
          Tennessee Militia*

*145 Drawings of United States Army
     flags captured during the War
     of 1812
     Manuscripts Division, Windsor
     Castle Library*

Fig. 148   The Flag of Levi Colbert
Oklahoma Historical Society

until 1841 that the infantry was authorized to carry the stars and stripes. Therefore it was not until the Mexican War that the stars and stripes were first carried into combat by American soldiers.

Two flags associated with Indians during the War of 1812 deserve some mention here. The first of these is the flag made by the ladies of Nashville for the Nashville Battalion of Tennessee militia in its campaign against the Creek Indians in 1813. It depicts a brown eagle with a blue ribbon in its beak. Along the bottom of the flag is the motto "God Armeth the Patriot." Surrounding the head of the eagle are thirteen five-pointed gold stars edged in black thread (Figure 147).

The second flag associated with Indians is one carried by the Chickasaw division who fought with General Andrew Jackson at the battle of New Orleans in January 1815. At the beginning of this battle the standard-bearer was killed and Levi Colbert, a Chickasaw member of the division, rushed forward, recovered the flag, and carried it throughout the fight. Colbert was the son of Logan Colbert, a white man who had come into the Chickasaw country before the American Revolution, and had married a full-blooded Chickasaw girl. The Chickasaws and the Choctaws were among the tribes of Indians approached by Tecumseh, the great Shawnee chief, in an effort to organize all the Indians west of the Alleghenies to eliminate the Americans in the region and to block further white settlements. Both the Chickasaws and the Choctaws refused to participate, for they felt themselves bound by treaties with the Americans. Their stance encouraged other tribes to resist the entreaties of Tecumseh, and most certainly helped to defeat his ambitious plans. The Chickasaws and Choctaws both fought with the Americans at New Orleans.

After the battle, General Jackson presented the Chickasaw flag to Levi Colbert and recommended that the entire Chickasaw division be cited for distinguished service. Colbert subsequently received a medal from President John Quincy Adams in 1825. The flag was presented to the Oklahoma Historical Society by descendants of Colbert in 1940 (Figure 148). It consists of a blue woolen canton on which a brown spread eagle is painted. The eagle's eyes have red pupils and a red tongue can be seen. It has four arrows in its right talon, a green olive branch in its left, and a shield between. Thirteen red and white stripes adorn the lower part of the shield. Above the eagle's head are nine

Fig. 149   The Battle Near the City of New
Orleans; *engraving by Francisco
Scacki*
Chicago Historical Society

small rectangles that must originally have been gold in color, but are now tan
with red pin stripes. There is a blue plume-like design above the wings.
Twenty-five stars now adorn the flag. During the War of 1812 it would have
had only fifteen, so stars were added to bring the flag up to date as of 1836,
when Arkansas was admitted to the Union. There are thirteen red and white
stripes, which vary in width but are about 3¾ inches wide. The flag itself
measures forty-six inches wide by eighty inches long.

No discussion of military flags at the battle of New Orleans would be
complete without some notice of the flags that appear in prints commemorating
the battle. An engraving by Francisco Scacki shows the battle from a perspective behind the British lines. On the horizon are the American lines over which
three large flags are waving. In the center is a red and white striped flag with
an eagle in the canton surrounded by stars. At the top of the flag pole is a
Liberty Cap. The artist has depicted a flag with about twenty stripes and
seventeen stars in a circle around the eagle. To the right and left of this flag
and at the ends of the American line are two flags with many stripes. Instead
of a canton there is a light area to the right of center surrounded by what
appear to be laurel wreaths. In the center of these wreaths is a single large

179

Fig. 150 *The Battle of New Orleans; engraving by Louis-Philibert Debucourt (detail)*
Library of Congress

star. It is not known what the basis for these designs was, but presumably the single star flags are products of the artist's imagination. The engraving is believed to have been published in the United States in 1815 (Figure 149).

A tremendous panorama of the battle that depicts the ferocity of the fighting in front of the American position was painted by Hyacinthe Laclotte, presumably in 1815. Laclotte was described as an "architect and assistant engineer in the Louisiana Army," probably a Creole volunteer. His painting was used by a famous Paris engraver, Louis-Philibert Debucourt, as the basis for a colored aquatint of the battle. A detail from this aquatint shows the stars and stripes on the parapet. The flag appears to have fifteen stripes and fifteen stars arranged in a 5–5–5 pattern (Figure 150).

Another painting of the battle from the perspective of the British lines was done by William Edward West. West was studying in Philadelphia under Thomas Sully between 1807 and 1819, and presumably made the painting during the years 1815–19. It was the basis for an engraving by Joseph Yeager of Philadelphia, probably issued soon after the war. The engraving of the battle is

Fig. 151 Battle of New Orleans; *engraving*
  by Joseph Yeager
  Library of Congress

of less interest here than the miniature portrait of Jackson below it amid the title. Jackson is flanked by two flags and an array of arms. The flags appear to have fifteen stripes and a star arrangement that seems to indicate fifteen stars in three rows of five (Figure 151).

The Peace of Ghent, ending the War of 1812, was the inspiration for an allegorical painting by Madame Anthony Plantou. Her *Peace of Ghent 1814 and Triumph of America* depicts the figure of America, in a cross between Indian and Roman garb, riding in a chariot through a cheering crowd past a monument on which is inscribed the names of heroic and victorious army and navy officers. America holds a bow in her left hand and a flag pole in her right. The pole carries the stars and stripes and is decorated with a Liberty Cap. The red stripes of the flag are painted more narrowly than the white, and there appear to be about twenty-five altogether. The five-pointed stars are arranged in a horizontal pattern in an apparent effort to show a flag of eighteen stars. Madame Plantou's painting was the basis for an engraving by Alexis Chataigner; it is believed to have been published in Paris in 1815 (Figure 152).

181

Fig. 152   Peace of Ghent, 1814 and
Triumph of America; *engraving*
by Alexis Chataigner
Chicago Historical Society

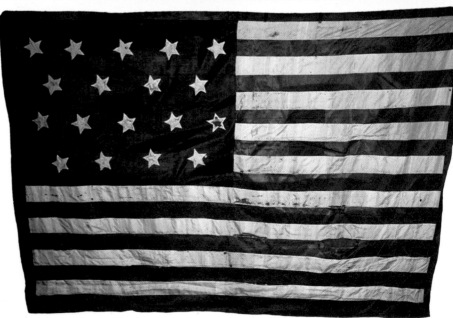

Fig. 153   *The Baton Rouge Flag*
Smithsonian Institution, courtesy
Louisiana State Museum

While the War of 1812 was raging, a curious little book entitled *Flags of Nations* was published in Venice in the Armenian language. The United States flag is depicted with sixteen stripes, a red stripe at the top and a white stripe at the bottom. The stars are arranged in a circle, with one star in the middle. In addition, this book shows a flag with a tree on a white background and a legend, presumably "An Appeal to Heaven." This suggests that some of the flags of the colonial era, about which Consul General O'Brien was so concerned in 1798, were still in use in the Mediterranean at the time of the War of 1812.

The Flag Act of 1818

On December 11, 1816, Indiana was admitted to the Union. This was the fourth state admitted since the passage of the flag law of 1794, but as yet there was no formal recognition of the growth of the Union in the flag itself. As the new states came into the Union, it had become customary for persons displaying the flag to add a stripe and a star. As a result, flags in use in various parts of the country had no uniform number of stars or stripes. A striking example of this tendency is the flag of eighteen stars and stripes still preserved in the Louisiana State Museum (Figure 153).

According to a family letter preserved with the flag, Colonel Philip Hicky was in charge of the arsenal at Baton Rouge at the time of Louisiana's admission to the Union on April 30, 1812. The colonel wanted a flag for the occasion, but it would take too long to get one from Washington. So he arranged to have one made on the Hope plantation by the women of Baton Rouge, headed by Mrs. Ann Mather Hicky, the colonel's wife. Red and white silk dresses were supposed to have been used to make the flag, and indigo was used as a dye to make the color blue for the canton. The flag was used at Baton Rouge until a regular one was received from Washington.

After Indiana was admitted to the Union, Congressman Peter H. Wendover of New York introduced a resolution in the House of Representatives that "a Committee be appointed to inquire into the expediency of altering the flag of the United States." A committee was appointed, and it reported a bill on January 2, 1817. The matter was not acted upon, probably because it was too late in the Fourteenth Congress, which adjourned on March 3, 1817. But during the time the matter was before the committee, Wendover called Captain Samuel Chester Reid, U.S.N., who was in Washington at the time. Reid had won fame during the War of 1812 by defending his small privateer ship, the *General Armstrong*, against the attack of two hundred armed British sailors in twelve boats in the neutral port of Fayal in the Azores. Wendover asked Reid to design a flag that would allow for the increase of the number of states without destroying the distinctive character of the flag. Wendover was especially concerned about this matter, for the committee was considering increasing both the stars and the stripes.

Reid recommended that the stripes be reduced to thirteen for the original states, and that the number of stars representing the whole number of states be formed into one great star in the union. One star would be added for each new state, thereby giving significance to the national motto, *E pluribus unum*, one out of many. The committee liked his suggestion and adopted it. A bill was reported on January 2, 1817, but it did not pass.

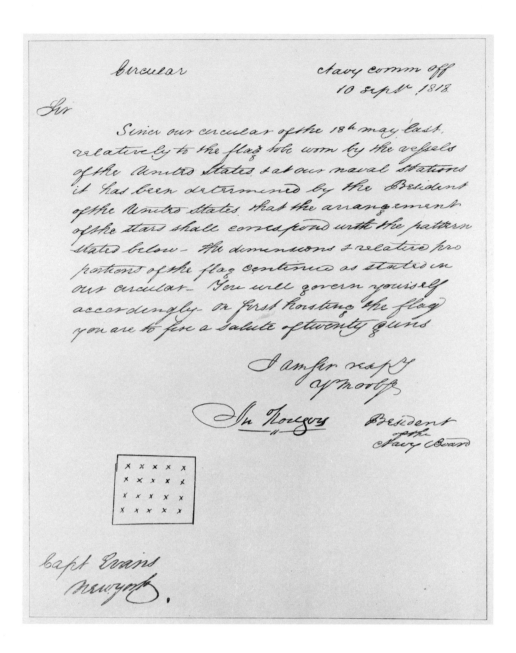

Wendover took up the matter again on December 16, 1817, by introducing a resolution to appoint a new committee "to inquire into the expediency of altering the flag of the United States, and that they have leave to report by bill or otherwise." By way of justification, Wendover pointed out that, except for those used by the Navy, the flags in general use varied greatly and did not agree with the act of 1794: the building in which Congress sat flew a flag with nine stripes while the Navy Yard flew one with eighteen. Wendover won his point, and a committee was appointed.

On January 6, 1818, the committee reported a bill to alter the flag that was substantially the same as that recommended at the last session of Congress. The matter came before the House on March 24, and it resolved itself into a committee of the whole to consider the measure. The real difference between this bill and the previous one was that now there was no mention of forming a great star. The bill provided that there be a union of twenty stars, white on a blue field, and that upon the admission of each new state into the Union one star be added to the union of the flag on the fourth of July following its date of admission. The earlier proposal to reduce the stripes to thirteen red and white stripes remained. Various members of the House discussed the question of the stripes and stars. The bill passed the House.

The Senate took up the bill on March 31, and passed it by unanimous consent. President James Monroe signed the bill on April 4, 1818, and it became law. In its final form the law read:

That from and after the fourth day of July next, the flag of the United States be thirteen horizontal stripes, alternate red and white; that the union be twenty stars, white, in a blue field.

Section 2. *And be it further enacted,* That on the admission of every state into the Union, one star be added to the union of the flag; and that such addition shall take effect on the fourth of July next succeeding such admission.

The third flag law thus established the design of the United States flag.

Following the usual procedure of officially announcing changes in the flag, the Navy published the change in the arrangement of the twenty stars in a circular letter dated May 18, 1818. The letter, signed by Captain John Rodgers, the president of the Board of Navy Commissioners, also stated that "The size of the flag must be in the proportion of 14 feet in width × 24 feet in length— the field of the union must be ⅓rd of the length of the flag, & 7⁄13ths of its depth so that from the top to the bottom of the union there will be seven stripes and six stripes from the bottom of the union to the bottom of the flag. The manner of arranging the stars, you will perceive by the subjoined sketch." Then, using *x*'s for stars, Rodgers depicted a canton in which the twenty stars were arranged in four staggered horizontal lines that contained five stars on each line. Lines one and three had the stars begin near the hoist end of the canton, lines two and four began with indented stars and ended with stars near the fly end of the canton.

This star arrangement did not please President Monroe, so he changed the design to one of four symmetrical rows of five stars each. The change was announced to the Navy by a new circular letter of Captain Rodgers of September 10, 1818 (Figure 154). He noted that the change "has been determined by the President of the United States" and that the dimensions and proportions announced earler remained the same. Rodgers also gave the officers a change in protocol: "On first hoisting the flag you are to fire a salute of twenty guns." It had become a custom for the Army to fire a salute of guns corresponding to the number of states in the Union. This was now adopted by the Navy. It had long been customary in most navies to fire salutes based on the rank of the person saluted. These always involved an uneven number of guns, for an even number was considered unlucky.

By 1818, the basic pattern for the evolution of the flag was established: Congress authorizes the admission of states into the Union; their entrance is reflected in the flag by the addition of a star on the next fourth of July; the arrangement of stars is determined by the president. The act of 1818 was the first time that it was specified that the stripes in the flag should be horizontal.

The passage of time showed that while the law was followed, official and unofficial flags evolved differently. Official flags tended to follow the basic horizontal arrangement of the stars. But with unofficial flags, it was the flagmaker and not the president who determined the design of the stars. As the Union grew, flag makers exercised considerable ingenuity in designing flags with a wide variety of star arrangements. Many of these were very colorful and individualistic, but they conveyed anything but a sense of a uniform design. Yet in their richness of design and diversity of pattern they were a fitting symbol for the wide array of restless people who were building a nation.

Notes

Modern accounts of the causes of the War of 1812 and the major events in that conflict are Harry L. Coles, *The War of 1812* (Chicago, 1965); Patrick C. T. White, *A Nation on Trial: America and the War of 1812* (New York, 1965); Reginald Horsman, *The War of 1812* (New York, 1969); and J. Mackay Hitsman, *The Incredible War of 1812: A Military History* (Toronto, 1965). On the battle between the *Chesapeake* and the *Shannon* see also Hugh F. Pullen, *The Shannon and the Chesapeake* (Toronto, 1970). Details on the Fort Hill and Fort McHenry flags are in the accession papers for those objects in the Smithsonian Institution. Copies of these papers are in the Division of Naval History, Smithsonian Institution. The British attack on Stonington, Conn., is described in Preble's *History of the Flag of the United States of America* (Boston, 1880). For a full account of the attack on Fort McHenry see Walter Lord, *The Dawn's Early Light* (New York, 1972). An older account is in Benson J. Lossing, *The Pictorial Field Book of the War of 1812* (New York, 1868). The making of the Fort McHenry flag is recounted in Preble and in Mary-Paulding Martin, *The Flag House Story* (Baltimore, 1970). Details on the publication history of Francis Scott Key's "The Star Spangled Banner" can be found in P. William Filby and Edward G. Howard, *Star Spangled Books* (Baltimore, 1972).

Background information on Levi Colbert and his flag are in the War of 1812 folder in the Furlong Flag Files in the Division of Naval History, Smithsonian Institution. Information on the artists and prints that commemorated events in the War of 1812 may be found in Donald Mugridge, ed., *An Album of American Battle Art, 1775–1918* (Washington, 1947) and in Wendy J. Shadwell, *American Printmaking: The First 150 Years* (Washington, 1969). The Armenian flag book published in Venice in 1813 is in the Anne S. K. Brown Military Collection, Brown University. Information on the Baton Rouge flag is in the Furlong Flag Files. The story of the enactment of the Flag Act of 1818 may be found in the *Annals of Congress* from the second session of the 14th Congress to first session of the 15th Congress. A biographical sketch of Captain Samuel Reid may be found in the *Dictionary of American Biography*. The papers of Samuel Chester Reid are in the Library of Congress. Copies of the Circular Letters of Captain John Rodgers, U.S.N., can be found in the outgoing letters of the Board of Navy Commissioners, Record Group 45, entry 212, National Archives.

CHAPTER 11

The Increase of the Stars

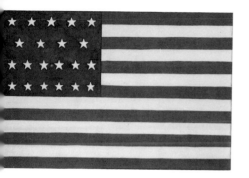

Fig. 155   An artist's conception of the ap-pearance of a twenty-one star flag

Following the end of the War of 1812, the United States and Great Britain undertook negotiations to resolve their outstanding points of conflict. One of these was the question of the boundary between the United States and Canada. The Convention of 1818 adjusted the poorly defined northern boundary of the Louisiana Purchase. A new line was drawn from the Lake of the Woods along the 49th parallel to the Rocky Mountains. Beyond the mountains lay the Oregon country embracing present-day British Columbia, Washington, and Oregon. This territory was to be open to both Britons and Americans for ten years.

Illinois pressed for admission to the Union, which it attained on December 3, 1818. Under the formula established by the flag act of 1818, the twenty-first star was added to the flag on July 4, 1819. In official flags the change was made by arranging the stars in a 5–4–6–6 pattern (Figure 155). An unofficial version may be seen in a watercolor painting entitled *Ship Macon Newyork & Savannah packet Cap. D. C. Porter,* and inscribed "Nivelet." It shows a flag with twenty stars in the shape of a large star and a slightly larger twenty-first star in the center of the big star. While this painting is dated from either 1827 or 1834, there is no reason to believe that the flag depicted was not authentic.

Expansion of American Interests: the South

In the early years of the nineteenth century the attention of American politi-cians became focused on developments in the south. At the time of the negotiations for the purchase of the Louisiana Territory, the United States tried to buy East and West Florida. While Florida was under British sovereignty between 1763 and 1783, it was divided into separate provinces with the Apalachicola River the boundary. An American diplomat argued that the repossession of East and West Florida by Spain in 1783 reintegrated that territory into Louisiana. Spain was not willing to accept this interpretation, and the French preferred to keep the boundaries vague. When the United States took over Louisiana Territory in 1803, it did not include East or West Florida, but President Jefferson was determined to have those areas eventually.

Responding to President Jefferson's suggestion, Congress passed the Mobile Act in 1804. This law said that the territory ceded by France "and also all the navigable waters, river, creeks, bays, and inlets, lying within the United States, which empty into the Gulf of Mexico, east of the river Mississippi, shall be annexed to the Mississippi district." The law gave the president the power to establish a separate customs district there with a port of entry. While this law did not explicitly place West Florida under the Mobile Act, it was a claim to the territory and Spain resented it. The United States now pursued a diplomatic policy to persuade Spain to part with the territory.

While the diplomats talked, American settlers entered the territory of West Florida. In 1804 a group of these settlers declared their independence from Spain and attempted to capture Grand Pre. They raised a flag consisting of seven white and blue stripes and two stars in a blue field. The two stars apparently stood for East and West Florida. The Spanish authorities quickly put down the revolt, but the spirit that prompted it did not die.

In 1810 another insurrection took place in the Baton Rouge district. This time President James Madison proclaimed the rightful occupation of the region between the Iberville and Perdido rivers, but actually occupied the area only as far east as the Pearl River. Thus the United States was careful not to interfere with the Spanish garrisons in Mobile and Pensacola. Spain was now allied with Great Britain in a war against Napoleon in Europe, and the British government protested the American action. Congress met in a secret session on January 15, 1811, and passed a resolution that the United States could not see any part of Florida territory pass into the hands of any foreign power without serious disturbance. It authorized the president to take custody of East Florida if it was in danger of being occupied by a foreign power.

President Madison hesitated and looked to the settlers there to gravitate toward the protection of the United States. In an effort to hasten this process, General George Mathews tried to stimulate an uprising by American settlers against Spanish authority. On March 13, 1812, a group of ten residents of East Florida announced their grievances against Spain and in a manifesto they declared their independence. They invited all like-minded men in the province to join them. At Rose's Bluff, about four miles above the border town of St. Mary's, Georgia, the rebels erected an improvised flag pole and raised their flag on it. This flag consisted of a soldier in blue against a white background. The soldier carried a bayonet on his musket, which was thrust forward in the act of charging. Below the soldier was the motto: "Salus populi, lex suprema." Some of the observers on the scene who had a background in the classics pointed out to the rebels that the word "salus" meant safety, health or welfare in Latin. In a revolution there would be little of that. The rebels then changed the motto on the flag to read: "Vox populi, lex suprema," or "the voice of the people, the supreme law." The majority of the frontiersmen declaring their independence had little appreciation of the nuances of the Latin language. To them the flag was simply a piece of cloth with a man on it and a slogan whose substance was that the voice of the people was the law of the land. That seemed good enough.

Within a few days the rebel force numbered about 180 men. They set out for Amelia Island in the Amelia River between the border of Georgia and Florida. Here they captured the town of Fernandina on the west side of the island. The Spanish flag was hauled down and the rebel flag raised on March 17, 1812. General Mathews's rebels moved against St. Augustine, but they were not strong enough to take it without the assistance of the United States Army and Navy units in the area. Such aid was not forthcoming. The Madison administration told General Mathews that his actions were unauthorized and that it disapproved. But it also told the Spanish authorities that it did not want the rebels punished for their actions. So Fernandina was evacuated and East Florida remained in Spanish hands.

But in West Florida the United States was prepared to act. Congress annexed West Florida west of the Pearl River in April 1812 and added it to the state of Louisiana. A month later the Congress annexed the eastern half of the territory of Mississippi. On June 25, 1812, a week after the declaration of war against Great Britain, the Congress secretly authorized President Madison to take possession of the territory "lying south of the Mississippi Territory (and) the State of Georgia." Madison chose not to use this authority, and when the war with Great Britain ended in 1815 East Florida was still ruled by Spain.

Once again the diplomats took up the question of the future of the Floridas. Western settlers were concerned about the fact that the Spanish-held Floridas were a base from which hostile Indians operated against American border areas. Spain's inability to restrain these Indians prompted General Andrew Jackson to lead an armed force into the region. Jackson seized the Spanish fort at St. Marks in April 1818, hauled the flag and replaced it with the stars and stripes. Two British subjects, charged with inciting the Indians, were tried and executed. Within a few weeks, Jackson had captured every important post in Florida except St. Augustine. He deposed the Spanish governor and replaced him with an American. The diplomatic uproar that followed led President Monroe to return the captured territory, but the actions of Jackson were defended on the grounds of self defense.

Jackson's actions and the American posture convinced Spain that it should part with the territory. Under the terms of the Adams-Onis Treaty signed in Washington in 1819, the United States acquired East Florida and the validation of its seizure of West Florida. It also clarified the western boundary of the Louisiana Purchase and acquired Spain's claim to the Oregon country.

Since 1817 the Mississippi Territory had been divided into Mississippi and the Alabama Territory. Alabama was admitted to the Union as the twenty-second state on December 14, 1819. The Union and the power in the Senate was balanced between eleven free and eleven slave states at a time when the subject of slavery was becoming a matter of growing concern in the north. This delicate political and sectional balance was threatened when Maine sought admission as a free state. Missouri also asked for admission. Only if it were permitted to enter as a slave state would the sectional balance be maintained. If both Missouri and Maine entered the Union as free states, the sectional balance in the Senate would be lost and the future of slavery placed in jeopardy.

From February 1819 to March 1820 the problem of statehood for Missouri was debated in the Congress. In the end a solution was reached under what was to become known as the Missouri Compromise, which allowed Missouri to enter the Union as a slave state and Maine as a free state. For the rest of the territory embraced under the Louisiana Purchase, slavery was forbidden in states formed north of the line of 36 degrees, 30 minutes, and permitted only south of that line. Under these terms, Maine entered the Union on March 13, 1820. The following July 4 the stars in the flag were increased to twenty-three, for Alabama and Maine. Although there was no official twenty-two star flag, for Alabama, such flags may have been made.

Fig. 156   A twenty-four star eagle type flag

Missouri entered the Union on August 10, 1821. The following July 4, the stars in the flag numbered twenty-four. The standard arrangement of the stars was four rows of six stars each. Preserved in the Smithsonian Institution is a badly worn example of what was once a twenty-four star flag. This is the original "Old Glory," so named by Captain William Driver of Salem, Massachusetts, in 1824 when his mother and female friends presented him with the results of their handiwork in the form of the flag. As a merchant captain, Driver carried the flag with him on a number of voyages. Twice it went around the world, once it went to Australia, and once to Pitcairn's Island, where Driver met the descendants of the mutineers of H.M.S. *Bounty.* When Driver retired from the sea in 1837, he took the flag with him to his new home in Nashville, Tennessee. Here it was his custom to fly the flag over his property on holidays.

In 1860 Mrs. Driver and one of the captain's daughter's took the flag apart, cut off the raveled and frayed seams, replaced the old stars and added new ones to bring the flag up-to-date with the number of states in the Union. When the flag was sewn together again it had thirty-four stars, and Captain Driver added an anchor to the lower right hand corner to commemorate his sea service. The flag was destined to play a dramatic role in Nashville during the Civil War, but that story properly belongs to a later portion of this narrative.

A twenty-four star flag of the eagle type is in the custody of the Smithsonian's Military History Division (Figure 156). This has an eagle and a shield painted on the blue bunting canton, as well as twenty-four stars. The flag measures seventy-eight inches long by forty-four inches wide. This flag is

190

of some significance, as it indicates that the eagle-in-canton design, first used late in the Revolutionary War, was still in use on the eve of the Mexican War. The specific association of this flag is not known, but it may have been used by a militia unit.

Meanwhile in 1834 the Army attempted for the first time to describe design requirements for flags in the General Regulations of the Army. These regulations reflected practices then in force. The national color of infantry regiments was to be a blue flag with the arms of the United States and the regimental name and number. A second color was to be the regimental standard, with a white field and the name and number of the regiment in the center in gold or yellow on a blue scroll. Both flags were to be 6 feet wide and 6½ feet long and each was to have a fringe of yellow silk and black and yellow cords and tassels. The standard of dragoon units was similar in design to those of the infantry, but had smaller dimensions.

Artillery regiments were also to have two silk colors with the same dimensions as those of the infantry. The regimental color had a yellow field with two crossed cannon in the center, and the letters *U.S.* as well as the name and number of the unit. But for the national color, artillery regiments received a stars and stripes flag with the unit designation in gold letters on the center stripe. Thus for the first time the stars and stripes were used as a national color for the regiments of one branch of the Army.

The Northwest

The flag of twenty-four stars is associated with the continuing projection of American interests into areas beyond its political boundaries. One such extension of interests occurred in regard to Russia and the Pacific Northwest.

Between 1728 and 1741 Captain Vitus Bering, a Dane in Russian service, carried out a series of voyages under the auspices of Peter the Great that resulted in the discovery of the Bering Strait, the exploration of the Aleutian Islands, and the finding and naming of Mount St. Elias on the American side. Traders and trappers followed Bering to these regions, and in 1763 Kodiak Island was discovered. A settlement was made there in 1784.

When the British Captain Cook explored the northwest coast of North America in 1778, he traveled to Norton Sound north of the Yukon and touched at Unalaska where he found Russian settlers. Private companies and traders operating in Alaska robbed, abused, and killed the natives. To stop these excesses, the Russian government established a semiofficial corporation known as the Russian-American Company to trade in the area. The headquarters of the company was established at Kodiak, but was transferred to Sitka in 1805. The company was also given a flag to fly over its installations. This was a tricolor, the top portion of which was a wide band of white with the double-headed imperial eagle in the middle. Below the white band were two narrower stripes of blue and red (Figure 157).

In the early years of the nineteenth century the Russian-American Company was associated with the growth of the fur trade in California. It began when Count Nikoli Rezanov came to Spanish-held San Francisco in 1806 to negotiate for food for the Russian colonies. He also wanted to establish a base for the capture of sea otters. This had been so successful a business operation in the

Fig. 157   Flag of the Russian-American
Company, 1806–1861

north that the Russians wished to seek the animals farther down the coast. The
Spanish were agreeable, and about seventy-five miles north of San Francisco a
fort was eatablished in 1812 at a small harbor above the Slavianka or Russian
River. Fort Ross, as the settlement became known, soon grew to fifty buildings
outside the fort itself. None of this was of any concern to most Americans until
the czar of Russia expressed an interest in the region in a dramatic way.

In 1821 the czar issued an imperial edict by which he assumed the power to
exclude all but Russian subjects from trading or fishing within one hundred
Italian miles* of the northwest coast of North America as far south as 51 degrees
north latitude. Both Great Britain and the United States protested this expression of Russian sovereignty. For a time after that the czar dropped the matter
while he dealt with internal problems in Russia. Later, in July 1823, Secretary
of State John Quincy Adams told the Russian minister at Washington that the
United States would contest the right of Russia to any territorial establishment
on this continent. Not surprisingly, the Russians did not accept this interpretation, but in 1824 the two governments agreed to a treaty that set limits on any
new colonial establishments in this hemisphere. The southern boundary of
Alaska was set at 54 degrees 40 minutes. A year later Great Britain accepted
this same boundary and drew another line from there to the Arctic Ocean
which continues to be the boundary of Alaska.

While the Russian matter was still pending, Secretary Adams received word
of a British proposal for a joint Anglo-American declaration on the status of the
Spanish colonies in the Western Hemisphere that had revolted against Spanish

---

* Presumably a reference to the Roman mile, which was originally 5,000 feet. In about 1500 the Roman
mile was changed to 5,280 feet.

rule. Fears that Spain might attempt to regain these colonies, with or without the help of France, prompted the British offer. Rather than join with the British in such a declaration, President Monroe decided to make his own announcement of American interests in the Western Hemisphere. In a message to Congress in December 1823, Monroe stated that the United States would regard it as an unfriendly act if any European power attempted to intervene in the political system of the American continents, or if it attempted to acquire new territory there. For its part, the United States would not participate in the politics or wars of the European powers on matters relating to themselves. These sentiments, embraced in what became known as the Monroe Doctrine, attempted to lay the groundwork for the erection of an American system in the Western Hemisphere. The Monroe administration was careful not to commit itself to any agreements with the Latin American governments. In the end, it was British diplomatic activity and the British Navy that removed the threat of any European intervention in Latin American affairs, but the Monroe Doctrine became a major principle of American foreign policy.

Texas

Another projection of American interests beyond its boundaries came in regard to Texas. Between 1825 and 1830 American immigrants streamed into Texas. At first they were welcomed, but the Mexican government soon found out that it had a large population of unassimilated foreigners within its boundaries. Laws were passed restricting further immigration and colonization. American settlers in Texas resented both these restrictions and the Mexican government's efforts to exert better control over its territory.

Meanwhile, the United States government attempted to buy all or parts of Texas, but the Mexicans resolutely rejected these offers. Americans in Texas revolted against Mexican rule in 1835. From the adjoining southern states volunteers went to Texas to assist the revolt; many of these men carried the stars and stripes flag with them. Neutrality laws restricting such actions were not enforced. The Texans won their autonomy in 1836 and a year later petitioned for annexation to the United States.

For President Martin Van Buren the Texas offer posed grave problems. Texas was still at war with Mexico, a country with which the United States had a treaty of amity. The annexation of an independent republic was also a matter whose constitutionality was in doubt. There was also the fact that the admission of Texas would mean the slave states would be increased by one or more new states. Accordingly, the annexation offer was rejected. Texas was destined to continue as a nation for eight years—its independence recognized by Great Britain, Holland, Belgium, and the United States.

Four flags are associated with the years that Texas was an independent republic. The first, in use from March to December 1836, consisted of a blue field with a large white five-pointed star in the center, and the letters of the word Texas placed between each of the points of the star. A second flag, used from December 1836 to January 1839 and described as the national standard, had a blue field with a yellow five-pointed star in the center. A third version, inspired by the stars and stripes, was used by the Texas navy. This had a square blue canton with a single white, five-pointed star in the center, and

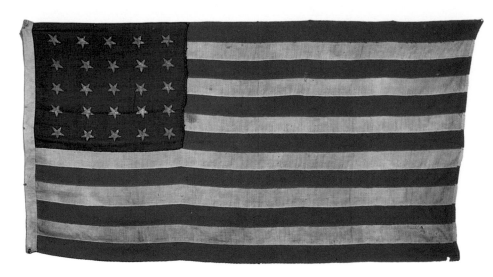

thirteen red and white horizontal stripes that began and ended with a red
stripe. This flag was in use from April 1836 to about the end of December
1845. The fourth flag became the state flag after Texas joined the Union. In
use from January 1839 to the present, it is a tricolor, with a blue vertical stripe
along the hoist from the top to the bottom edge and a single white five-pointed
star in the center. Attached to the blue are two broad horizontal stripes, a
white on top and a red below.

Admission of New States

By this time the growth of the antislavery agitation was affecting virtually every
aspect of national life. Arkansas sought admission to the Union in 1836, which,
if granted, would give the proslavery forces a majority of two votes in the
Senate. Therefore, it was again necessary to admit both a free and a slave state.
Michigan was chosen for the pairing. Michigan's acceptance was delayed by a
land dispute with Ohio, so Arkansas entered the Union on June 15, 1836. The
following July 4, the flag grew to twenty-five stars (Figure 158).

It is doubtful that very many twenty-five star flags were made, for it was
known that Michigan would soon enter the Union and render that star pattern
obsolete. Michigan was admitted on January 26, 1837, and on July 4 of that
year the stars in the flag increased to twenty-six.

The most common star arrangement was a 7–6–6–7 pattern. Two examples
of a twenty-six star flag are represented in the private collection of Boleslaw
and Marie Mastai. One is a block printed cotton flag and the other is a printed
silk. Power woven cotton, probably of American manufacture, was used to
make the twenty-seven inch flag. In the case of the silk flag, the fabric is
twenty-nine inches long, and the stars are arranged to form one big star.

Only a few years passed before the south again had a state seeking admission
to the Union—Florida. This time Iowa was slated to be the free area to be
paired, but there was a delay and Florida was admitted on March 3, 1845. The
stars in the flag were officially increased to twenty-seven the next July 4, but it
is unlikely that many flags with this design were made.

By this time Texas was again seeking admission, and many southern politi-
cians were determined that it be accepted. The election of 1844 was largely

Fig. 159   A twenty-nine star flag (artist's conception)

fought on this issue. Although the election of James K. Polk was not a true mandate for annexation, it was interpreted this way. The outgoing president, John Tyler, signed the joint resolution of the Congress approving annexation, and on December 29, 1844, Texas entered the Union. Twenty-eight star flags became official on July 4, 1845. The conventional horizontal star pattern was 7–7–7–7.

Iowa had been awaiting the pleasure of Congress on its application for some time. Finally, on December 26, 1846, it was admitted as a free state. A flag of twenty-nine stars, arranged in a 8–6–7–8 pattern, was the conventional design (Figure 159). In actual practice it is likely that flag makers had difficulty in staying abreast of official requirements. For the average person who might wish to display a flag on appropriate occasions, there was probably no aversion to flying one with less than the official number of stars.

The Mexican War

Another factor that undoubtedly contributed to the lag in displaying official flags of the proper number of stars was the outbreak of the Mexican War. Relations with Mexico had been tense and strained since the admission of Texas to the Union. A major factor in this situation was the dispute about the border between Texas and Mexico. The United States sent troops into the disputed area in 1846, and they were fired upon by Mexican troops. This incident provided President Polk with a convenient pretext to ask Congress for a declaration of war. Congress declared war on Mexico on May 13, but both the incident that provoked it and the war itself were occasions for bitter political divisions. Southerners tended to favor and support the war. Northerners saw it as an unjustifiable conflict and a naked attempt to extend slave territory. These sentiments were crystallized in the summer of 1846 when Representative David Wilmot of Pennsylvania offered a proviso to a pending appropriation bill that would bar slavery from all lands acquired as a result of the war. Although the proviso in its original form was defeated, it raised anew the problem of slavery in the territories and sharpened sectional divisions to the point of disunion.

The Mexican War has a special relevance for the history of the flag, for it was the first conflict in which the stars and stripes were carried into battle by American troops (Figure 160). The Army regulations adopted in 1834 stated that the garrison flag was to be the national flag, and authorized the carrying of that flag by the artillery troops. Regulations adopted in 1841 authorized infantry regiments to carry the stars and stripes as well as their regimental color. A white flag, originally authorized for infantry use in 1834, was eliminated. A blue flag, previously used as a national color, now became the regimental flag. Cavalry units were authorized to use the stars and stripes on guidons in 1862, but did not receive the right to use the stars and stripes flag until 1895.

The battles of the Mexican War inspired several lithographers to record the heroic deeds. While flags appear in these prints, many are drawn so that an accurate count of the stars is not possible. Virtually all show flags with stars in horizontal rows. A striking exception is the *Death of Major Ringgold, of the Flying Artillery, at the Battle of Palo Alto, May 8, 1846* (Figure 161). This hand colored lithograph, apparently made by Louis Nagel, was printed and issued

195

by James S. Baille, who had colored prints for Nathaniel Currier before establishing his own business in New York. Beyond the dying Ringgold there is a cannon and a flag of twenty-three six-pointed stars arranged as concentric ovals.

The Acquisition of California

The outbreak of the Mexican War was followed by important developments in California. Captain John C. Frémont was leading his third surveying expedition in the west when he moved his men into California in January 1846 and established a camp in the Salinas Valley. General José Castro, the Mexican military commandant at Monterey, ordered Frémont to leave the area. Instead, he built a fortified position on the top of Gavilan Mountain over which he hoisted a United States flag.

The flag flown by Frémont was a very distinctive one, consisting of a white canton on which was painted a blue eagle bearing a red and white calumet or pipe of peace in its left claw, and nine blue arrows in its right claw. Above and below the eagle are twenty-seven five-pointed stars outlined in blue. Since Frémont was to explore territory outside the borders of the United States and in territory claimed by Spain, it had been decided that he would not carry the stars and stripes flag. Instead, his wife, Jessie Benton Frémont, designed and made this flag. It was an adaptation of the eagle-in-canton flags carried by

196

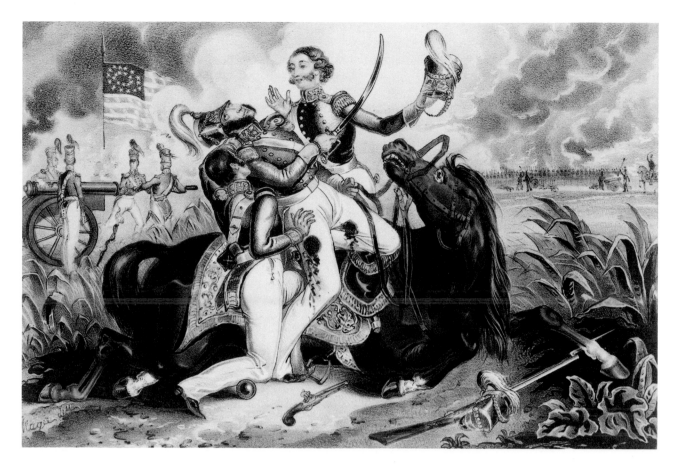

Fig. 161 Death of Major Ringgold
Library of Congress

Fig. 162 *The Fremont Flag*
Southwest Museum, Los Angeles

Army regiments. The peace pipe in the eagle's claws was a symbol readily understood by the Indians and more appropriate than the traditional olive branch. This flag is preserved in the Southwest Museum in Los Angeles (Figure 162).

197

The Mexicans sent a superior force against him, and Frémont withdrew to Klamath Lake on the Oregon frontier. Here he was overtaken by Lieutenant Archibald H. Gillespie of the United States Marine Corps, with dispatches and news from Washington. The extent of the news that Frémont received is not known, but immediately afterward he led his force back to California and worked to precipitate a revolt between the American settlers and the Mexican authorities. The so-called "Bear Flag Revolt" followed. The Bear Flag had a white field with a bear and a star colored with berry juice, and the words "California Republic." A red stripe decorated the bottom of the flag. It was raised at Sonoma on June 14, 1846. Frémont reached Sonoma eleven days later and gave his support to the uprising. On July 5, the local settlers chose him to represent them in the direction of the affairs of the newly born republic.

Elsewhere events were taking place that insured that the republic would have a short life. Commodore John D. Sloat, U.S.N. landed a force at Monterey on July 2, raised the stars and stripes, and declared California to be a part of the United States. Other naval units occupied San Francisco, Sonoma, and Sutter's Fort on the Sacramento River. The Bear Flag Republic gave way before the United States. On August 17, Commodore Robert F. Stockton, U.S.N. issued a proclamation stating that California was annexed to the United States and declaring himself the governor. Further fighting was necessary before the Mexican forces were defeated and American power consolidated.

Mexico was losing territory in other areas as well. Moving from Fort Leavenworth (in what later became Kansas), an American army under General Stephen W. Kearny occupied Las Vegas and Santa Fe in August 1847. The territory was annexed and a provisional government was established.

To bring the unpopular Mexican War to a close as rapidly as possible, an American army under General Winfield Scott landed in Mexico and fought its way to the capital city by the fall of 1847. In February 1848 a treaty of peace was signed with Mexico whereby the United States acquired California and New Mexico territories and all Mexican claims to Texas north of the Rio Grande. At that time the territories of California and New Mexico included more than the states that bear those names. It was a vast domain that also embraced parts of Utah, Nevada, Arizona, and Colorado. The peace treaty established a new boundary line with Mexico.

New States and the Problem of Slavery

New states were still being carved out of older territories in the midwest. Wisconsin, consisting of the last remaining portion of the old Northwest Territory, was admitted to the union as the thirtieth state on May 29, 1848. Thirty-star flags became official on July 4, 1848, although it is doubtful if many were produced by that date. The most logical horizontal arrangement was five rows of six stars in each row.

The same year that the treaty of peace was ratified, the world heard news of the discovery of gold in California. People flocked to the region in hopes of quick wealth. The rapid growth of population made it necessary to establish a formal territorial government and to look forward to eventual statehood. But these questions raised anew the problem of slavery in the territories, for California lay both north and south of the old Missouri Compromise line.

Fig. 164 A thirty-two star flag (artist's conception)

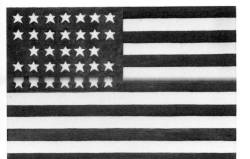

Fig. 165 A thirty-three star flag (artist's conception)

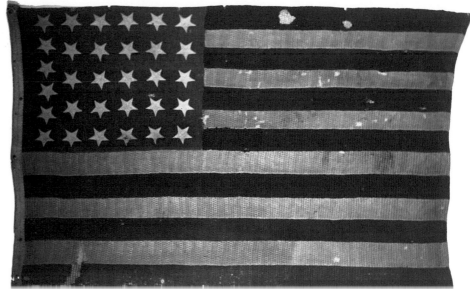

Fig. 163 The thirty-one-star flag of Commodore Matthew C. Perry used on expedition to Japan, 1853–54
U.S. Naval Academy Museum

After a great deal of political argument, the Congress worked out a formula whereby California would be admitted as a free state, and Texas, New Mexico, and Utah organized without restrictions in regard to slavery. These and other compromise measures were the ingredients of a political settlement that maintained the appearance of peace between pro- and antislavery forces in the Union for another decade. California was represented on the flag on July 4, 1851, when the stars were increased to thirty-one. The standard method for representing this number in horizontal lines was the 7–5–6–6–7 arrangement, although there were often variations (Figure 163).

Unofficial flags reflected imaginative variations, such as the so-called "seeded" design of uneven and crowded stars in a rough 6–6–5–5–6–3 pattern. There was also the outer and inner square design with a larger star in the center. Another variation used the stars to form a star design which had a larger star in its center. A pentagon design had a larger star in the center and regular sized stars in each of the four corners.

The number of free states in the Union was enlarged on May 11, 1858, when Minnesota was admitted. In accord with the law, the star for the new state was added to the flag on July 4, making the total thirty-two (Figure 164). It is not likely that many flags of this design were made, for on February 14, 1859, Oregon entered the Union and the flag was changed to thirty-three stars the following July 4 (Figure 165).

The customary design for this flag was a 7–7–5–7–7 pattern. There are, however, examples of more imaginative designs, such as that of the great star made up of individual stars, and the "Parenthesis Flag" whose design emphasizes a single star in the center surrounded by four stars in a curved pattern inside a six-star curve with a triangle of three stars in each of the corners of the canton. Perhaps the most unusual design is the homemade one of the Dodge family using two sizes of stars. There is a small star in the center of the canton, surrounded by a ring of twelve stars of the same size. This circle is surrounded by a circle of twelve larger stars. Large stars are also placed in each

199

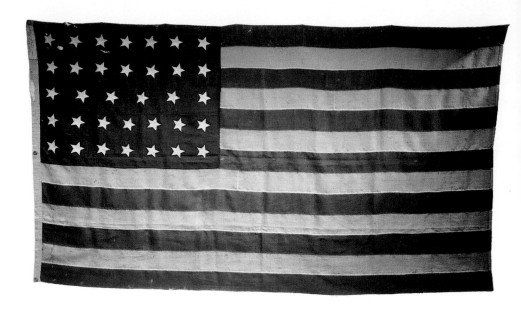

Fig. 166   A thirty-four star flag

of the corners of the canton, and between them on the top, bottom and sides is a star the size of those in the center of the canton. This homemade flag is also unusual for having only ten stripes, with a red one on top and a white one on the bottom, and for its teal blue canton and burgundy stripes.

The future of slavery in the territories continued to have a great influence on the political life on the nation. Both sides tried to capture Kansas for their cause. After much strife, Kansas entered the Union as a free state on January 29, 1861. Six months later the flag had its thirty-fourth star (Figure 166).

Public rejoicing over the admission of Kansas was overshadowed by the fact that the stability of the Union itself was now in doubt. Following the election of Abraham Lincoln as president in November 1860, South Carolina passed an ordinance of secession dissolving its allegiance to the Union. Within six weeks Alabama, Florida, Georgia, Louisiana, Mississippi, and Texas had followed South Carolina's example. These states organized themselves into the Confederate States of America and chose Jefferson Davis as their first president.

Notes

General information on the growth of the Union may be found in most standard history textbooks and in encyclopedia articles relating to specific states. Illustrations of flag designs at various periods may be found in Eggenberger and in a chapter in Grace R. Cooper's book on thirteen-star flags. A description of the painting *Ship Macon Newyork & Savannah packet* also appears in Cooper's book. Additional illustrations of star patterns can be found in Donald Mugridge, *Album of American Battle Art*, in M.V. and Dorothy Brewington, *The Marine Paintings and Drawings in the Peabody Museum* (Salem, 1968), and in Boleslaw and Marie Mastai, *The Stars and the Stripes* (New York, 1973). For the flag raised by General George Mathews over Amelia Island, Florida, see Rembert W. Patrick, *Florida Fiasco* (Athens, 1954). On flags in the Army see Quaife, Weig, and Appleman, *History of the United States Flag.*

200

CHAPTER **12**

Toward a More Perfect Union

In 1861 seven southern states, having severed their connections with the federal Union, established a separate political system. The Confederacy raised a new flag, the stars and bars. This consisted of a blue canton or union in which the states were represented by a circle of five-pointed stars, and a field of three wide horizontal stripes of red, white, and red. Although never formally authorized by the Confederate Congress, this was accepted as the first official flag of the Confederacy (Figure 167).

Within the Confederacy, officials soon began taking over the property of the United States government. In South Carolina this was resisted by Major Robert Anderson, who commanded federal troops stationed in Charleston Harbor. Anderson moved his troops to Fort Sumter and waited. President Abraham Lincoln resolved to supply the fort and so notified the South Carolina officials. The attempt failed. Shortly after this the South Carolina forces opened fire and forced the fort to surrender on April 14, 1861. Major Anderson and his troops were allowed to depart for the north. With him Anderson took the garrison flag that had flown during the two-day bombardment, and the smaller post flag. After he arrived in Washington these were officially presented to him by the War Department. Anderson kept them for the rest of his life, and his widow

Fig. 167   The first type of Confederate flag; flag worn by the C.S.S. Virginia
Chicago Historical Society

kept them until her death in 1905. In accordance with her will they were
returned to the War Department, which displayed them in Washington for
many years. In 1955 the Department of the Army transferred them to the
Department of the Interior. They are now preserved at the Fort Sumter
National Monument in Charleston harbor.

Of special interest is the garrison flag, whose thirty-three stars are not
arranged in a traditional horizontal pattern. Instead they follow a vertical
arrangement with the longest row in the center of the canton. The vertical
pattern is 5–3–5–7–5–3–5 (Figure 168).

Upon receiving news of the surrender of Fort Sumter in 1861, President
Lincoln issued a proclamation declaring that a state of insurrection existed, and
asking for 75,000 volunteers to put it down. Lincoln's call for troops forced
other slave states to take sides. Between April and June the legislatures in
Virginia, Arkansas, North Carolina, and Tennessee passed ordinances of secession. The Confederate states now numbered eleven. In July the capital of the
Confederacy was moved from Montgomery, Alabama, to Richmond, Virginia.

The United States government was confident that the secession movement
would quickly collapse before a show of force. But when Union forces were
defeated by the Confederates in the first battle of Bull Run in July 1861,
Lincoln and other northern leaders realized that the war would not be easily
won.

The battle of Bull Run also led to a change in the Confederate flag. Amidst
the smoke of battle and in the absence of a breeze, it was difficult to
distinguish the stars and bars from the stars and stripes. Consequently, a new
Confederate battle flag was designed by General Pierre G. T. Beauregard. It
consisted of a red field with a blue cross of St. Andrew edged with a narrow
white band. Arranged along the blue cross were twelve five-pointed stars, three
on each arm of the cross and one in the center (Figure 169). While there were
only eleven states in the Confederacy, Beauregard hoped that at least one of the
border states where there were strong pro-southern sentiments—Maryland,
Kentucky, or Missouri—would join. The presence of federal troops prevented

this, although in each of those states southern sympathizers did support the Confederate forces.

This new version of the stars and bars battle flag served the Confederate Army for the rest of the war. But for the use of the Confederate Navy and maritime service, as well as the government, the squared battle flag was not adequate. A new flag was designed, using the battle flag as a canton on a white field (Figure 170). This second version of the Confederate national flag was adopted on May 1, 1863. While it had the advantage of being recognized as a distress signal if flown upside down, its disadvantage was that in a calm the canton would be hidden and the white field might be mistaken for a flag of surrender. In an effort to prevent such an occurrence, the Confederate Congress authorized the addition of a wide red vertical stripe at the end of the white fly. This third Confederate national flag was adopted on March 4, 1865, only thirty-six days before General Robert E. Lee surrendered to General Ulysses S. Grant. Therefore the official life of the third Confederate flag was short.

Meantime, there had been a secessionist movement within the Confederacy itself. Pro-Union citizens in the western portion of Virginia had been enabled to secede from the state when Union troops defeated Confederate forces in that region. These Virginians organized a government and elected a governor in June 1861. In February 1862 a constitution for the proposed state of West Virginia was adopted by popular vote, and on June 20, 1863, West Virginia entered the Union. The following July 4, a thirty-fifth star was officially added to the flag (Figure 171). Until the end of the war, however, many flags with thirty-four stars remained in use, for wartime exigencies made it necessary to defer a complete changeover to quieter times.

Fig. 171   A thirty-five star flag

Since President Lincoln did not recognize the right of the southern states to dissolve their ties with the Union, it was appropriate that official flags should still have a star for each of the Confederate states. There were, it is true, some northerners who wanted the flag to embody a visual distinction between secessionist states and those that were loyal, but their views apparently never commanded much attention. Nevertheless, the Civil War was notable for the patriotic fervor it generated, much of which manifested itself in a preoccupation with flags. Certain entirely unofficial flags were produced that had striking designs.

Captain Driver's "Old Glory"

There are a number of flag stories associated with events in the Civil War, but one of the most famous and long remembered concerned the raising of the stars and stripes over Nashville, Tennessee, in 1862 by Captain William Driver.

The captain had settled in Nashville after many years at sea. One of his most prized possessions was the flag that he had named "Old Glory" when it was presented to him as a young man. Driver was in the habit of displaying his thirty-four-star flag on his home on patriotic occasions. But after Tennessee seceded from the union on June 8, 1861, the last state to join the southern Confederacy, the pro-Union Driver family felt uneasy in Nashville. The captain heard reports that pro-Confederate persons in the area had threatened to destroy his flag. So he had the flag sewn into a comforter to hide and preserve it.

For the Driver family, the days of tension came to an end on February 25, 1862, when advance units of the Union army reached Nashville. On hand to greet them was Captain Driver. He brought a captain of an Ohio Regiment to his home, and in the officer's presence he tore open the comforter to reveal the flag. Driver folded the flag, carried it in his arms, and escorted by a group of soldiers, headed for the state house. There he climed to the dome and raised his flag over the city. As he did so, he is reported to have said: "Thank God! I lived to raise Old Glory on the dome of the Capitol of Tennessee; I am now ready to die and go to my forefathers." Until that moment, the term "Old Glory" was simply Driver's personal name for the flag. The publicity surrounding his action brought him fame and gave national standing to his private nickname. Thereafter, "Old Glory" was recognized as a synonym for the United States flag.

204

Fig. 172 "Old Glory" or the Driver Flag

Fig. 173 A thirty-six star flag (artist's conception)

"Old Glory" flew over the capitol of Tennessee overnight. Driver stayed with it. Then, fearful that the strong winds would damage the flag, he took it down and substituted another United States flag for it. The flag was returned to the Driver home where it remained until 1873, when he gave it to his daughter, Mary Jane Roland, prior to her returning home to Nevada after a visit. Mrs. Roland kept the flag until 1922, when she gave it to President Warren G. Harding. The president gave it to the Smithsonian Institution, where it remains. The flag is made of worsted bunting and measures nine feet five inches by seventeen feet. For many years it has been in a poor state of preservation (Figure 172). As this book goes to press, however, plans are underway to restore and exhibit "Old Glory."

Aftermath of War

The ending of the war focused national attention on two questions: what should be done about the freed slaves, and what should be done about permitting the former Confederate states to resume their role in the life of the nation. On the first matter, the Thirteenth Amendment, abolishing slavery, was sent by Congress to the state legislatures for their ratification. As for the southern states, Congress devised a plan whereby they would be "reconstructed" and thus made eligible to return to the Union with all former rights restored. One requirement was ratification of the Thirteenth Amendment. The Radical Republican leaders in Congress, who did not share Lincoln's view that the southern states had never been out of the Union, regarded them as "conquered provinces" on which they could impose any terms they wished.

While these Radical Republicans had acquired considerable power, as the war neared its end they were concerned about support for the Thirteenth Amendment in the north and west. Their search for extra votes led them to accelerate the statehood process for Nevada Territory, which was admitted to the Union on October 31, 1864, even though it lacked sufficient population under the normal rules. On July 4, 1865, the stars in the official flag increased to thirty-six (Figure 173). Nevada ratified the Thirteenth Amendment along

205

Fig. 174   A thirty-seven star flag (artist's
            conception)

Fig. 175   A Centennial flag

with twenty-six other states, and it took effect on December 18, 1865.

The ratification of the Thirteenth Amendment proved to be only one facet of the struggle over Reconstruction. President Andrew Johnson hoped to restore the Union under the moderate formula Lincoln had devised. But Congress had its way, passing the first Reconstruction Act in March 1866. This act divided the south into five military districts subject to martial law. To gain readmittance to the Union each state was compelled to call a constitutional convention with delegates chosen by universal manhood suffrage. These conventions were to establish new state governments that would guarantee Negro suffrage and ratify the Fourteenth Amendment, making the Negro a citizen. This reconstruction act was followed by three others. It was not until 1877 that the last federal troops were withdrawn from South Carolina and Louisiana, thus signaling the end of Reconstruction. So, while the continued use of the flag with its full complement of stars implied acceptance of Lincoln's assertion that the Confederate states had never been out of the Union, in point of fact it was more than a dozen years after the end of the war before all eleven once again became full participants in the Union.

While national politics was being largely dominated by bitter disputes over Reconstruction, the expansion of the national domain during these same postwar years went forward with relatively little fanfare. In 1867 the United States was able to purchase Alaska from the government of Imperial Russia for the sum of $7,200,000. Contemporary discussions in Congress and the press underscored the ignorance of most Americans about Alaska and how irrelevant its acquisition seemed to them. Only gradually would the significance of this tremendous bargain become evident.

Indifference toward the huge territory of Alaska was matched by a total lack of interest in the island of Midway, likewise acquired in 1867. Here, again, only time would show the strategic value of this tiny dot of land in the Pacific.

On the other hand, there was great immediate interest in the admission of Nebraska to the Union. Congress had authorized admission in 1864, but when Nebraskans finally submitted a state constitution it appeared to limit the franchise to white men. President Johnson therefore vetoed it, even though Nebraskans insisted they did not intend to bar nonwhites from voting. Eventually Congress overrode the veto and Nebraska entered the Union on March 1, 1867. On July 4, the thirty-seven star flag became official (Figure 174).

Several design possibilities now presented themselves. One method involved placing the stars in a 8–7–7–7–8 horizontal pattern. A more striking and original conception, though its design was reminiscent in part of the Confederate flag, centers about twenty-one stars in the form of the cross of St. Andrew. A triangle of five stars is located on its side in the area within the arm of the cross adjacent to the hoist. The opposite area of the canton uses three stars on a vertical line and two stars in a horizontal line and extending toward the center of the cross. Finally, the triangular spaces above and below the center of the cross contain three stars each in the shape of triangles. The Mastai collection which contains this flag also contains one that uses the design of an inner and outer oval made of stars.

The Centennial and New Western States

In 1876 the United States celebrated the centennial of its independence. The centennial intensified popular interest in the flag, and many reproductions of earlier designs were manufactured, especially thirteen-star flags. Fanciful designs also enjoyed a vogue; one entrepreneur marketed a flag with a canton on which eighty stars with rays were printed to form the numbers *1776* and *1876* (Figure 175).

As the nation celebrated its one-hundredth birthday, Colorado petitioned for admission to the Union. On August 1, 1876, it became the thirty-eighth state, and on July 4, 1877, the flag with that number of stars became official. One method of accommodating the new star was to stagger rows of stars in a 8–7–8–7–8 pattern. Another horizontal pattern had a 7–6–6–6–6–7 design. At least one flag exists with stars arranged in a double oval, one inside the other, a star in each corner of the canton, and a large star in the center. Still another unofficial design had the stars arranged in vertical rows of 7–6–6–6–6–7.

The centennial of the nation seems to have inspired an outburst of imaginative and unusual star designs. It also engendered great publicity for the Betsy Ross story and its firm implantation in American folklore. Many flags were produced with thirteen stars in a circle for the so-called "Betsy Ross" flag.

Other tremendously popular souvenir items were prints of the famous scene *The Spirit of 76*. This was originally painted for the centennial by Archibald M. Willard, who subsequently did two other renditions. Reproductions of these paintings were sold for at least fifty years, and there was a resurgent interest in the painting and its history during the bicentennial in 1976.

An expedition under Lieutenant Adolphus W. Greely (1881–84) took a thirty-eight star flag to the highest latitude theretofore reached by man, 83

Fig. 176   A thirty-eight star flag used by the Adolphus Greely expedition

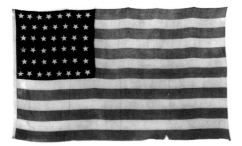

Fig. 177   A forty-four star flag

degrees, 24 minutes (Figure 176). Greely and his party got to within 497 miles of the North Pole—a goal that would continue to inspire brave men for years thereafter.

By the late 1880s several western states were petitioning for admission to the Union. On February 22, 1889, President Grover Cleveland signed a bill that provided for the admission of North Dakota, South Dakota, Montana, and Washington, and these territories became states in November. Flag makers generally anticipated forty-two stars by July 4, 1890. But on July 3 Idaho was admitted, and the next day forty-three stars became the official number. It is doubtful, however, whether there were many correct flags on that Independence Day. No doubt there was some hasty improvisation, but even that was soon rendered obsolete. On July 10 President Benjamin Harrison approved a bill admitting Wyoming, so that on July 4, 1891, the official number of stars totalled forty-four (Figure 177). After that the push for statehood quieted down for a few years, and flag makers were able to get caught up with the proper number of stars. For many American families the transition from the old flag to the new probably meant replacing a thirty-eight star flag with one of forty-four stars. One method of depicting the stars on the new flag was the horizontal pattern of 8–7–7–7–7–8, with the rows of seven stars staggered.

The Annexationist Struggle in Hawaii

In January 1893 Americans living in the Hawaiian Islands revolted and deposed Queen Liliuokalani. With the help of John L. Stevens, the United States minister to the Kingdom of Hawaii, a provisional government was set up. At the request of its leaders Stevens raised the stars and stripes over the government building in Honolulu on February 1, 1893, proclaiming Hawaii as a protectorate of the United States. The flag he raised had thirty-eight stars arranged in a pattern of 8–7–8–7–8. It is still preserved in the Public Archives of Hawaii. A treaty of annexation was signed on February 15, and submitted to the Senate.

Before it could be acted upon, the administration of Benjamin Harrison went out of office and the new president, Grover Cleveland, took over. Five days after his inauguration Cleveland withdrew the Hawaiian treaty from the Senate until he could probe the matter. He sent John H. Blount to Honolulu to investigate the annexation movement. Blount reported that the revolution was started mainly by American aliens with the support of Minister Stevens. Blount's report helped to dampen the annexationist sentiment in the United States and the stars and stripes were hauled down in Honolulu. The American sailors and Marines, whose presence in the city lent support to the revolutionaries, were ordered back to their ships.

The president's efforts to undo the work of the annexationists was hampered by Queen Liliuokalani's desire to punish the plotters. Cleveland instructed the new American minister to Hawaii to secure pledges from the queen that she would be lenient with the conspirators before allowing her to return to the throne. At first the queen refused, and the annexationists did not intend to give up the government. Cleveland placed the matter before the Congress. The Senate agreed unanimously that Hawaii should manage its own affairs without outside interference. On July 4, 1894, the Republic of Hawaii was proclaimed, and Cleveland recognized it on August 8. The American leaders of the new

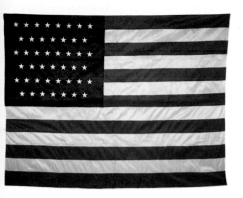

Fig. 178 A forty-five star flag

republic actively propagandized the citizens of the United States for the annexation of the Hawaiian Islands, but the measure had no chance while Cleveland was in office.

After William McKinley replaced Cleveland in the White House, the annexationists signed a new treaty on June 16, 1897, but Democrats in the Senate prevented its ratification. The matter remained pending until the Spanish-American War, when imperialism and patriotic fervor brought about a change of heart on the issue. A joint resolution in favor of annexation easily passed and was signed by McKinley on July 7, 1898. When the news reached Honolulu, a flag of forty-five stars was raised in August 1898. This flag is still preserved in Honolulu.

While the agitation over Hawaii was taking place, the Territory of Utah was ready to enter the Union. Since the annexation of that territory after the Mexican War there had been periodic disputes between the Mormon political leadership and the federal government. One of the most troublesome issues involved the Mormon belief in polygamy. Eventually, however, a compromise was reached and Utah was admitted to the Union on January 4, 1896. On July 4 the stars in the official flag increased to forty-five (Figure 178). A horizontal design to accommodate the new star followed a 8–7–8–7–8–7 pattern.

The Spanish-American War

The forty-five star flag became official at the time of a growing American concern about the island of Cuba. In 1895 there was a new uprising against Spanish authority and harsh attempts to put it down. These events were avidly covered in the American press. A concern in governmental circles for the safety of American lives and property in Cuba led to the sending of the U.S.S. *Maine* to Havana. While in the harbor, the *Maine* was blown up with a heavy loss of life. A subsequent investigation by the Navy Department concluded that the *Maine* had been destroyed by an external explosion, and the finger of guilt was pointed at Spain.

In the midst of a great deal of public uproar, the Congress declared war on Spain as of April 21, 1898. It was a short war. On May 1, the American fleet in the Pacific defeated the Spanish squadron at Manila Bay. Subsequently the United States took possession of the Philippines and of Guam.

Another naval victory was won in July against Spanish ships at Havana. An invasion of the island of Cuba led to the capture and occupation of that island by the Americans. Puerto Rico was also seized. The Spanish government asked for peace terms on July 26. Under the terms of the Treaty of Paris, concluded on December 10, Spain ceded the Philippines, Guam, and Puerto Rico to the United States. All claims and title to Cuba were given up by Spain, and it assumed the liability for the Cuban debt. Cuba remained under the control of a United States Army administration until 1902. Although Cuba became independent at that time the United States maintained a quasi-protectorate over the island until 1934. A treaty with the Cuban government giving the United States the right to maintain a naval base at Guantanamo remains in effect to this day.

In the Philippines, the overthrow of Spanish rule was followed by a challenge to American authority. Emilio Aguinaldo, a Philippine insurrectionist leader, had expected the United States to turn the islands over the the Filipinos after the Spanish-American War. When the United States decided to keep the

Fig. 179 Formal transfer of Hawaiian sovereignty to the United States, August 12, 1898
Leslie's Weekly, *September 15, 1898*

islands, Aguinaldo and his followers waged war against the American occupying forces. Organized resistance to American rule ended in 1899, but guerrilla warfare continued until 1902.

During the Spanish-American War the Hawaiian Islands were annexed to the United States by a joint resolution of Congress on July 7, and officially transferred on August 12, 1898 (Figure 179). A United States expedition, enroute to the Philippines in 1899, claimed possession of Wake Island, a small bit of land 2,325 miles west of Honolulu, and formally occupied the island in 1900. Thus, within a few years of the adoption of the forty-five star flag, it was raised over a wide-ranging collection of territories.

In 1900 the forty-five star flag was carried into China by a small force of American soldiers and Marines, part of an international expedition sent to relieve the foreign legations in Peking during the Boxer Rebellion. The flag was also carried by the United States fleet in its cruise around the world between 1907 and 1909.

Laws Regarding the Flag

Along with the growth of the Union came an increased concern about actions that showed a disrespect for the flag. In 1897 South Dakota became the first state to pass a law protecting the flag from mutilation through political or commercial advertising. Other states enacted similar laws. Some were chal-

210

lenged and struck down as unconstitutional; in other cases the protection of the flag was upheld.

One of the most important challenges came from a Nebraska brewer who tried to market a bottle of beer with a picture of the flag on the label. The Nebraska courts found him guilty of violating the state law against such practices. The case was appealed to the United States Supreme Court. In its ruling on *Halter* v. *Nebraska* the Supreme Court upheld the constitutionality of the Nebraska law. Justice John Marshall Harlan said in part:

"By the statute in question the State has in substance declared that no one subject to its jurisdiction shall use the flag for purposes of trade and traffic, a purpose wholly foreign to that for which it was provided by the Nation. Such a use tends to degrade and to cheapen the Flag in the estimation of the people, as well as to defeat the object of maintaining it as an emblem of National power and National honor. And we cannot hold that any privilege of American citizenship or that any right of personal liberty is violated by a state enactment forbidding the Flag to be used as an advertisement on a bottle of beer."

This decision reinforced the growing propensity of Americans to treat the stars and stripes as an object of veneration. On February 20, 1905 the Congress passed a law prohibiting the registry of any trademark that consisted of "the Flag or coat of arms or other insignia of the United States or any simulation thereof, or of any State or municipality or of any foreign nation." Still, national legislation lagged behind state actions in regard to flag profanation. But the wide disparity in state laws, and the challenges to them, led the proponents of flag legislation to seek a common method of defining abuses. This search led eventually to a National Conference of Commissioners of Uniform State Laws in 1917, and to the drafting of a Uniform Flag Act. The drafters of the act hoped that all state legislatures would enact the proposed law, and thereby create a nationwide uniformity. But by 1980 only fifteen states had enacted the proposed legislation.

New Stars and Standardized Designs

On November 16, 1907, Oklahoma was admitted to the Union as the forty-sixth state. When the question of changing the flag came up, the secretary of the Navy asked the secretary of war to establish a joint board of Army and Navy officers to recommend a new star arrangement. Admiral George Dewey, the hero of the battle of Manila Bay, was chosen as the senior member of the board. The plan it submitted, adopted without the formal approval of President Theodore Roosevelt, featured stars in a 8–7–8–8–7–8 horizontal arrangement (Figure 180). Probably the most famous event associated with the use of the forty-six star flag was the discovery of the North Pole by Cmdr. Robert E. Peary on April 6, 1909. Peary photographed a group of Eskimos and Matthew Henson, his American Negro associate, with the stars and stripes and other flags at the pole (Figure 181). The news of the flag-raising at the top of the world was received by telegraph on September 6, and stimulated much public interest in the frozen north.

Two years later public attention turned to the southwest where Arizona and New Mexico were seeking admission to the Union. In 1910 the Congress had

Fig. 180   A forty-six star flag

Fig. 181   The stars and stripes at the
North Pole
National Geographic Society

passed the necessary enabling legislation, but various delays held up the admission of New Mexico until January 6, 1912, and of Arizona until February 14. This meant that two new stars would be added to the flag on July 4. The Joint Army-Navy Board headed by Admiral Dewey met again and worked out the star arrangement. There were forty-eight stars in six horizontal rows of eight. This arrangement became official on July 4, 1912 (Figure 182).

The concern for standardized design evidenced in the work of the Army-Navy Board led to two mandates by President Taft. The first, an executive order dated June 24, specified the relative proportions of the entire flag as well as the star arrangement. It also stipulated that a single point of each star was to be upward. This order was the outgrowth of an investigation by the Army-Navy Board which had found that the executive branch had flags in sixty-six different sizes and proportions. The number of approved sizes was limited to twelve.

On October 29, 1912, President Taft issued a second executive order that modified the earlier one. The position and size of each star was to be in accordance with the Navy Department plan. Presidential approval was given to the longstanding practice of using thirteen-star flags on small boats of the Navy.

During the presidency of Woodrow Wilson these executive orders were revoked and a new one substituted on May 29, 1916. This changed the earlier orders in only one substantive way, ending the Navy practice of using thirteen-star flags in boats. It also specified a standard design for the flag of the chief executive. Prior to this time, the Army and Navy and other departments had different flags for use in connection with a visit by the president. Wilson asked Assistant Secretary of the Navy Franklin D. Roosevelt and Commodore Byron McCandless, an aide to the secretary of the Navy, to devise a standard design. They recommended the presidential coat of arms on a blue field with a white star in each of the four corners, and President Wilson accepted this. In the course of his work with the Navy Department, Roosevelt discovered that there was no flag for the assistant secretary of the Navy, so he promptly designed one that was adopted.

212

Fig. 182   A forty-eight star flag

Fig. 183   Flag-making shop in the Brooklyn
Navy Yard, July 1917
Library of Congress

The Forty-Eight Star Flag

The flag of forty-eight stars is associated with many momentous events in history (Figure 183). Two weeks after the United States entered World War I on the side of the Allies, its flag was hoisted over the highest spire of the British Parliament building—the first foreign flag ever to fly there. During the war the stars and stripes was carried to France and later to the Rhineland during the postwar occupation of Germany. It was used in Russia during the Allied interventions at Murmansk and in Siberia. It waved in Paris during the discussions that led to the Treaty of Versailles and to the establishment of the League of Nations. It covered the coffin of the unknown soldier when he was buried at Arlington National Cemetery on November 11, 1921.

The flag of forty-eight stars was also carried by Lieutenant Commander Richard E. Byrd, U.S.N. (Retired) on the first airplane flight over the North Pole, on May 9, 1926. Bird dropped the specially weighted flag at the spot he calculated to be the top of the earth. On November 29, 1929, Byrd made a flight over the South Pole to honor the memory of Floyd Bennet, a former chief aviation pilot in the United States Navy and the pilot on Byrd's North Pole flight. Byrd dropped an American flag weighted with a stone from Bennet's grave.

The forty-eight star flag is associated with the depression years of the 1930's, with the bonus marchers, and with many events during the presidency of Franklin D. Roosevelt. The Roosevelt administration also took further steps in the direction of standardization. In 1934 the exact shades of red, white, and blue to be used were specified and given numbers in the Federal Standard Stock Catalog. Henceforth there would be no reason for any color discrepancy between flags manufactured by private firms and those made under government contract.

Fig. 184 *Flag over the U.S.S.* Yorktown,
October 1944
U.S. Navy

During World War II the forty-eight star flag was carried to every fighting front from the Arctic to the deserts of North Africa, from the jungles of Burma and New Guinea to the major cities of Western Europe (Figure 184). The flag that flew over the United States Capitol on December 7, 1941, the day of the attack on Pearl Harbor, was subsequently raised over the captured enemy capitals of Rome, Berlin, and Tokyo. One of the most famous flag raisings involved a group of United States Marines on Mount Suribachi during the fight over Iwo Jima in the Pacific (Figure 185). The stars and stripes was attached to a piece of pipe and elevated for a second time over the mountain on February 23, 1945. This particular raising was captured by news photographer Joe Rosenthal in a dramatic moment. The picture subsequently inspired the scene to be commemorated in bronze in the Marine Corps Memorial in Washington, D.C.

Fig. 185   On Iwo Jima, replacing the small flag first raised on Mount Suriba-chi by a larger flag, February 23, 1945
U.S. Marine Corps

The Flag Code and the Pledge of Allegiance

It was not until 1942 that Congress codified the existing rules and customs pertaining to the use of the flag. World War I had seen an increase in patriotic feeling and a concern about the need for proper respect for the flag. For many years patriotic groups had been expressing concern about standardizing procedures for its display. The Army and Navy had evolved their own customs but there remained wide divergences in civilian practices. On June 14, 1923, four months after the War Department had issued a circular on flag usage, representatives of sixty-eight patriotic and civic organizations met in Washington, D.C., to draft a uniform code of flag etiquette. They accepted most of the War Department's code, and subsequently the department published this code in pamphlet form.

215

Almost twenty years passed, however, before a flag code became national law. On June 22, 1942, Congress passed a joint resolution, which was subsequently amended by a joint resolution of December 22, 1942, that became Public Law 829, Chapter 806, 77th Congress, 2d session. This law not only prescribed exact rules for the use and display of the flag, but also embodies sections on the playing of the national anthem and on the pledge of allegiance. Later, on June 14, 1959, President Eisenhower approved a Congressional resolution to amend the flag code. By the terms of Public Law 396, 83rd Congress, 2d session, the pledge of allegiance was revised to include the words "under God" after the word "Nation," so it now reads: "one Nation under God indivisible, with liberty and justice for all."

It has long been customary for school children to recite the pledge of allegiance in their classrooms. In 1940 this practice was challenged by the parents of two children in the Minersville, Pennsylvania, school district on the grounds that it was offensive to members of the Jehovah's Witnesses religious sect. The two children were expelled from school for refusing to salute the flag in the daily exercise. Eventually the case went to the United States Supreme Court. In *Minersville School District* v. *Gobitis,* the Court upheld the school board, ruling that the ritual flag salute was intended to build a sense of national unity, and that "national unity is the basis of national security." The Court argued that "the ultimate foundation of a free society is the binding tie of cohesive sentiment." Since the state legislature saw the flag salute as a means toward achieving cohesive sentiment, the law ought to be respected.

No doubt the justices were influenced by the patriotic spirit of the times, on the rise since the outbreak of World War II in Europe in 1939. Yet the decision was not in keeping with the tradition of protecting dissident minorities from coercion. It was not destined to stand for long. In 1943 a similar case in West Virginia was appealed to the Supreme Court. This time some of the justices changed their mind. In *West Virginia State Board of Education* v. *Barnette* the majority ruled that a refusal to salute the flag did not interfere with the rights of others, and that the West Virginia law was contrary to the First Amendment. As a result of this decision, state laws requiring a compulsory flag salute were declared unconstitutional.

The New Presidential Flag

A concern about flags during the war years also led to a change in the presidential flag. When Congress created the five-star military ranks, general of the Army and fleet admiral, in December 1944, President Roosevelt decided that it was no longer appropriate for the presidential flag to display only four stars. He asked his former collaborator, Commodore McCandless, to design a new presidential flag. McCandless sent several designs based on earlier American flags to Roosevelt, but Roosevelt died without seeing them. His successor, Harry S Truman, saw the sketches in June 1945 and suggested to McCandless that the flag have forty-eight stars arranged in a circle around the coat of arms. McCandless had a new design to show Truman in August 1945, following his return from the Potsdam Conference. Truman was pleased, and sought reactions from the War and Navy departments.

While the matter was being reviewed in the War Department, Arthur E.

Fig. 186   The Presidential flag

DuBois, the chief of the heraldic section of the office of the quartermaster general, pointed out that the eagle used on the presidential seal and coat of arms was not in accordance with that on the Great Seal. Truman therefore asked DuBois to redesign the presidential seal, arms, and flag so that they conformed both to the Great Seal and to proper heraldic custom. Truman also decided that the eagle on the new design should be in full color instead of in white as formerly. The new presidential flag consisted of a brown eagle facing the viewer's left, with white tail feathers, white head and neck, and a yellow beak, bearing the red, white, and blue shield on its chest. The eagle grasps a green olive branch in its right talon and white arrows in its left. In its beak it holds a white banner on which the words "E Pluribus Unum" are printed in black. Radiating above the eagle's head are a series of golden rays that pass through thirteen round cumulus clouds of varied sizes that taper away evenly to the right and left in a small arc. Surrounding the eagle is a circle of forty-eight stars. The background is blue. An executive order dated October 25, 1945, prescribed for the first time the design of the president's coat of arms and seal, and provided for the change in the presidential flag (Figure 186). President Truman explained the changes in his news conference of October 25.

Night and Day Display of the Flag

During and after World War II there was a renewed interest in having the flag fly both night and day at special locations. The first instance seems to have been in 1861 in Taos, New Mexico, when Kit Carson and Captain Smith H. Simpson, concerned about the formation of the Confederate States, nailed the

217

stars and stripes to the flag pole in the town plaza as a symbol of loyalty to the Union. Other citizens kept watch over the flag pole day and night to see that the flag was not removed. And so a tradition was born that continues to this day.

In 1894 Congress passed legislation providing for the daily hoisting of the flag over the east and west fronts of the Capitol. During World War I, in response to popular sentiment, these flags were kept flying both night and day, and the custom has continued since 1918. On the other hand, flags are flown over the Senate and House wings of the Capitol only when those bodies are in session.

Sometime before World War I it became customary to fly the flag both night and day, as a mark of special honor, over the grave of Francis Scott Key in Mount Olivet Cemetery, Frederick, Maryland. During the next few years two other communities adopted the practice. Between 1917 and 1952 the flag flew twenty-four hours a day on Mount Stover, near Colton, California. In the latter year the flag pole was destroyed by some mining work and was not replaced. During World War I the citizens of Deadwood, South Dakota, adopted the practice of flying the flag continuously on top of the Brown Rocks near the city. This practice was abandoned after the war, but was revived during World War II and has continued since then.

On the fifteenth anniversary of Armistice Day, citizens of the city of Worcester, Massachusetts, dedicated a memorial to the dead of World War I. Because it seemed in keeping with the sentiment of the memorial to display the stars and stripes continuously, a ninety-foot pole was erected for the purpose; the flag has flown there since November 11, 1933.

These long-established local customs were given official sanction in a Joint Resolution of Congress of December 22, 1942. After World War II the practice spread. On July 2, 1948, President Truman proclaimed that the flag was to be displayed around the clock at Fort McHenry National Monument and Historic Shrine, Baltimore. Since May 30, 1949, the flag has flown continuously over the monument marking the site of Francis Scott Key's birthplace, Terra Rubra Farm, Carroll County, Keymar, Maryland. On March 26, 1954, Congress granted permission to fly the flag twenty-four hours a day over Flag House Square in Baltimore. A replica of the fifteen-star flag that flew over Fort McHenry during the War of 1812 is also displayed here both night and day. On July 12, 1961, President John F. Kennedy authorized the flag to be flown day and night at the Marine Corps Memorial in Arlington, Virginia, across the river from Washington, D.C. Thus the flag is now flown day and night at four places by presidential proclamation.

Another indication of a growing public interest in ceremonies relating to the flag was the establishment of Flag Day, first proclaimed by President Woodrow Wilson on June 14, 1916—the anniversary of the Flag Resolution of 1777. While Flag Day was celebrated in various communities for years after Wilson's proclamation, it was not until August 3, 1949, that President Truman signed an act of Congress designating June 14 of each year as National Flag Day.

Statehood for Alaska and Hawaii

During the presidency of Dwight D. Eisenhower longstanding questions about Alaska and Hawaii were resolved. Hawaii had been a territory since 1900,

Fig. 187 A forty-nine star flag

Alaska since 1912. Judge James Wickersham, the territorial delegate of Alaska to the United States Congress, introduced the first statehood bill for Alaska on March 30, 1916. It did not pass. A bill for statehood for Hawaii was introduced in the Congress in 1919 and it also failed. But these rejections did not end the desire for statehood in either territory. In 1933 Alaska's delegate introduced another statehood bill that also failed. Similar bills were introduced in every Congress thereafter.

The great increase in domestic and foreign air travel following World War II, as well as America's far-flung military commitments after that conflict, helped to bring home to the citizens of the United States the shrinking size of the world. Prejudices against admitting Alaska and Hawaii because they were not a part of the continental United States no longer seemed to have relevance in an age of air travel. Yet there was opposition to the statehood measures in both the major political parties. Democrats thought that Hawaii would be a Republican stronghold, and Republicans were afraid that Alaska would go Democratic. Southerners felt that the two new states would support the cause of racial integration then being discussed in the Congress and in the land. In the case of Hawaii, there was also the additional argument that the island's economy would be dominated by the International Longshoremen's and Ware-housemen's Union—a union that allegedly had a large number of Communists in its membership. Still others objected to the fact that only one-third of the population of Hawaii belonged to the Caucasian race. Nevertheless, the Democratic party's platform in both the elections of 1948 and 1952 pledged immediate statehood to Alaska and Hawaii. The Republican platform of 1952 urged immediate statehood for both territories "under an equitable enabling act."

Respect for the Flag

There was also a renewal of interest in laws to enforce respect for the flag. During World War I various states passed laws forbidding verbal abuse of the flag. Congress enacted similar legislation in 1917, but it expired in 1921. Four years later the Attorney General of the United States gave an opinion that in the absence of a national law against flag profanation, the states could act on the question. He added that if Congress wished to assume control it had the power under the Constitution to do so. In 1947 Congress enacted legislation that applied to the District of Columbia. But while this law forbade acts whereby a flag might be defaced, it did not attempt to ban words that might be considered disrespectful.

When Eisenhower won the election of 1952 he took steps to fulfill his party's pledges. Believing that Hawaii had a better case, Eisenhower called upon the Congress in his first State of the Union message to grant it statehood. Congress did nothing for the statehood prospects of either territory. In January 1957 Eisenhower recommended to Congress statehood for both Hawaii and Alaska. At this time there was a special interest in the future of Alaska, for oil was discovered on the Kenai Peninsula. Committees in both the Senate and the House of Representatives presented Alaska statehood bills in the summer of 1957. One of these passed the House in May 1958 and the Senate in June. On July 7, 1958, Eisenhower signed the bill granting statehood to Alaska. It was formally admitted to the Union on January 3, 1959 (Figure 187).

219

Fig. 188   *President Eisenhower and the*
fifty-star flag
U.S. Army

The first forty-nine star flag was made in the Army Quartermaster Depot at Philadelphia, and was used in the White House ceremony when Eisenhower signed the proclamation admitting Alaska to the Union. Subsequently this flag was carried to Philadelphia by Senator Hugh Scott of Pennsylvania, who gave it to the mayor of Philadelphia to raise over Independence Hall on July 4. After these ceremonies Scott gave the flag to his colleague, Senator Ernest Gruening of Alaska, who, in turn, delivered it to Governor William A. Eagan to be flown over the state capitol at Juneau. This flag was later given to the Alaskan State Museum for preservation.

Once Alaska was in the Union, the movement to admit Hawaii intensified, and President Eisenhower signed the Hawaiian Statehood Bill on March 18, 1959. Subsequently, on August 21, he signed a proclamation formally admitting Hawaii into the Union. That same day Eisenhower signed an executive order adding the fiftieth star to the flag as of July 4, 1960. The arrangement of the stars was changed from seven staggered rows of seven to nine alternate rows of six and five. The new flag was previewed by President Eisenhower on the day he signed the executive order (Figure 188). The fifty-star flag was raised over Iolani Palace in Honolulu, the state capitol, on July 4, 1960. Beside it flew the old flag of the Kingdom of Hawaii, which had become the territorial flag in 1903, and now became the state flag. In accordance with a precedent established with the admission of Alaska, at 12:01 A.M. on Monday, July 4, 1960, the fifty-star flag was formally raised over Fort McHenry by the secretary of the interior. The next day this flag was flown over Federal Hall in New York City, and then it was donated to the Fort McHenry Museum.

Fig. 189   *The stars and stripes on the moon*
National Aeronautics and Space
Administration

The Flag on the Moon

Undoubtedly the most momentous event thus far associated with the fifty-star flag was its raising on the moon. On Sunday, July 20, 1969, Colonel Neil A. Armstrong and Colonel Edwin E. Aldrin, Jr., safely landed their spacecraft on the moon while Colonel Michael Collins stayed with the Apollo 11 mother craft. Because of atmospheric conditions on the moon, the flag that Armstrong and Aldrin left there was mounted in a wire frame (Figure 189). A duplicate of this flag is preserved in the National Air and Space Museum, Smithsonian Institution, Washington, D.C.

As the United States celebrated the bicentennial of its independence in 1976, an unmanned American space craft, marked with the United States flag, made a successful landing on Mars and sent the first pictures of that mysterious planet back to the earth. Thus, in the course of its two-hundred-year history, the flag that was to represent a new constellation among the nations of the world was carried not only to the far corners of the globe, but also out into the universe.

Back on earth another kind of probing had been going on for years. This was the effort to determine the limits of free speech and the relationship of the flag to symbolic acts. The 1950's and the early years of the 1960's saw a number of public action and demonstrations in support of civil rights. In the trials that followed the arrests of participants in such activities, symbolic expressions were recognized as legal. The Supreme Court stated that the First and Fourteenth Amendments to the Constitution protected those individuals who were communicating ideas by marching, picketing, and patroling on streets and highways.

During the Vietnam War some of those opposed to that conflict argued that the burning of draft cards was a form of symbolic speech, and that laws prohibiting it were constitutional. The Supreme Court disagreed and upheld the convictions of draft card burners.

Apparently prompted by the burning of draft cards, Congress decided to amend the law dealing with flag profanation in the District of Columbia. On July 5, 1968 it passed a law "to prohibit desecration of the flag, and for other purposes," which became the major federal legislation on the subject. The law states that: "Whoever knowingly casts contempt upon any flag of the United States by publicly mutilating, defacing, defiling, burning, or trampling upon it shall be fined not more than $1,000 or imprisoned for not more than one year, or both." The constitutionality of this law was soon challenged.

On January 20, 1969, while waiting for the start of the inaugural parade in Washington, D.C., Thomas Wayne Joyce removed a small American flag from a stick he was carrying, tore the fabric so that it could be tied to his right index finger, and waved his right hand above his head in a *V* sign. A detective who witnessed the act arrested Joyce for mutilating a flag and a District of Columbia court found him guilty. In appealing his case, Joyce argued that the law against desecration was too broad and unconstitutionally vague, and that it abridged his freedom of speech. The United States Court of Appeals of the District of Columbia rejected these arguments. It ruled that there was a difference between physical acts and free speech, and that the United States had a substantial, genuine and important interest in protecting the flag.

Sixteen months after Joyce's action a flag was burned in Arizona as part of a protest against the war in Vietnam. On May 6, 1970 a group of students assembled in the R.O.T.C. building at the University of Arizona. Sharon K. Crosson and another woman carried a fifty-star United States flag into the gathering. Mrs. Crosson put the flag on the floor, sprayed it with a substance from a can, and lighted it with a match. Several of the bystanders also threw lighted matches on the flag. These actions were observed by undercover agents of the Arizona Department of Public Safety, and Mrs. Crosson was arrested, tried and convicted for publicly burning a United States flag. She was sentenced to four months in jail and fined. Crosson appealed her case and the District Court of Arizona found that her action was symbolic speech, agreeing with her contention that the state law against flag desecration should be declared unconstitutional.

The case was then referred to the United States Court of Appeals, 9th District, which on May 26, 1972, ruled against Mrs. Crosson. It struck down the argument about symbolic speech, and found her guilty of violating the federal law against flag desecration. It ruled that the law was not unconstitutionally vague, and that the sentence did not constitute cruel and unusual punishment. So, in both the Joyce and Crosson cases the courts upheld the federal law against flag desecration.

With the end of the Vietnam War in 1975 public protests by Americans that involved acts of disrespect to the flag became rare. The Bicentennial years, and especially the public celebrations in 1976 and 1977, provided an opportunity for Americans to reflect upon their heritage and on the ideas and symbols that united them. In 1976 Congress further clarified points in the laws regarding individual conduct during the playing of the national anthem and the manner of delivering the Pledge of Allegiance, and issued a recodification of rules and customs regarding the flag, including provisions for its display over twenty-four hour periods.

Displaying the flag in public over individual, business and local government properties became very important following the seizure of the United States Embassy in Teheran, Iran, in 1979. Americans were offended by television pictures of Iranians burning the United States flag and they were outraged and humiliated when Iranian militants forcibly detained fifty-two American citizens in Iran for more than a year. Throughout that ordeal American homes and American communities showed their continued concern for their countrymen by displaying the flag. When the captives were finally released and returned home in February 1981 they received a tumultuous welcome that was underscored by a lavish display of flags.

What does the flag symbolize? Over the years statesmen, legislators, judges and citizens have given various definitions. To Justice Felix Frankfurter of the United States Supreme Court it was "the symbol of our national life." At least two federal courts defined it as "the symbol of our national unity, transcending all internal differences, however large, within the framework of the Constitution." Robert G. Ingersoll required a paragraph to define what the flag symbolized. For him, it was, among other things, "the emblem of equal rights. It means free hands, free lips, self-government, and the sovereignty of the individual. . . ." During a 1967 debate in the House of Representatives over the flag profanation law, it also took a Congressman a full paragraph to define the symbolism of the flag. These difficulties suggest that perhaps Woodrow Wilson was closest to the mark when in 1917 he defined the flag as "the emblem of our unity, our power, our thought and purpose as a nation. It has no other character than that which we give it from generation to generation."

For many Americans their sentiments about the flag are not something that they can or choose to define. They are as individual as personality, as private as a family matter, and as personal as religion.

Notes

The political pattern of the growth of the union is recounted in standard textbook accounts as well as in encyclopedia articles and books on the various states. Flag information on the various states may be found in Quaife, Weig and Appleman, in Eggenberger, and in books by Grace R. Cooper. Artistic and unusual star patterns are illustrated in the work of Boleslaw and Marie Mastai, *The Stars and the Stripes.*

Legal and constitutional questions relating to the flag can be conveniently reviewed in Alfred H. Kelly and Winfred A. Harrison, *The American Constitution: Its Origins and Development,* 3d ed. (New York, 1963). The *Statutes at Large* contain the texts of the laws and executive orders printed in the *Federal Register.* Most flag books carry the text of the flag code of 1942, amended 1959, as an appendix.

For information on the presidential flag see Quaife, Weig and Appleman, and for the change during President Truman's administration see *Public Papers of the Presidents of the United States: Harry S. Truman, 1945* (Washington, 1961), document 175 and note 1.

For a discussion of the question of flag profanation see Emmet V. Mittlebeeler, "Flag Profanation and the Law," *Kentucky Law Journal,* 60 (1972), 885–930. On *Joyce v. United States* see *U.S. Court of Appeals, District of Columbia Circuit,* vol. 147, pp. 128–49. For the details of the flag burning in Arizona see *Crosson v. Silver, Federal Supplement,* vol. 319, pp. 1084–90; and *U.S. v. Crosson, Federal Reporter,* 2d ser., vol. 462, pp. 96–111.

Conclusion

Out of the American protests against Parliamentary regulations following the end of the Seven Years War, there emerged a desire to express deeply held sentiments by symbols. For a time cries of "Wilkes and Liberty" and "45" sufficed, but these were replaced by an emphasis on the single word "Liberty" and the formation of organizations known as the Sons of Liberty. These Sons of Liberty manifested their sentiments by the use of Liberty trees, the erection of Liberty poles, and the flying of Liberty flags of various designs.

The use of red and white striped flags symbolizing the unity of the thirteen colonies began shortly before the Revolution. It was an attractive symbol, and one that European artists and illustrators continued to use both during and after the Revolution. These stripes were combined with the British Union Jack to produce the Continental or Grand Union flag that waved over Esek Hopkins's flagship and George Washington's headquarters at the siege of Boston. It was a flag that was widely used at sea, and it received the first foreign recognition when Danish officials at St. Croix and the Dutch authorities on the island of St. Eustatius acknowledged it.

Almost a year passed after the Declaration of Independence before a new flag was adopted by the Continental Congress. Even then the adoption was gradual and subject to varied interpretations. Evidence of its use over military installations comes very late in the war.

A tendency toward many variations in the star pattern and in the dimensions of the flag was evident during much of the nineteenth century. The Flag Act of 1818 fixed the number of horizontal stripes at thirteen, and set the precedent that the star arrangement was determined by the president. While official flags tended to use flags with stars in horizontal arrangements, unofficial flags, especially those used in the merchant marine, used a wide and colorful variety of star patterns. But by the late nineteenth century the increase in the number of stars to be arranged tended to make even the unofficial flags follow a pattern of horizontal lines. The use of the stars and stripes by the Army was a gradual process. Artillery units were given the flag in 1834, infantry units in 1841, and cavalry organizations in 1845. The stars and stripes was not carried into battle by the United States Army until the Mexican War.

An executive order issued in 1912 established the relative proportions of the flag and the star arrangement. Later, when Alaska and Hawaii entered the Union, those stars were added to the flag, adapting the traditional horizontal arrangement.

225

Public interest in the history and display of the flag grew slowly. The circumstances surrounding the Civil War led to a great deal of public manifestation of sentiment for the national flag. These feelings were revived again during the centennial celebrations of 1876, and were popularized by the legend that Betsy Ross made the first stars and stripes flag. Despite historical refutations through the years, the legend is still presented as fact in many schools.

American involvement in the Spanish-American War and in World War I and World War II stimulated patriotic sentiments and interest in the flag. In 1942 Congress codified various rules and customs concerning the flag and the pledge of allegiance. The years since World War II have seen the refinement of various laws and regulations concerning the flag. As Americans celebrated the two-hundredth anniversary of their independence they learned that their flag had been landed on Mars. On the earth and in the United States, the two-hundredth anniversary of the adoption of the stars and stripes flag found most Americans concerned about it only on national holidays or on occasions when it was publicly insulted. Otherwise it had become an accepted part of the decoration of most public buildings and a symbol regarded as appropriate to almost any setting where the citizens gather together.

If modern Americans did not speak of the flag in the same poetic and romantic terms as their 19th century forebears, it is clear that it is still regarded with affection and respect. For many it connotes a sense of unity, and a reminder of the best instincts of the people and the nation.

The History of the Pledge of Allegiance to the Flag

"I pledge allegiance to the flag of the United States of America and to the Republic for which it stands, one Nation under God, indivisible, with liberty and justice for all."

The original pledge was drawn up in the office of *The Youth's Companion* magazine in Boston and appeared in the issue for September 8, 1892. It was published to celebrate the 400th anniversary of the discovery of America, and was first used in the public schools to celebrate Columbus Day, October 12, 1892. The pledge was re-printed in leaflet form, and thousands were sent by the magazine to schools throughout the country to mark the anniversary.

Several years later a controversy developed among the descendants of two former staff members of the *Youth's Companion*, Francis Bellamy and James Upham, as to who was the author of the pledge. To resolve the question, Colonel James A. Moss, U.S. Army (Retired) and the United States Flag Association of Washington, D.C., appointed a committee of experts in 1939. The committee consisted of two professors of American history, Charles C. Tansill and Bernard Mayo, and a professor of political science, W. Reed West. The committee weighed carefully the evidence presented by the opposing families, and decided unanimously in favor of Bellamy.

When first published, the pledge read "my flag" rather than "the flag of the United States." When representatives of various patriotic organizations came together on June 14, 1923, for the first National Flag Conference, a change in the wording was adopted. The rationale for the change was that it prevented ambiguity among foreign-born children and adults, who might have the flag of their native land in mind when reciting the pledge.

The pledge received the official recognition of Congress in an Act approved on June 22, 1942. The phrase "under God" was added to the pledge by an act of Congress passed on June 14, 1954. At that time, President Dwight D. Eisenhower said that "in this way we are reaffirming the transcendence of religious faith in America's heritage and future; in this way we shall constantly strengthen those spiritual weapons which forever will be our country's most powerful resource in peace and war."

The Meaning of the Colors in the Flag

Sentimental writers and orators sometimes ascribe meanings to the colors in the flag. The practice is erroneous, as are statements on this subject attributed to George Washington and other founders of the country.

Charles Thomson, Secretary of the Continental Congress, reporting to Congress on the Seal of the United States, stated: "The colours of the pales [the vertical stripes] are those used in the flag of the United States of America; White signifies purity and innocence, Red, hardiness & valour, and Blue, the color of the Chief [the broad band above the stripes] signifies vigilence, perseverance & justice."

The American's Creed

"I believe in the United States of America as a Government of the people by the people, for the people, whose just powers are derived from the consent of the governed; a democracy in a Republic; a sovereign Nation of many sovereign States; a perfect Union, one and inseparable; established upon those principles of freedom, equality, justice, and humanity for which American patriots sacrificed their lives and fortunes.

I therefore believe it is my duty to my Country to love it; to support its Constitution; to obey its laws; to respect its flag, and to defend it against all enemies."

The American's Creed was the result of a nationwide contest for writing a National Creed, which would be a brief summary of the American political faith founded upon things fundamental in American history and tradition. The contest was the idea of Henry Sterling Chapin, Commissioner of Education of New York State. Over three thousand entries were received, and William Tyler Page was declared to be the winner. James H. Preston, the mayor of Baltimore, presented an award to Page in the House of Representatives Office Building on April 3, 1918. The speaker of the House of Representatives and the commissioner of education of the state of New York accepted the Creed for the United States, and the proceedings relating to the award were printed in the *Congressional Record* of April 13, 1918. It was a time when patriotic sentiments were very much in vogue. The United States had been a participant in World War I only a little over a year at the time the Creed was adopted.

The author of the Creed, William Tyler Page, was a descendant of John Page, who had come to America in 1650 and had settled in Williamsburg, Virginia. Another ancestor, Carter Braxton, had signed the Declaration of Independence. Still another ancestor, John Tyler, was the tenth president of the United States. William Tyler Page had come to Washington at the age of thirteen to serve as a Capitol page. Later he became an employee of the Capitol building and served in that capacity for almost sixty-one years. In 1919 he was elected clerk of the House. Thirteen years later, when the Democrats again became a majority party, they created for Page the office of minority clerk of the House of Representatives. He held this position for the remainder of his life.

Referring to the Creed, Page said: "It is the summary of the fundamental principles of the American political faith as set forth in its greatest documents, its worthiest traditions, and its greatest leaders." His wording of the Creed used passages and phrases from the Declaration of Independence, the Preamble to the Constitution, Lincoln's Gettysburg Address, and Daniel Webster's reply to Robert Y. Hayne in the Senate in 1830.

Laws and Legal Developments Regarding the Flag

U. S. Code. 1976 Edition; Vol. 1, pp. 277–279

The following sections of previous laws were codified and enacted into positive law by Congress on July 30, 1947, and subsequently amended by a law of October 31, 1951. Other additions were made by an Executive Order of January 3, 1959, later replaced by an Executive Order of August 21, 1959; and by an amendment to section 3 on July 5, 1968.

TITLE 4 *Flag and Seal, Seat of Government, and the States*

CHAPTER 1—THE FLAG

Section 1. Flag; stripes and stars on

The flag of the United States shall be thirteen horizontal stripes, alternate red and white; and the union of the flag shall be forty-eight stars, white in a blue field.
(Source: Act of July 30, 1947, *U.S. Statutes at Large,* vol. 61, p. 642, chapter 389)

EXECUTIVE ORDER NO. 10834. PROPORTIONS AND SIZES OF FLAGS AND POSITION OF STARS August 24, 1959.

WHEREAS the State of Hawaii has this day been admitted into the Union; and

WHEREAS section 2 of title 4 of the United States Code [section 2 of this title] provides as follows: "On the admission of a new State into the Union one star shall be added to the union of the flag; and such addition shall take effect on the fourth day of July then next succeeding such admission."; and

WHEREAS the Federal Property and Administrative Services Act of 1949 (63 Stat. 377), as amended, authorizes the President to prescribe policies and directives governing the procurement and directives governing the procurement and utilization of property by executive agencies; and

WHEREAS the interests of the Government require that orderly and reasonable provision be made for various matters pertaining to the flag and that appropriate regulations governing the procurement and utilization of national flags and union jacks by executive agencies be prescribed:

NOW, THEREFORE, by virtue of the authority vested in me as President of the United States and as Commander in Chief of the armed forces of the United States, and the Federal Property and Administrative Services Act of 1949, as amended, it is hereby ordered as follows:

Part I—Design of the Flag

Section 1. The flag of the United States shall have thirteen horizontal stripes, alternate red and white, and a union consisting of white stars on a field of blue.

Sec. 2. The positions of the stars in the union of the flag and in the union jack shall be as indicated on the attachment to this order, which is hereby made a part of this order.

Sec. 3. The dimensions of the constituent parts of the flag shall conform to the proportions set forth in the attachment referred to in section 2 of this order.

Part II—Regulations Governing Executive Agencies

Sec. 21. The following sizes of flags are authorized for executive agencies:

Size	Dimensions of flag	
	Hoist (width)	Fly (length)
	Feet	*Feet*
(1)	20.00	38.00
(2)	10.00	19.00
(3)	8.95	17.00
(4)	7.00	11.00
(5)	5.00	9.50
(6)	4.33	5.50
(7)	3.50	6.65
(8)	3.00	4.00
(9)	3.00	5.70
(10)	2.37	4.50
(11)	1.32	2.50

Sec. 22. Flags manufactured or purchased for the use of executive agencies:

(a) Shall conform to the provisions of Part I of this order, except as may be otherwise authorized pursuant to the provisions of section 24, or except as otherwise authorized by the provisions of section 21, of this order.

(b) Shall conform to the provisions of section 21 of this order, except as may be otherwise authorized pursuant to the provisions of section 24 of this order.

Sec. 23. The exterior dimensions of each union jack manufactured or purchased for executive agencies shall equal the respective exterior dimensions of the union of a flag of a size authorized by or pursuant to this order. The size of the union jack flown with the national flag shall be the same as the size of the union of that national flag.

Sec. 24. (a) The Secretary of Defense in respect of procurement for the Department of Defense (including military colors) and the Administrator of General Services in respect of procurement for executive agencies other than the Department of Defense may, for cause which the Secretary or the Administrator, as the case may be, deems sufficient, make necessary minor adjustments in one or more of the dimensions or proportionate dimensions prescribed by this order, or authorize proportions or sizes other than those prescribed by section 3 or section 21 of this order.

(b) So far as practicable, (1) the actions of the Secretary of Defense under the provisions of section 24(a) of this order, as they relate to the various organizational elements of the Department of Defense, shall be coordinated, and (2) the Secretary and the Administrator shall mutually coordinate their actions under that section.

Sec. 25. Subject to such limited exceptions as the Secretary of Defense in respect of the Department of Defense, and the Administrator of General Services in respect of executive agencies other than the Department of Defense, may approve, all national flags and union jacks now in the possession of executive agencies, or hereafter acquired by executive agencies under contracts awarded prior to the date of this order, including those so possessed or so required by the General Services Administration for distribution to other agencies, shall be utilized until unserviceable.

Part III—General Provisions

Sec. 31. The flag prescribed by Executive Order No. 10798 of January 3, 1959, shall be the official flag of the United States until July 4, 1960, and on that date the flag prescribed by Part I of this order shall become the official flag of the United States; but this section shall neither derogate from section 24 or section 25 of this order nor preclude the procurement, for executive agencies, of flags provided for by or pursuant to this order at any time after the date of this order.

Sec. 32. As used in this order, the term "executive agencies" means the executive departments and independent establishments in the executive branch of the Government, including wholly-owned Government corporations.

Sec. 33. Executive Order No. 10798 of January 3, 1959, is hereby revoked.

DWIGHT D. EISENHOWER

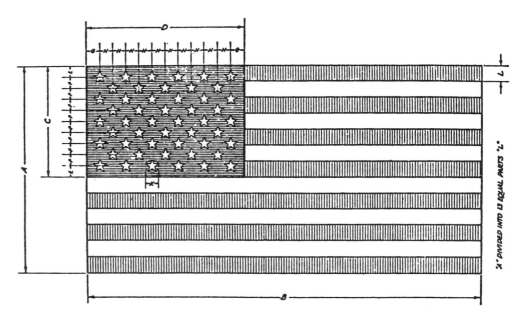

Standard proportions

Hoist (width) of flag 1.0	Fly (length) of flag 1.9	Hoist (width) of Union 0.5385 (7/13)	Fly (length) of Union 0.76	0.054	0.054	0.063	0.063	Diameter of star 0.0616	Width of stripe 0.769 (1/13)
A	B	C	D	E	F	G	H	K	L

(Source: *Federal Register*, vol. 24, p. 6865)

Section 2. Flag; additional stars

On the admission of a new State into the Union one star shall be added to the union of the flag; and such addition shall take effect on the fourth day of July then next succeeding such admission.

(Source: Act of July 30, 1947, *U.S. Statutes at Large*, vol. 61, p. 642, chapter 389).

Section 3. Use of flag for advertising purposes; mutilation of flag ·

Any person who, within the District of Columbia, in any manner, for exhibition or display, shall place or cause to be placed any word, figure, mark, picture, design, drawing, or any advertisement of any nature upon any flag, standard, colors, or ensign of the United States of America; or shall expose or cause to be exposed to public view any such flag, standard, colors, or ensign upon which shall have been printed, painted, or otherwise placed, or to which shall be attached, appended, affixed, or annexed any word, figure, mark, picture, design, or drawing, or any advertisement of any nature; or shall manufacture, sell, expose for sale, or to public view, or give away or have in possession for sale, or to be given away or for use for any purpose, any article or substance being an article of merchandise, or a receptacle for merchandise or article or thing for carrying or transporting merchandise, upon which shall have been printed,

painted, attached, or otherwise placed a representation of any such flag, standard, colors, or ensign, to advertise, call attention to, decorate, mark, or distinguish the article or substance on which so placed shall be deemed guilty of a misdemeanor and shall be punished by a fine not exceeding $100 or by imprisonment for not more than thirty days, or both, in the discretion of the court. The words "flag, standard, colors, or ensign", as used herein, shall include any flag, standard, colors, ensign, or any picture or representation of either, or of any part or parts of either, made of any substance or represented on any substance, of any size evidently purporting to be either of said flag, standard, colors, or ensign of the United States of America or a picture or a representation of either, upon which shall be shown the colors, the stars and the stripes, in any number of either thereof, or of any part or parts of either, by which the average person seeing the same without deliberation may believe the same to represent the flag, colors, standard, or ensign of the United States of America.
(Source: Act of July 30, 1947, *U.S. Statutes at Large*, vol. 61, p. 642, chapter 389; and July 5, 1968, *U.S. Statutes at Large*, vol. 82, p. 291, Public Law 90-381, section 3)

TITLE 18 *Crimes and Criminal Procedure*

U.S. Code, 1976 Edition, Vol. 4, p. 1100

Chapter 33—Emblems, Insignia and Names

Section 700. Desecration of the flag of the United States; penalties

(a) Whoever knowingly casts contempt upon any flag of the United States by publicly mutilating, defacing, defiling, burning, or trampling upon it shall be fined not more than $1,000 or imprisoned for not more than one year, or both.

(b) The term "flag of the United States" as used in this section, shall include any flag, standard, colors, ensign, or any picture or representation of either, or of any part or parts of either, made of any substance or represented on any substance, of any size evidently purporting to be either of said flag, standard, colors, or ensign of the United States of America, or a picture or a representation of either, upon which shall be shown the colors, the stars and the stripes, in any number of either thereof, or of any part or parts of either, by which the average person seeing the same without deliberation may believe the same to represent the flag, standards, colors, or ensign of the United States of America.

(c) Nothing in this section shall be construed as indicating an intent on the part of Congress to deprive any State, territory, possession, or the Commonwealth of Puerto Rico of jurisdiction over any offense over which it would have jurisdiction in the absence of this section.
(Source: Act of July 5, 1968, *U.S. Statutes at Large*, vol. 82, p. 291, Public Law 90-381, section 1)

The following collection of laws, sections of laws and Presidential proclamations have been brought together under a single title in the *U.S. Code*. The original citations of the component parts are in the source notes. Amendments through 1976 are reflected in the text below.

TITLE 36 *Patriotic Societies and Observances*

U.S. Code, 1976 edition, vol. 9, pp. 540–545.

CHAPTER 10—PATRIOTIC CUSTOMS

Section 170. National anthem; Star-Spangled Banner

The composition consisting of the words and music known as The Star-Spangled Banner is designated the national anthem of the United States of America.
(Source: Act of March 3, 1931, *U.S. Statutes at Large*, vol. 46, p. 1508, chapter 436).

Section 171. National anthem; Star-Spangled Banner; conduct during playing

During the rendition of the national anthem when the flag is displayed, all present except those in uniform should stand at attention facing the flag with the right hand over the heart. Men not in uniform should remove their headdress with their right hand and hold it at the left shoulder, the hand being over the heart. Persons in uniform should render the military salute at the first note of the anthem and retain this position until the last note. When the flag is not displayed, those present should face toward the music and act in the same manner they would if the flag were displayed there.
(Source: Sections 171 to 178 were originally a part of the Act of June 22, 1942, *U.S. Statutes at Large*, vol. 56, p. 380, chapter 435. This act was amended by the Act of July 7, 1976, *U.S. Statutes at Large*, vol. 90, pp. 810–813, Public Law 94-344, section 1).

Section 172. Pledge of allegiance to the flag; manner of delivery

The Pledge of Allegiance to the Flag, "I pledge allegiance to the Flag of the United States of America, and to the Republic for which it stands, one Nation under God, indivisible, with liberty and justice for all," should be rendered by standing at attention facing the flag with the right hand over the heart. When not in uniform men should remove their headdress with their right hand and hold it at the left shoulder, the hand being over the heart. Persons in uniform should remain silent, face the flag, and render the military salute.

Section 173. Display and use of flag by civilians; codification of rules and customs; definition

The following codification of existing rules and customs pertaining to the display and use of the flag of the United States of America is established for the use of such civilians or civilian groups or organizations as may not be required to conform with regulations promulgated by one or more executive departments of the Government of the United States. The flag of the United States for the purpose of this chapter shall be defined according to sections 1 and 2 of Title 4 and Executive Order 10834 issued pursuant thereto.

Section 174. Time and occasions for display

(a) Displays on buildings and stationary flagstaffs in open; night display
It is the universal custom to display the flag only from sunrise to sunset on buildings and on stationary flagstaffs in the open. However, when a patriotic effect is desired, the flag may be displayed twenty-four hours a day if properly illuminated during the hours of darkness.

234

(b) Manner of hoisting

The flag should be hoisted briskly and lowered ceremoniously.

(c) Inclement weather

The flag should not be displayed on days when the weather is inclement, except when an all weather flag is displayed.

(d) Particular days of display

The flag should be displayed on all days, especially on New Year's Day, January 1; Inauguration Day, January 20; Lincoln's Birthday, February 12; Washington's Birthday, third Monday in February; Easter Sunday (variable); Mother's Day, second Sunday in May; Armed Forces Day, third Saturday in May; Memorial Day (half-staff until noon), the last Monday in May; Flag Day, June 14; Independence Day, July 4; Labor Day, first Monday in September; Constitution Day, September 17; Columbus Day, second Monday in October; Navy Day, October 27; Veterans Day, November 11; Thanksgiving Day, fourth Thursday in November; Christmas Day, December 25; and such other days as may be proclaimed by the President of the United States; the birthdays of States (date of admission); and on State holidays.

(e) Display on or near administration building of public institutions

The flag should be displayed daily on or near the main administration building of every public institution.

(f) Display in or near polling places

The flag should be displayed in or near every polling place on election days.

(g) Display in or near schoolhouses

The flag should be displayed during school days in or near every schoolhouse.

VALLEY FORGE STATE PARK, PENNSYLVANIA; DISPLAY OF FLAG
Public Law 94-53, July 4, 1975, 89 Statutes 259, provided:

"That, notwithstanding the rule or custom pertaining to the display of the flag of the United States of America between sunrise and sunset, as set forth in section 2(a) of the joint resolution, entitled, 'Joint resolution to codify and emphasize existing rules and customs pertaining to the display and use of the flag of the United States of America', approved June 22, 1942 (30 U.S.C. 174(a)) [subsec. (a) of this section], the flag of the United States of America may be flown for twenty-four hours of each day on the grounds of the National Memorial Arch in Valley Forge State Park, Valley Forge, Pennsylvania. The flag may not be flown pursuant to the authority contained in this Act [this note] during the hours from sunset to sunrise unless it is illuminated."

FLAG HOUSE SQUARE, BALTIMORE, MARYLAND; DISPLAY OF FLAG; TIME

Act Mar. 26, 1954, ch. 109, 68 Stat. 35, provided:

"That notwithstanding any rule or custom pertaining to the display of the flag of the United States of America as set forth in the joint resolution entitled 'Joint resolution to codify and emphasize existing rules and customs pertaining to the display and use of the flag of the United States of America', approved June 22, 1942, as amended [sections 171 to 178 of this title], authority is hereby conferred on the appropriate officer of the State of Maryland to permit the flying of the flag of the United States for twenty-four hours of each day in Flag House Square, Albemarle and Pratt Streets, Baltimore, Maryland.

Sec. 2. Subject to the provisions of section 3 of the joint resolution of June 22, 1942, as amended [section 175 of this title], authority is also conferred on the appropriate officer of the State of Maryland to permit the flying of a replica of the flag of the United States which was in use during the War of 1812 for twenty-four hours of each day in Flag House Square, Albemarle and Pratt Streets, Baltimore, Maryland."

LEXINGTON, MASSACHUSETTS; DISPLAY OF FLAG

Public Law 89–335. Nov. 8, 1965, 79 Stat. 1294, provided: "That, notwithstanding any rule or custom pertaining to the display of the flag of the United States of America as set forth in the joint resolution entitled 'Joint resolution to codify and emphasize existing rules and customs pertaining to the display and use of the flag of the United States of America', approved June 22, 1942 (36 U.S.C. 171–178), the flag of the United States of America be flown for twenty-four hours of each day on the green of the town of Lexington, Massachusetts. The flag may not be flown pursuant to the authority contained in this Act during the hours from sunset to sunrise unless it is illuminated."

DISPLAY OF FLAGS AT THE WASHINGTON MONUMENT
Proclamation No. 4064
July 6, 1971, *Federal Register,* Volume 36, p. 12967

The Washington Monument stands day and night as America's tribute to our first President. The fifty American flags that encircle the base of the Monument represent our fifty states and, at the same time, symbolize our enduring Federal Union.

As this Nation's 200th year approaches, I believe that it would do all Americans well to remember the years of our first President and to recall the enduring ideals of our Nation.

As an expression of our rededication to the ideals of America and in accordance with the joint resolution of Congress of June 22, 1942 (56 Stat. 377), as amended by the joint resolution of December 22, 1942, (56 Stat. 1074), which permits the flag to be displayed at night "upon special occasions when it is desired to produce a patriotic effect," it is appropriate that our national colors henceforth be displayed day and night at the Washington Monument.

NOW, THEREFORE, I, RICHARD NIXON, President of the United States of America, do hereby proclaim that, effective July 4, 1971 the fifty flags of the United States of America displayed at the Washington Monument in the District of Columbia be flown at all times during the day and night, except when the weather is inclement.

The rules and customs pertaining to the display of the flag as set forth in the joint resolution of June 22, 1942, as amended [section 173 et seq. of this title], are hereby modified accordingly.

IN WITNESS WHEREOF, I have hereunto set my hand this sixth day of July, in the year of our Lord nineteen hundred seventy-one, and of the Independence of the United States of America the one hundred ninety-sixth.

RICHARD NIXON

DISPLAY OF FLAG AT UNITED STATES CUSTOMS PORT OF ENTRY
Proclamation No. 4131
May 5, 1972, *Federal Register,* Volume 37, p. 9311

The flag of the United States should be one of the first things seen at our Customs ports of entry, both by American citizens returning from abroad and by travelers from other countries.

As the symbol of our country and our freedoms, the national colors of the United States provide a welcome greeting of warm promise.

Many people, however, enter our country at night when the flag is not flown, because of the nearly universal custom of displaying it only from sunrise to sunset.

Authority exists to amend that custom. A Congressional joint resolution of June 22, 1942 (56 Stat. 377), as amended (36 U.S.C 173–178), permits the flag to be displayed at night "upon special occasions when it is desired to produce a patriotic effect."

I believe it is appropriate that returning citizens and visitors from other countries be welcomed by our flag whether they arrive at their ports of entry by night or by day.

NOW, THEREFORE, I, RICHARD NIXON, President of the United States of America, do hereby proclaim that the flag of the United States of America shall hereafter be displayed at all times during the day and night, except when the weather is inclement, at United States Customs ports of entry which are continually open.

The rules and customs pertaining to the display of the flag, as set forth in the joint resolution of June 22, 1942, as amended, are hereby modified accordingly.

IN WITNESS WHEREOF, I have hereunto set my hand this fifth day of May, in the year of our Lord nineteen hundred seventy-two, and of the Independence of the United States of America the one hundred ninety-sixth.

RICHARD NIXON

Section 175. Position and manner of display

The flag, when carried in a procession with another flag or flags, should be either on the marching right; that is, the flag's own right, or, if there is a line of other flags, in front of the center of that line.

(a) The flag should not be displayed on a float in a parade except from a staff, or as provided in subsection (i) of this section.

(b) The flag should not be draped over the hood, top, sides, or back of a vehicle or a railroad train or a boat. When the flag is displayed on a motorcar, the staff shall be fixed firmly to the chassis or clamped to the right fender.

(c) No other flag or pennant should be placed above or, if on the same level, to the right of the flag of the United States of America, except during church services conducted by naval chaplains at sea, when the church pennant may be flown above the flag during church services for the personnel of the Navy. No person shall display the flag of the United Nations or any other national or international flag equal, above, or in a position of superior prominence or honor to, or in place of, the flag of the United States at any place within the United States or any Territory or possession thereof: *Provided*, That nothing in this section shall make unlawful the continuance of the practice heretofore followed of displaying the flag of the United Nations in a position of superior prominence or honor, and other national flags in positions of equal prominence or honor, with that of the flag of the United States at the headquarters of the United Nations.

(d) The flag of the United States of America, when it is displayed with another flag against a wall from crossed staffs, should be on the right, the flag's own right, and its staff should be in front of the staff of the other flag.

(e) The flag of the United States of America should be at the center and at the highest point of the group when a number of flags of States or localities or pennants of societies are grouped and displayed from staffs.

(f) When flags of States, cities, or localities, or pennants of societies are flown on the same halyard with the flag of the United States, the latter should always be at the peak. When the flags are flown from adjacent staffs, the flag of the United States should be hoisted first and lowered last. No such flag or pennant may be placed above the flag of the United States or to the United States flag's right.

(g) When flags of two or more nations are displayed, they are to be flown from separate staffs of the same height. The flags should be of approximately equal size. International usage forbids the display of the flag of one nation above that of another nation in time of peace.

(h) When the flag of the United States is displayed from a staff projecting horizontally or at an angle from the window sill, balcony, or front of a building, the union of the flag should be placed at the peak of the staff unless the flag is at half staff. When the flag is suspended over a sidewalk from a rope extending from a house to a pole at the edge of the sidewalk, the flag should be hoisted out, union first, from the building.

(i) When displayed either horizontally or vertically against a wall, the union should be uppermost and to the flag's own right, that is, to the observer's left. When displayed in a window, the flag should be displayed in the same way, with the union or blue field to the left of the observer in the street.

(j) When the flag is displayed over the middle of the street, it should be suspended vertically with the union to the north in an east and west street or to the east in a north and south street.

(k) When used on a speaker's platform, the flag, if displayed flat, should be displayed above and behind the speaker. When displayed from a staff in a church or public auditorium, the flag of the United States of America should hold the position of superior prominence, in advance of the audience, and in the position of honor at the clergyman's or speaker's right as he faces the audience. Any other flag so displayed should be placed on the left of the clergyman or speaker or to the right of the audience.

(*l*) The flag should form a distinctive feature of the ceremony of unveiling a statue or monument, but it should never be used as the covering for the statue or monument.

(m) The flag, when flown at half-staff, should be first hoisted to the peak for an instant and then lowered to the half-staff position. The flag should be again raised to the peak before it is lowered for the day. On Memorial Day the flag should be displayed at half-staff until noon only, then raised to the top of the staff. By order of the President, the flag shall be flown at half-staff upon the death of principal figures of the United States Government and the Governor of a State, territory, or possession, as a mark of respect to their memory. In the event of the death of other officials or foreign dignitaries, the flag is to be displayed at half-staff according to Presidential instructions or orders, or in accordance with recognized customs or practices not inconsistent with law. In the event of the death of a present or former official of the government of any State, territory, or possession of the United States, the Governor of that State, territory, or possession may proclaim that the National flag shall be flown at half-staff. The flag shall be flown at half-staff thirty days from the death of the President or a former President; ten days from the day of death of the Vice President, the Chief Justice or a retired Chief Justice of the United States, or the Speaker of the House of Representatives; from the day of death until interment of an Associate Justice of the Supreme Court, a Secretary of an executive or military department, a former Vice President, or the Governor of a State, territory, or possession; and on the day of death and the following day for a Member of Congress. As used in this subsection—

(1) the term "half-staff" means the position of the flag when it is one-half the distance between the top and bottom of the staff;

(2) the term "executive or military department" means any agency listed under sections 101 and 102 of Title 5; and

(3) the term "Member of Congress" means a Senator, a Representative, a Delegate, or the Resident Commissioner from Puerto Rico.

(n) When the flag is used to cover a casket, it should be so placed that the union is at the head and over the left shoulder. The flag should not be lowered into the grave or allowed to touch the ground.

(*o*) When the flag is suspended across a corridor or lobby in a building with only one main entrance, it should be suspended vertically with the union of the flag to the observer's left upon entering. If the building has more than one main entrance, the flag should be suspended vertically near the center of the corridor or lobby with the union to the north, when entrances are to the east and west or to the east when entrances are to the north and south. If there are entrances in more than two directions, the union should be to the east.

DISPLAY OF FLAG AT HALF-STAFF UPON DEATH OF CERTAIN OFFICIALS AND FORMER OFFICIALS
Proclamation No. 3044
March 1, 1954, *Federal Register*, Volume 19, p. 1235

WHEREAS it is appropriate that the flag of the United States of America be flown at half-staff on Federal buildings, grounds, and facilities upon the death of principal officials and former officials of the Government of the United States and the Governors of the States, Territories, and possessions of the United States as a mark of respect to their memory; and

WHEREAS it is desirable that rules be prescribed for the uniform observance of this mark of respect by all executive departments and agencies of the Government, and as a guide to the people of the Nation generally on such occasions:

NOW, THEREFORE, I, DWIGHT D. EISENHOWER, President of the United States of America and Commander in Chief of the armed forces of the United States, do hereby prescribe and proclaim the following rules with respect to the display of the flag of the United States of America at half-staff upon the death of the officials hereinafter designated:

1. The flag of the United States shall be flown at half-staff on all buildings, grounds, and naval vessels of the Federal Government in the District of Columbia and throughout the United States and its Territories and possessions for the period indicated upon the death of any of the following-designated officials or former officials of the United States:

(a) The President or a former President: for thirty days from the day of death.

The flag shall also be flown at half-staff for such period at all United States embassies, legations, and other facilities abroad, including all military facilities and naval vessels and stations.

(b) The Vice President, the Chief Justice or a retired Chief Justice of the United States, or the Speaker of the House of Representatives: for ten days from the day of death.

(c) An Associate Justice of the Supreme Court, a member of the Cabinet, a former Vice President, the Secretary of the Army, the Secretary of the Navy, or the Secretary of the Air Force: from the day of death until interment.

2. The flag of the United States shall be flown at half-staff on all buildings, grounds, and naval vessels of the Federal Government in the metropolitan area of the District of Columbia on the day of death and on the following day upon the death of a United States Senator, Representative, Territorial Delegate, or the Resident Commissioner from the Commonwealth of Puerto Rico, and it shall also be flown at half-staff on all buildings, grounds, and naval vessels of the Federal Government in the State, Congressional District, Territory, or Commonwealth of such Senator, Representative, Delegate, or Commissioner, respectively, from the day of death until interment.

3. The flag of the United States shall be flown at half-staff on all buildings and grounds of the Federal Government in a State, Territory, or possession of the United States upon the death of the Governor of such State, Territory, or possession from the day of death until interment.

4. In the event of the death of other officials, former officials, or foreign dignitaries, the flag of the United States shall be displayed at half-staff in accordance with such orders or instructions as may be issued by or at the direction of the President, or in accordance with recognized customs or practices not inconsistent with law.

5. The heads of the several departments and agencies of the Government may direct that the flag of the United States be flown at half-staff on buildings, grounds, or naval vessels under their jurisdiction on occasions other than those specified herein which they consider proper, and that suitable military honors be rendered as appropriate.

IN WITNESS WHEREOF, I have hereunto set my hand and caused the Seal of the United States of America to be affixed

DONE at the City of Washington this 1st day of March in the year of our Lord nineteen hundred and fifty-four, and of the Independence of the United
[SEAL]   States of America the one hundred and seventy-eighth.

DWIGHT D. EISENHOWER

239

Section 176. Respect for flag

No disrespect should be shown to the flag of the United States of America; the flag should not be dipped to any person or thing. Regimental colors, State flags, and organization or institutional flags are to be dipped as a mark of honor.

(a) The flag should never be displayed with the union down, except as a signal of dire distress in instances of extreme danger to life or property.

(b) The flag should never touch anything beneath it, such as the ground, the floor, water, or merchandise.

(c) The flag should never be carried flat or horizontally, but always aloft and free.

(d) The flag should never be used as wearing apparel, bedding, or drapery. It should never be festooned, drawn back, nor up, in folds, but always allowed to fall free. Bunting of blue, white, and red, always arranged with the blue above, the white in the middle, and the red below, should be used for covering a speaker's desk, draping the front of the platform, and for decoration in general.

(e) The flag should never be fastened, displayed, used, or stored in such a manner as to permit it to be easily torn, soiled, or damaged in any way.

(f) The flag should never be used as a covering for a ceiling.

(g) The flag should never have placed upon it, nor on any part of it, nor attached to it any mark, insignia, letter, word, figure, design, picture, or drawing of any nature.

(h) The flag should never by used as a receptacle for receiving, holding, carrying, or delivering anything.

(i) The flag should never be used for advertising purposes in any manner whatsoever. It should not be embroidered on such articles as cushions or handkerchiefs and the like, printed or otherwise impressed on paper napkins or boxes or anything that is designed for temporary use and discard. Advertising signs should not be fastened to a staff or halyard from which a flag is flown.

(j) No part of the flag should ever be used as a costume or athletic uniform. However, a flag patch may be affixed to the uniform of military personnel, firemen, policemen, and members of patriotic organizations. The flag represents a living country and is itself considered a living thing. Therefore, the lapel flag pin being a replica, should be worn on the left lapel near the heart.

(k) The flag, when it is in such condition that it is no longer a fitting emblem for display, should be destroyed in a dignified way, preferably by burning.

Section 177. Same; conduct during hoisting, lowering or passing of flag

During the ceremony of hoisting or lowering the flag or when the flag is passing in a parade or in review, all persons present except those in uniform should face the flag and stand at attention with the right hand over the heart. Those present in uniform should render the military salute. When not in uniform, men should remove their headdress with their right hand and hold it at the left shoulder, the hand being over the heart. Aliens should stand at attention. The salute to the flag in a moving column should be rendered at the moment the flag passes.

Section 178. Same; modification of rules and customs by President

Any rule or custom pertaining to the display of the flag of the United States of America, set forth in sections 171 to 178 of this title, may be altered, modified, or repealed, or additional rules with respect thereto may be prescribed, by the Commander in Chief of the Armed Forces of the United States, whenever he deems it to be appropriate or desirable; and any such alteration or additional rule shall be set forth in a proclamation.

THE FLAG OF THE UNITED STATES

Proclamation No. 2605

February 21, 1944, *Federal Register*, Volume 9, 1957; 58 *U.S. Statutes at Large* Volume 58, p. 1126

The flag of the United States of America is universally representative of the principles of the justice, liberty, and democracy enjoyed by the people of the United States; and

People all over the world recognize the flag of the United States as symbolic of the United States; and

The effective prosecution of the war requires a proper understanding by the people of other countries of the material assistance being given by the Government of the United States:

NOW, THEREFORE, by virtue of the power vested in me by the Constitution and laws of the United States, particularly by the Joint Resolution approved June 22, 1942, as amended by the Joint Resolution approved December 22, 1942 [sections 171–178 of this title], as President and commander in Chief, it is hereby proclaimed as follows:

1. The use of the flag of the United States or any representation thereof, if approved by the Foreign Economic Administration, on labels, packages, cartons, cases, or other containers for articles or products of the United States intended for export as lend-lease aid, as relief and rehabilitation aid, or as emergency supplies for the Territories and possessions of the United States, or similar purposes, shall be considered a proper use of the flag of the United States and consistent with the honor and respect due to the flag.

2. If any article or product so labelled, packaged or otherwise bearing the flag of the United States or any representation thereof, as provided for in section 1, should, by force of circumstances, be diverted to the ordinary channels of domestic trade, no person shall be considered as violating the rules and customs pertaining to the display of the flag of the United States, as set forth in the Joint Resolution approved June 22, 1942, as amended by the Joint Resolution approved December 22, 1942 (U.S. C.Supp. II, Title 36, secs. 171–178) [sections 171–178 of this title], for possessing, transporting, displaying, selling or otherwise transferring any such article or product solely because the label, package, carton, case, or other container bears the flag of the United States or any representation thereof.

Bibliography

I. Manuscript Collections

Ann Arbor, Michigan. William Clements Library, University of Michigan. Papers of Sir Henry Clinton.

Baltimore. Maryland Historical Society. Francis Hopkinson papers.

Boston, Massachusetts Historical Society. Heath papers.

———. George Henry Preble papers.

Cambridge, England. Pepysian Library, Magdalen College, Cambridge University. Lieutenant Graydon's Manuscript.

Cambridge, Massachusetts. Houghton Library, Harvard University. Stark manuscripts.

Hartford. Connecticut Historical Society. Silas Deane papers.

Ithaca, New York. Cornell University Library. Henry Vanderlyn Letter Book, 1810–1824.

New Haven, Connecticut. Sterling Library, Yale University. Webb papers.

New York City. New-York Historical Society. Gansevoort-Lansing papers

———. Grider collection.

———. Tomilson collection.

Philadelphia, American Philosophical Society. Gratz collection.

Philadelphia. Pennsylvania Historical Society. Gratz collection.

———. Wharton Account Books.

Providence. Rhode Island Historical Society. Esek Hopkins papers.

Stafford, Staffordshire, England. William Salt Library. Dartmouth papers.

Washington, D.C. Library of Congress. British Transcripts: Admiralty 1/484; British Museum Additional Manuscripts, 22206; Colonial Office 5/126.

———. John Paul Jones papers.

———. Samuel Chester Reid papers.

———. George Washington papers.

Washington, D.C. National Archives. Record Group 360. Papers of the Continental Congress.

———. Record Group 93. Revolutionary War records.

———. Record Group 93. War Department collection of Revolutionary War records.

Washington, D.C. National Museum of American History, Smithsonian Institution. Furlong flag files.

242

II. Newspapers and Periodicals

Annual Register [London], 1775–83
Baltimore American, February 1908
Bennington (Vt.) *Daily Banner*, August 15, 17, 1877
Boston Weekly News-Letter, May 23, 1754
Bradford's Pennsylvania Journal, 1775
Dunlap's Pennsylvania Packet or General Advertiser, 1777–78
Gaines New York Mercury Gazette, 1777
The Gentleman's Magazine [London], 1775, 1777–78
Indiana History Bulletin 4, 1926–27
Ladies Magazine [London] 7, 1776
Middlesex Journal and Evening Advertiser, 1775
New England Chronicle, 1775
New Hampshire Freeman's Journal, 1777
New York Journal and General Advertiser, September 8, 1777
North Carolina Gazette, 1877
Pennsylvania Evening Post, 1777–78
Pennsylvania Gazette, 1776, 1777, 1783
Pennsylvania Packet, 1781–83
South Carolina and American General Gazette, October 1777
The (Baltimore) *Sun Magazine*, December 24, 1975
The (Nashville) *Tennessean*, July 25, September 5, and October 17, 1976
Town's Pennsylvania Evening Post, August 24, 1776
Vermont Centennial, August 30 and September 4, 1877
Virginia Gazette, September 12, 1797

III. Books and Flag Sheets

Allard, Carel. *Nieuwe Hollandsche Scheeps-Bouw.* Amsterdam: C. Allard, 1695.

The American Heritage Book of the Revolution. New York: American Heritage Publishing Company, 1958.

Ammon, Harry. *James Monroe: The Quest for National Identity.* New York: McGraw-Hill Book Company, 1971.

Andrews, Charles M. *The Colonial Period of American History*, Vol. I. New Haven: Yale University Press, 1934.

Arnold, Samuel Greene. *History of the State of Rhode Island and Providence Plantations.* 2 vols. New York: D. Appleton, 1859–60.

Avery, Elroy McKendree. *A History of the United States and Its People.* 8 vols. Cleveland, Ohio, and Tarrytown, N.Y.: The Burrows Brothers Company, 1905–15.

Bailey, Francis. *Pocket Almanac for 1784.* Boston: T. and J. Flett, 1783.

Barnes, John S., ed. *Fanning's Narrative, Being the Memoirs of Nathaniel Fanning, A Naval Officer of the Revolution, 1778–1783. New York: Naval Historical Society,* 1912.

Barrows, John. *The Life, Voyages, and Exploits of Sir Francis Drake.* London: J. Murray, 1861.

Beaumont, John. *The Present State of the Universe*. 3d ed. London: B. Motte, 1701.

Beck, Alverda S. *The Letter Book of Esek Hopkins, Commander-in-Chief of the United States Navy, 1775–1777*. Providence: Rhode Island Historical Society, 1932.

Beck, Alverda S., ed. *The Correspondence of Esek Hopkins, Commander-in-Chief of the United States Navy*. Providence: Rhode Island Historical Society, 1933.

Bibbins, Ruthella Bernard. *The Baltimore Book. Flag House Guide to Historic Landmarks of Baltimore*. 2d ed. Baltimore: Flag House Association, 1929.

Bolton, Herbert E. *Coronado, Knight of Pueblos and Plains*. New York: Whittlesey House, 1949.

Bolton, Herbert E., ed. *Spanish Exploration in the Southeast, 1542–1706*. New York: Charles Scribner's Sons, 1911.

Bouton, Nathaniel, et al., eds. *Documents and Records Relating to the Province of New Hampshire*. 7 vols. Concord, N.H.: E.A. Jenks, 1867–73.

Bouton, Nathaniel, comp. *State Papers. Documents and Records Relating to the State of New Hampshire during the Period of the American Revolution, from 1776 to 1783*. Concord, N.H.: E.A. Jenks, 1874. Reprint, New York: AMS Press, 1973.

Bowles, Carrington. *Bowles's Universal Display of the Naval Flags of All Nations in the World*. London: Carrington Bowles, 1760, 1783, 1801.

Brewington, M.V. and Dorothy. *The Marine Paintings and Drawings in the Peabody Museum*. Salem, Mass.: The Peabody Museum, 1968.

Britten, Evelyn Barrett. *Chronicles of Saratoga*. Brooklyn, N.Y.: Gerald J. Rickard, 1959.

Brown, Abram English. *History of the Town of Bedford, Middlesex County, Massachusetts*. Bedford: Abram E. Brown, 1891.

Browne, William Hand, ed. *Archives of Maryland: Proceedings of the Council of Maryland, 1693–1696/7*. Vol. 20. Baltimore: Maryland Historical Society, 1910.

Carter, Clarence, ed. *The Territory of Orleans, 1803–1812*. Vol. 9, *Territorial Papers of the United States*. Washington: U.S. Government Printing Office, 1940.

A Collection of the Principal Flags of All Nations in the World: From the Best Authorities. Bungay, England: Brightly and Childs, 1813.

Commonwealth of Pennsylvania. *Colonial Records of Pennsylvania, 1683–1790*. 16 vols. Philadelphia and Harrisburg: Theo Fenn Co., 1852–53.

Corbett, Sir Julian, ed. *Papers Relating to the Navy during the Spanish War, 1585–1587*. London: Naval Records Society, 1898.

Covens and Mortier. *Tables des Pavillons*. Amsterdam: Covens and Mortier, 1711.

Cox, Isaac Joselin. *The West Florida Controversy, 1798–1813: A Study in American Diplomacy*. Baltimore: Johns Hopkins University Press, 1918.

Cutler, Alfred H. *The Continental "Great Union" Flag*. Somerville, Mass.: Somerville School Committee, 1929.

Davis, Gherardi. *Regimental Colors in the War of the Revolution*. New York: The Gilliss Press, 1907.

Dawson, Henry B. *Battles of the United States, By Sea and Land*. 2 vols. New York: Johnson, Fry and Company, 1858.

Dawson, Henry B. *The Sons of Liberty in New York*. Poughkeepsie, N.Y.: Platt & Schran, 1859. Reprint, New York: Arno Press, 1969.

Desjardins, Gustave A. *Recherches sur les drapeaux français*. Paris: A. Morel & Cie., 1874.

Dexter, Franklin Bowditch, ed. *The Literary Diary of Ezra Stiles, D.D., L.L.D., President of Yale College*. 3 vols. New York: Charles Scribner's Sons, 1901.

Drake, Samuel Adams. *Burgoyne Invasion of 1777; With an Outline Sketch of the American Invasion of Canada, 1775–76*. Boston: Lea & Shepard, 1889.

Edwards, Major T.J. *Standards, Guidons and Colours of the Commonwealth Forces*. Aldershot, England: Gale & Polden Ltd., 1953.

Eggenberger, David. *Flags of the U.S.A.*, New York: Thomas Y. Crowell Co., 1964.

Farrand, Max, ed. *Memoirs of Benjamin Franklin. Parallel Text Edition Comprising the Texts of Franklin's Original Manuscripts*. Berkeley: University of California Press, 1949.

Filby, P. William, and Edward G. Howard, comps. *Star Spangled Books*. Baltimore: Maryland Historical Society, 1972.

Fitzpatrick, John C., ed. *George Washington's Accounts of Expenses while Commander in Chief of the Continental Army, 1775–1783*. Boston: Houghton Mifflin Company, 1917.

———. *The Diaries of George Washington*. 4 vols. Boston: Houghton Mifflin Company, 1925.

———. *The Writings of George Washington from the Original Manuscript Sources, 1775–1799*. 39 vols. Washington: U.S. Government Printing Office, 1931–44.

Flags of the World. Venice: Monastery of St. Lazarus, 1813.

Force, Peter, comp. *American Archives*. 4th ser., 6 vols.; 5th ser., 3 vols. Washington: M. St. Clair Clarke and Peter Force, 1837–53.

Ford, Worthington C. *Defenses of Philadelphia in 1777*. Brooklyn, N.Y.: Historical Printing Club, 1897.

Ford, Worthington C. et al., eds. *Journals of the Continental Congress, 1774–1789*. 34 vols. Washington: U.S. Government Printing Office, 1904–37.

Foster, Herbert Darling. *Stark's Independent Command at Bennington*. Manchester, N.H.: Standard Book Company, 1908.

Franklin, Benjamin. *Plain Truth, Or Serious Considerations on the Present State of the City of Philadelphia, and the Province of Pennsylvania*. Philadelphia: B. Franklin, 1747.

Freeman, Douglas Southall. *George Washington: A Biography*. 6 vols. New York: Charles Scribner's Sons, 1948–54.

Gipson, Lawrence Henry. *The British Empire Before the American Revolution*. 15 vols. Caldwell, Idaho, and New York: The Caxton Press and Alfred A. Knopf, Inc., 1939–69.

Gjerset, Knut. *History of the Norwegian People*. 2 vols. New York: Macmillan Company, 1932.

Greenwood, Isaac J. *Captain John Manley*. Boston: C.E. Goodspeed, 1915.

—————. *The Revolutionary Services of John Greenwood of Boston and New York, 1775–1783*. New York: The DeVinne Press, 1922.

Guthman, William H. *March to Massacre: A History of the First Seven Years of the United States Army, 1784–1791*. New York: Alfred A. Knopf, Inc., 1975.

Hallenbeck, Cleve. *Alvar Nunez Cabeza De Vaca. The Journey and Route of the First European to Cross the Continent of North America, 1534–1536*. Glendale, Calif.: Arthur H. Clark, 1940.

Hamilton, Schuyler. *The History of the National Flag of the United States of America*. Philadelphia: Lippincott, Grambo, and Co., 1852.

—————. *Our National Flag, The Star Spangled Banner. The History of it*. New York: George A. Lockwood and Son, 1887.

Harrison, Peleg Dennis. *The Stars and Stripes and Other American Flags Including Their Origin and History*. Boston: Little, Brown & Co., 1906.

Hastings, George E. *The Life and Works of Francis Hopkinson*. Chicago: University of Chicago Press, 1926.

Hazard, Samuel, ed. *Colonial Records of Pennsylvania*. 16 vols. Harrisburg: T. Fenn & Co., 1851–60.

Hazard, Samuel, et al., eds. *Pennsylvania Archives*. 9th ser., 138 vols. Philadelphia and Harrisburg: J. Severns & Co., 1852–1949.

Heitmen, Francis B. *Historical Register of Officers of the Continental Army during the War of the American Revolution, April 1775 to December 1783*. Washington: U.S. Government Printing Office, 1893.

Hitsman, J. Mackay. *The Incredible War of 1812: A Military History*. Toronto: University of Toronto Press, 1965.

Horsman, Reginald. *The War of 1812*. New York: Alfred A. Knopf, Inc., 1969.

Hough, Franklin Benjamin. *The Siege of Charleston by the British Fleet and Army under the Command of Admiral Arbuthnot and Sir Henry Clinton, which Terminated with the Surrender of that Place on the 12th of May 1780*. Albany, N.Y.: J. Munsell, 1867.

Hubbard, William. *A General History of New England, From the Discovery to MDCLXXX [1680]*. 2d ed. Boston: C.C. Little & J. Brown, 1848.

Ingstad, Helge. *Westward to Vinland: The Discovery of Pre-Columbian Norse House-Sites in North America*. Translated by Erik J. Friis. New York: St. Martin's Press, 1969.

Jackson, Donald, ed. *Letters of the Lewis and Clark Expedition, with Related Documents, 1783–1854*. Urbana: University of Illinois Press, 1962.

—————. *Journals with Letters and Related Documents of Zebulon Pike*. 2 vols. Norman: University of Oklahoma Press, 1966.

Jackson, John W. *The Pennsylvania Navy, 1775–1781*. New Brunswick N.J.: Rutgers University Press, 1974.

Jackson, Melvin H. *Privateers in Charleston, 1793–1796*. Washington: Smithsonian Institution Press, 1969.

James, Alton J., ed. *George Rogers Clark Papers, 1771–1781*. Illinois Historical Collections, vol. 8. Springfield: Illinois State Historical Library, 1912.

James, Bartlett B., and J. Franklin Jameson, eds. *Journal of Jasper Danckaerts, 1679–1680*. New York: Charles Scribner's Sons, 1913.

Jennison, Peter S., ed. *The 1976–77 Official Vermont Bicentennial Guide*. Taftsville, Vt.: The Countryman Press, Inc., 1975.

John Carter Brown Library. *Report to the Corporation of Brown University, July 1, 1951.* Providence R.I.: Brown University Library, 1951.

Johnson, Amandus. *The Swedes on the Delaware, 1638–1664.* Philadelphia: The Lenapé Press, 1914.

Justice, Alexander. *A General Treatise of the Dominion and Laws of the Sea, Containing What is Most Valuable for the Subject in Ancient and Modern Authors.* London: S. and J. Sprint, 1705.

Karrow, Robert W., Jr., comp. *Mapping the American Revolutionary War.* Chicago: Newberry Library, 1974.

Klauber, Lawrence M. *Rattlesnakes: Their Habits, Life Histories, and Influence on Mankind.* 2 vols. Berkeley: University of California Press, 1956.

Knollenberg, Bernhard. *Origin of the American Revolution, 1759–1766.* New rev. ed. New York: Collier Books, 1961.

Knopf, Richard C. *Anthony Wayne: A Name in Arms.* Pittsburgh: University of Pittsburgh Press, 1959.

Labaree, Leonard W., and Whitfield Bell, Jr., eds. *The Papers of Benjamin Franklin.* 21 vols. New Haven: Yale University Press, 1959–.

Lee, Richard Henry. *Life of Arthur Lee.* 2 vols. Boston: Wells and Lilly, 1829.

Levering, Joseph Mortimer. *A History of Bethlehem, Pennsylvania, 1741–1892.* Bethlehem: Pennsylvania Times Publishing Company, 1903.

Lewis, Michael. *England's Sea Officers: The Story of the Naval Profession.* London: George Allen and Unwin, Ltd., 1948.

Lord, Walter. *The Dawn's Early Light.* New York: W. W. Norton & Co., Inc., 1972.

Lossing, Benson J. *The Pictorial Field Book of the Revolution.* 2 vols. New York: Harper Brothers, 1852.

————. *The Pictorial Field Book of the War of 1812.* New York: Harper Brothers, 1868.

Luzader, John F., Luis Torres, and Orville W. Carroll. *Fort Stanwix.* Washington: U.S. Government Printing Office, 1976.

McCandless, Byron, and Gilbert Grosvenor, eds. *The National Geographic Magazine, October 1917: Our Flag Number.* Washington: National Geographic Society, 1917.

Mahon, John K. *The War of 1812.* Gainesville: University of Florida Press, 1972.

Martin, Mary Paulding. *The Flag House Story.* Baltimore: The Star Spangled Flag House, 1970.

Mastai, Boleslaw and Marie. *The Stars and Stripes.* New York: Alfred A. Knopf, Inc., 1973.

Milne, Samuel A. *The Standards and Colours of the Army from the Restoration, 1666, to the Introduction of the Territorial System, 1881.* Leeds, England: Goodall and Suddick, 1893.

Mondhare. *Tableau de tous les pavillons que lon arbore sur les vaisseaux dans les quatres parties du monde avec une explication de tous les agres et manoeuvres des vaisseaux.* Paris :Mondhare, 1781.

Moore, Howard Parker. *A Life of General John Stark of New Hampshire.* New York: privately published, 1949.

Morgan, Edmund S. and Helen M. *The Stamp Act Crisis: Prologue to Revolution.* Chapel Hill: University of North Carolina Press, 1953.

Morison, Samuel Eliot. *Admiral of the Ocean Sea.* Boston: Little Brown & Co., 1942.

———. *John Paul Jones: A Sailor's Biography.* Boston: Little Brown & Co., 1959.

———. *Portuguese Voyagers to America in the Fifteenth Century.* Cambridge, Mass.: Harvard University Press, 1940.

———. *The European Discovery of America.* 2 vols. New York: Oxford University Press, 1971–74.

Morris, Richard B., ed. *John Jay: The Making of a Revolutionary. Unpublished Papers, 1745–1780.* Vol. 1. New York: Harper and Row, Publishers, 1975.

Morris, Robert. *The Truth about the American Flag.* Beach Haven, N.J.: Wynnehaven Publishing Company, 1976.

Mortier, Pieter. *De Franche Neptunus, of, Nieuwe Atlas van de Zeekaarten.* Amsterdam: Pieter Mortier, 1693.

Neeser, Robert W., ed. *Letters and Papers Relating to the Cruises of Gustavus Conyngham: A Captain of the Continental Navy.* New York: Naval History Society, 1915.

New England Historical and Geneological Society. *New England Historical and Geneological Register,* Vols. 1 to 50. Boston: New England Historical and Geneological Society, 1847–1932.

New York Common Council. *Manual of the Coporation of the City of New York, 1841/42–1870.* Compiled by S.J. Willis and D.T. Valentine. 28 vols. New York: J.W. Bell, 1842.

Norie, J.W. *Plates Descriptive of the Maritime Flags of All Nations: A New Edition.* London: J.W. Norie & Co., 1829.

O'Callaghan, Edmund B. *History of New Netherlands.* 2d ed. 2 vols. Philadelphia: G. S. Appleton, 1855.

O'Callaghan, Edmund B. and Berthold Fernow, eds. *Documents Relative to the Colonial History of the State of New York.* 4 vols. Albany, N.Y.: Weed, Parsons, and Company, 1849–51.

Patrick, Rembert W. *Florida Fiasco. Rampant Rebels on the Georgia-Florida Border, 1810–1815.* Athens: University of Georgia Press, 1954.

Patterson, Richard S. and Richardson Dougall. *The Eagle and the Shield: A History of the Great Seal of the United States.* Washington: U.S. Government Printing Office, 1978.

Paullin, Charles O. *The Navy of the American Revolution: Its Administration, Its Policy, and Its Achievements.* Cleveland: The Burrows Brothers Co., 1906.

Paullin, Charles O., ed. *Out-Letters of the Continental Marine Committee and Board of Admiralty, August 1776–September 1780.* 2 vols. New York: Naval History Society, 1914.

Perrin, William G. *British Flags. Their Early History and Their Development at Sea; With an Account of the Origin of the Flag as a National Device.* Cambridge: Cambridge University Press, 1922.

Preble, George H. *History of the Flag of the United States of America.* 2d rev. ed. Boston: A. Williams and Company, 1880.

Prescott, Benjamin Franklin. *The Stars and Stripes. The Flag of the United States of America; When, Where, and by Whom Was it First Saluted? The Question Answered.* Concord: The Republican Press Association, 1876.

Phillips, Philip Lee, comp. *A List of Geographical Atlases in the Library of Congress with Bibliographical Notes.* 7 vols. Washington: U.S. Government Printing Office, 1909–14.

Pullen, Hugh F. *The Shannon and the Chesapeake.* Toronto: McClelland and Stewart Ltd., 1970.

Quaife, Milo M., Melvin J. Weig, and Roy E. Appleman. *The History of the United States Flag.* New York: Harper and Row, Publishers, 1961.

Roland, Mary Driver. *Old Glory, The True Story.* New York: Mary D. Roland, 1918.

Sams, Conway W. *The Conquest of Virginia: The First Attempt; Being an Account of Sir Walter Raleigh's Colony on Roanoke Island.* Norfolk, Va.: Keyser-Doherty Printing Corporation, 1924.

Schenck, Pieter. *Schoun-Park aller Scheeps-Vlaggen.* Amsterdam: Pieter Schenck, 1711.

Schermerhorn, Frank Earle. *American and French Flags of the Revolution, 1775–1783.* Philadelphia: Pennsylvania Society of Sons of the Revolution, 1940.

Sellers, Charles Coleman. *The Artist of the Revolution: The Early Life of Charles Willson Peale.* 2 vols. Hebron, Conn.: Feather & Good, Publishers, 1939; Philadelphia: The American Philosophical Society, 1947.

————. *Portraits and Miniatures by Charles Willson Peale.* Philadelphia: American Philosophical Society, 1952.

Seutter, Matthaus. *Flaggen aller seefahrenden Potenzen und Nationen der gantzen Welt.* Augsburg: Tobias & Conrad Lotter, 1782.

Shadwell, Wendy J. *American Printmaking: The First 150 Years.* Washington: U.S. Government Printing Office, 1969.

Sheppard, John H. *The Life of Samuel Tucker, Commodore in the American Revolution.* Boston: Alfred Mudge and Son, 1868.

Sherburne, John Henry. *Life and Character of John Paul Jones, A Captain in the United States Navy during the Revolutionary War.* 2d ed. New York: Adriance, Sherman & Co., 1851.

Sierksma, Klaes, ed. *Flags of the World, 1669–1670: A Seventeenth Century Manuscript.* Amsterdam: S. Emmering, 1966.

Sizer, Colonel Theodore, ed. *Autobiography of John Trumbull.* 2 vols. New Haven: Yale University Press, 1953.

————. *Works of Colonel John Trumbull, Artist of the American Revolution.* New Haven: Yale University Press, 1950.

Smelser, Marshall. *Congress Founds the Navy, 1787–1798.* South Bend, Ind.: University of Notre Dame Press, 1959.

Smith, Whitney. *The Flag Book of the United States.* New York: William Morrow & Co., Inc., 1970.

Spargo, John. *The Stars and Stripes in 1777, An Account of the Birth of the Flag and its First Baptism of Victorious Fire.* (Bennington, Vt.: Bennington Battle Monument and Historical Assn., 1928.

Sprengel, M.C. *Allgemeines historisches Taschenbuch, oder Abriss der mertwürdigsten neven Welt-Begebenheiten, enthaltend für 1784 die Geschichte der Revolution von Nord America . . .* Berlin: Haude und Spener, 1783.

249

Stark, Caleb. *Memoir and Official Correspondence of General John Stark.* Concord, N.H.: G.P. Lyon, 1860.

Stevens, Benjamin Franklin, ed. *B.F. Stevens' Facsimiles of Manuscripts in European Archives Relating to America, 1773–1783.* 25 vols. London: Malby and Sons, 1889–95. Reprint, Wilmington, Del.: The Mellifont Press, 1970.

Stone, Edward Martin. *Our French Allies: Rochambeau and His Army.* Providence, R.I.: Providence Press Co., 1884.

Swanson, Neil H. *The Perilous Flight.* New York: Farrar and Rinehart, Inc., 1945.

Tarbox, Increase Niles. *Sir Walter Raleigh and His Colony in America.* Boston: The Prince Society, 1884.

Thomas, M. Halsey, ed. *The Diary of Samuel Sewall, 1674–1729.* 2 vols. New York: Farrar, Straus & Giroux, Inc., 1973.

Thurston, R.C. Ballard. *Origin and Evolution of the U.S. Flag.* House Doc. 258, 69th Congress, 1st session. Washington: U.S. Government Printing Office, 1926.

United States Congress. *Annals of Congress. Debates and Proceedings in the Congress of the United States, 1789–1824.* 42 vols. Washington: Gales and Seaton, 1834–56.

——————. *Congressional Record.* 65th Congress, 2d session. Washington: U.S. Government Printing Office, 1918.

United States Navy Department. *Naval Documents of the American Revolution.* Vols. 1–8. Edited by William Bell Clark and William James Morgan. Washington: U.S. Government Printing Office, 1964–.

——————. *Naval Documents Related to the Quasi-War between the United States and France.* 7 vols. Washington: U.S. Government Printing Office, 1935–38.

——————. *Naval Documents Related to the United States Wars with the Barbary Powers.* 7 vols. Washington : U.S. Government Printing Office, 1939–44.

Vermont Historical Society. *Collections of the Vermont Historical Society.* 2 vols. Montpelier: Printed for the Society, 1870–71.

Wallace, Willard M. *Appeal to Arms. A Military History of the American Revolution.* New York: Harper and Brothers, Publishers, 1951.

Waller, George. *The American Revolution in the West.* Chicago: Nelson Hall Co., 1976.

Walton, E.P., ed. *Records of the Council of Safety and Governor and Council of the State of Vermont, 1775–1836.* 8 vols. Montpelier: J. & M. Poland, 1873–80.

Ward, Christopher. *The War of the Revolution.* 2 vols. New York: Macmillan Company, 1952.

Watson, John F. *Annals of Philadelphia and Pennsylvania.* 2 vols. Philadelphia: E. Thomas, 1857.

Weatherwise, Abraham. *Weatherwise's Town and Country Almanack for the Year of Our Lord 1782.* Boston: Robert Hodge, 1781.

Wharton, Francis, ed. *The Revolutionary Diplomatic Correspondence of the United States.* 6 vols. Washington: U.S. Government Printing Office, 1889.

White, Patrick C.T. *A Nation on Trial: America and the War of 1812*. New York: John Wiley & Sons, Inc., 1965.

Willet, William M.W. *A Narrative of the Military Actions of Colonel Marinus Willet*. New York: G. & C. & H. Carvill, 1831.

Williamson, James A. *The Cabot Voyages and Bristol Discovery under Henry VII*. Cambridge: Cambridge University Press, 1962.

Wilson, Joseph Lapsley, ed. *Book of the First Troop of Philadelphia City*. Philadelphia: Hallowell Co., 1915.

Winship, George Parker. *The Coronado Expedition, 1540–1542*. Chicago: The Rio Grande Press, Inc., 1964.

IV. Articles

Allen, Francis O. "The Provincial or Colonial Flag of Pennsylvania." *Pennsylvania Magazine of History and Biography* 18 (1894–95): 249–52.

Balderston, Marion. "The Flag John Paul Jones Really Fought Under," *Huntington Library Quarterly* 33 (1969): 77–3.

Barraclough, Captain E.M.C. "Three Historic Flags," *The Flag Bulletin* 10 (1971): 69–73.

Bostonian Society. "Report of the Committee on the Rooms," *Proceedings of the Boston Society, 1894*, vol. 3 (1894): pp. 36–37.

Carson, Jane. "The First American Flag Hoisted in Old England," *William and Mary Quarterly*, 3rd ser, vol. 11 (1954), pp. 434–39.

Chapin, Howard M. "Colonial Military Flags," *The New England Quarterly* 4 (1931): 448–59.

———. "Colonial Military Flags," *Transactions of the Colonial Society of Massachusetts* 32 (1937): 306–07.

———. "Early Rhode Island Flags," *Rhode Island Historical Society Collections* 18 (1925): 129–40.

———. "The Early Use of Flags in New England," *Old Time New England* 21 (1930): 60–73.

———. "Notes on Colonial Flags," *Old Time New England* 24 (1934): 135–41.

Chartrand, René. "Les Drapeaux en Nouvelle-France," *Conservation Canada* 1 (1974): 24–26.

———. "The Flags of New France," *The Flag Bulletin* 15 (1976): 13–21.

Davies, Major T.R. "Some Notes on the Vexillum and the Cross of St. George," *The Flag Bulletin* 16 (1977): 84–88.

F., P. "Historical Notes: The American Flag," *Army and Navy Chronicle* 3 (1844): 82–89, 239, 832.

Fawcett, Sir Charles. "The Striped Flag of the East India Company and Its Connection With the American Stars and Stripes," *Mariner's Mirror* 23 (1937): 449–76.

Furlong, Rear Admiral William Rea. "The U.S. Flag Code and the U.N. Flag," *Daughters of the American Revolution Magazine* 86 (1952): 715–17.

Goodell, A.C., Jr. "The Centennial Anniversary of the Meeting of the Provincial Legislature in Salem, Oct. 5, 1774," *Essex Institute Historical Collec-*

tions 13 (1875): 1–91.

Gottleib, Theodore D. "The American Flag," *New Jersey Historical Society Proceedings* 57 (1939): 177–89.

Grosvenor, Gilbert and William J. Showalter. "Flags of the World," *National Geographic Magazine* 66 (1934): 338–96.

Hamilton, Schuyler. "The Stars in Our Flag," *Magazine of American History* 19 (1888): 150–53.

Herrick, H.W. "General Stark and the Battle of Bennington," *Harpers New Monthly Magazine* 55 (1877): 511–20.

Hipkiss, Edwin J. "The Paul Revere Liberty Bowl," *Bulletin of the* [Boston] *Museum of Fine Arts* 47 (1949): 19–21.

Holst, Donald W. "Regimental Colors of the Continental Army," *Military Collector and Historian* 20 (1968): 69–73.

Holst, Donald W. and Marko Zlatich. "A Return of Some Continental Army Regimental Colors of 1776," *Military Collector and Historian* 19 (1967): 109–15.

Ingstad, Helge. "Vinland Found," *National Geographic Magazine* 126 (1964): 708–34.

Jameson, J. Franklin. "St. Eustatius in the American Revolution," *American Historical Review* 8 (1903): 683–708.

Johnson, Henry P. "Evacuation of New York by the British, 1783," *Harper's Magazine* 67 (1883): 902–23.

L., J.H. "The 33rd Regiment of Foot, 1771–1785," *The Journal of the Society For Army Historical Research* 7 (1928): 243–47.

McCusker, John J., Jr. "The American Invasion of Nassau in the Bahamas," *The American Neptune* 25 (1965): 189–217.

Matthews, Albert. "Rattlesnake Colonel," *The New England Quarterly* 10 (1937): 341–45.

Melville, Colonel Phillips, USAF (Ret.). "First Official Salute to the American Flag," *De Halve Maen: Quarterly Magazine of the Dutch Colonial Period in America* 52 (1977): no. 1, pp. 7–, 14; no. 2, pp. 3–4, 13–14.

Mittlebeeler, Emmet V. "Flag Profanation and the Law," *Kentucky Law Journal* 60 (1972): 885–930.

Murfin, James V. "Relic of Revolution Questioned: 'Cowpens' Flag May be Younger Than Officials Claim," *The* [Baltimore] *Sun Magazine*, December 14, 1975, pp. 23, 26, 28.

"Paul Lunt's Book," *Massachusetts Historical Society Proceedings*, 1st ser., vol. 12 (1871–73): pp. 192–206.

Pennypacker, Morton. "Captain John Hulbert and His Flag of 1775," *New York History* 14 (1933): 356–69.

Quaife, Milo. "Flags Over Detroit," *Detroit Historical Museum Bulletin* 7 (1951): 5–9.

Rankin, Hugh F. "The Naval Flag of the American Revolution," *William and Mary Quarterly*, 3d ser., vol. 11 (1954), pp. 339–53.

Riley, Edward M. "St. George Tucker's Journal of the Seige of Yorktown, 1781," *William and Mary Quarterly*, 3d ser., vol. 5 (1948), pp. 375–95.

Sadtler, Helen Cruikshank. "Flags on the Moon," *The Flag Bulletin* 10 (1971): 98, 100, 102–6.

Shaw, Janet P., ed. "Account Book of Francis Bosseron," *Indiana Magazine of History* 25 (1929): 212–41.

Sizer, Colonel Theodore. "Trumbull's Yorktown and the Evolution of the National Flag," *Art Quarterly* 11 (1948): 356–59.

Smith, Whiteney. "The Bedford Flag," *The Flag Bulletin* 10 (1971): 43–54.

Sommer, Frank H. "Emblem and Device: The Origin of the Great Seal of the United States," *The Art Quarterly* 24 (1961): 57–76.

Spencer, Richard Henry. "The Provincial Flag of Maryland," *Maryland Historical Magazine* 9 (1916): 218–25.

Stevens, John Austin. "Bauman's Map of the Seige of Yorktown," *The Magazine of American History With Notes and Queries* 6 (1881): 54–55.

Thurston, R.C. Ballard. "Colors of the Illinois Campaign Under George Rogers Clark," *Indiana History Bulletin* 9 (1931–32): 230–39.

Wall, Alexander J. "The Flag with an Eagle in the Canton," *The New-York Historical Society Quarterly Bulletin* 17 (1933): 51–67.

Wcstcott, Allen. "Samuel Chester Reid." In *Dictionary of American Biography*, edited by Dumas Malone. New York: Charles Scribner's Sons, 1935. Vol. 8, pt. 1, pp. 480–81.

Williams, H.V. "The Moulton Flag," *Old Time New England* 24 (1934): 132–35.

Wycoff, George S. "The Stars and Stripes First Voyage Around the World," *The Nautical Gazette*, May 1940, pp. 13–14, 32–33.

Index